RAF fighter pilots at an airdrome in southern England scramble for their airplanes after being alerted to the approach of German attackers. At the height of the Battle of Britain, in August 1940, Britain's overworked pilots flew up to seven sorties per day, and were often on call around the clock in the bone-wearying struggle to fend off the numerically superior Luftwaffe.

THE BATTLE OF BRITAIN

WORLD WAR II · TIME-LIFE BOOKS · ALEXANDRIA, VIRGINIA

BY LEONARD MOSLEY
AND THE EDITORS OF TIME-LIFE BOOKS

THE BATTLE OF BRITAIN

Time-Life Books Inc.
is a wholly owned subsidiary of
TIME INCORPORATED

Founder: Henry R. Luce 1898-1967

Editor-in-Chief: Henry Anatole Grunwald
President: J. Richard Munro
Chairman of the Board: Ralph P. Davidson
Executive Vice President: Clifford J. Grum
Chairman, Executive Committee: James R. Shepley
Editorial Director: Ralph Graves
Group Vice President, Books: Joan D. Manley
Vice Chairman: Arthur Temple

TIME-LIFE BOOKS INC.

Managing Editor: Jerry Korn
Executive Editor: David Maness
Assistant Managing Editors: Dale M. Brown
(planning), George Constable, Martin Mann,
John Paul Porter, Gerry Schremp (acting)
Art Director: Tom Suzuki
Chief of Research: David L. Harrison
Director of Photography: Robert G. Mason
Assistant Art Director: Arnold C. Holeywell
Assistant Chief of Research: Carolyn L. Sackett
Assistant Director of Photography: Dolores A. Littles

Chairman: John D. McSweeney
President: Carl G. Jaeger
Executive Vice Presidents: John Steven Maxwell,
David J. Walsh
Vice Presidents: George Artandi (comptroller);
Stephen L. Bair (legal counsel); Peter G. Barnes;
Nicholas Benton (public relations);
John L. Canova; Beatrice T. Dobie (personnel);
Carol Flaumenhaft (consumer affairs);
James L. Mercer (Europe/South Pacific);
Herbert Sorkin (production); Paul R. Stewart
(marketing)

WORLD WAR II

Editorial Staff for *The Battle of Britain*
Editors: William K. Goolrick, Charles Osborne
Picture Editor/Designer: Charles Mikolaycak
Text Editor: Valerie Moolman
Staff Writers: Ruth Kelton, James Randall
Researchers: Josephine Reidy, Doris Coffin,
Mary Carroll Marden, Clara Nicolai,
Suzanne Wittebort
Editorial Assistant: Cecily Gemmell

Editorial Production
Production Editor: Douglas B. Graham
Operations Manager: Gennaro C. Esposito,
Gordon E. Buck (assistant)
Assistant Production Editor: Feliciano Madrid
Quality Control: Robert L. Young (director),
James J. Cox (assistant), Daniel J. McSweeney,
Michael G. Wight (associates)
Art Coordinator: Anne B. Landry
Copy Staff: Susan B. Galloway (chief),
Mary Ellen Slate, Celia Beattie
Picture Department: Susan Hearn
Traffic: Kimberly K. Lewis

Correspondents: Elisabeth Kraemer (Bonn);
Margot Hapgood, Dorothy Bacon, Lesley Coleman
(London); Susan Jonas, Lucy T. Voulgaris (New
York); Maria Vincenza Aloisi, Josephine du Brusle
(Paris); Ann Natanson (Rome). Valuable assistance
was also provided by: Karin B. Pearce (London);
Carolyn T. Chubet, Miriam Hsia, Christina
Lieberman (New York); Mimi Murphy (Rome).

The Author: LEONARD MOSLEY, a native of Manchester, England, served as a war correspondent in the Far East and in Europe, where his reporting won him an Order of the British Empire. Among his more than 20 books are: *On Borrowed Time,* a study of the diplomacy of the period preceding World War II; *Backs to the Wall,* an account of life in London during nearly five years of bombing; *The Last Days of the British Raj;* and biographies of Reich Marshal Hermann Göring, of Japanese Emperor Hirohito and of Charles A. Lindbergh.

The Consultants: A. E. CAMPBELL is Professor of American History at the University of Birmingham, England. He was formerly Fellow and Tutor of Modern History at Keble College, Oxford, and has been Visiting Professor at several American universities. He is the author of *Great Britain and the United States: 1895-1903.*

COL. JOHN R. ELTING, USA (Ret.), is a military historian and author of *The Battle of Bunker's Hill, The Battles of Saratoga* and *Military History and Atlas of the Napoleonic Wars.* He edited *Military Uniforms in America: The Era of the American Revolution, 1755-1795* and *Military Uniforms in America: Years of Growth, 1796-1851,* and was associate editor of *The West Point Atlas of American Wars.*

HANS-ADOLF JACOBSEN, Director of the Seminar for Political Science at the University of Bonn, is the co-author of *Anatomy of the S.S.,* and editor of *Decisive Battles of World War II: The German View.*

JAMES P. SHENTON, Professor of History at Columbia University, has lectured frequently on educational television. He is the author of *History of the United States from 1865 to the Present* and *Robert John Walker: A Politician from Jackson to Lincoln.*

Library of Congress Cataloguing in Publication Data

Mosley, Leonard, 1913-
    The Battle of Britain

    (World War II; v. 3)
    Bibliography: p. 204
    Includes index.
    1. Britain, Battle of, 1940. London—Bombardment, 1940.
I. Time-Life Books. II. Title. III. Series.
D756.5.B7M67   940.53'41   76-45540
ISBN 0-8094-2460-6
ISBN 0-8094-2459-2 (lib. bdg.)
ISBN 0-8094-2458-4 (retail ed.)

For information about any Time-Life book, please write:

Reader Information
Time-Life Books
541 North Fairbanks Court
Chicago, Illinois 60611

CONTENTS

HITLER'S NIBBLE AT THE CHANNEL

ALL CIVILIAN Pr
LEAVING
MUST REPORT
AT THE WEI

COURTEOUS CONQUEST OF POLITE LITTLE ISLANDS

This notice of military abandonment was signed by King George VI and posted around the Channel Islands two weeks before the Nazis arrived.

MESSAGE FROM THE KING TO THE BAILIFFS OF JERSEY AND GUERNSEY

For strategic reasons it has been found necessary to withdraw the Armed Forces from the Channel Islands.

I deeply regret this necessity and I wish to assure My people in the Islands that, in taking this decision, My Government has not been unmindful of their position. It is in their interest that this step should be taken in present circumstances.

The long association of the Islands with the Crown and the loyal service the people of the Islands have rendered to my ancestors and Myself are guarantees that the link between us will remain unbroken and I know that My people in the Islands will look forward with the same confidence as I do to the day when the resolute fortitude with which we face our present difficulties will reap the reward of Victory.

It was a Sunday morning at the end of June 1940, when the first armed German arrived on Guernsey, one of a group of tiny British islands set down in the English Channel just off the French coast. Landing a plane on Guernsey's grassy airfield, the German drew his pistol and alighted. Suddenly, three British planes buzzed by overhead. The interloper nervously scrambled back to his aircraft, dropping the revolver, and took off. Later that day, however, another German plane touched down, and this time three men got out. One carefully retrieved the gun; another announced to an unruffled policeman that they intended to take over the island.

Thus began Hitler's occupation of the Channel Islands, which was undertaken to create stepping stones for the invasion of Britain, and ended with the Islands being the only bits of native British territory to be seized by the Germans during World War II. By the general standards of Nazi takeovers, it was a strangely peaceable, polite conquest, at least in the early stages. The bobby at the airport was actually expecting both the airmen and the German ground troops who soon arrived by boat. So was just about everybody else in the Channel Islands. Since Jersey, Guernsey, Alderney and Sark were within 30 miles of France, newly conquered by Hitler, and nearly 80 miles from Britain, His Majesty's Government considered them indefensible—and so informed the residents *(left)*.

Not that the occupation lacked certain discomforts for the natives: a curfew; liquor prohibition; Nazi films in movie houses; the construction of bristling shore and antiaircraft defenses. But generally, the islanders, obeying their leaders, were careful to show no hostility. When one old Guernseyite stood in his doorway with a rifle threatening to "shoot the first German who tries to come in," his relatives gently disarmed him. And the Dame of Sark *(right)*, feudal ruler of her two-square-mile fief, was so relaxed with the invaders that it was hard to tell just who had conquered whom. When one of the visitors asked if she were not frightened, she sweetly replied, in German, "Is there any need to be afraid of German officers?"

The Dame of Sark, the hereditary head of the Channel Island bearing the same name, meets with German officers in the courtyard of her estate.

Home Circle Library

BUSINESS AS USUAL
— AT —
Old Gate House
AND THE BRIDGE,
ST. SAMPSON'S.

Evening Press

SWELLING THE FRUIT

Use Frain's Blood and Bone, Blood and Fish, Aeroplane Organic and Special Fertiliser with a cross feed of Aeroplane Insignicisr or Aeroplane Extra Special Fertiliser.

W. Holmes & Son Ltd.
ESPLANADE. 'Phone 763 (5 lines)

No. 10,972   REGISTERED AT THE G.P.O.   POSTAGE 1d.   AS A NEWSPAPER   GUERNSEY, MONDAY, JULY 1, 1940   TELEPHONE 1400 (FIVE LINES)   GRATIS

ORDERS OF THE COMMANDANT OF THE GERMAN FORCES IN OCCUPATION OF THE ISLAND OF GUERNSEY

(1)—ALL INHABITANTS MUST BE INDOORS BY 11 P.M. AND MUST NOT LEAVE THEIR HOMES BEFORE 6 A.M.

(2)—WE WILL RESPECT THE POPULATION IN GUERNSEY; BUT, SHOULD ANYONE ATTEMPT TO CAUSE THE LEAST TROUBLE, SERIOUS MEASURES WILL BE TAKEN AND THE TOWN WILL BE BOMBED.

(3)—ALL ORDERS GIVEN BY THE MILITARY AUTHORITY ARE TO BE STRICTLY OBEYED.

(4)—ALL SPIRITS MUST BE LOCKED UP IMMEDIATELY, AND NO SPIRITS MAY BE SUPPLIED, OBTAINED OR CONSUMED HENCEFORTH. THIS PROHIBITION DOES NOT APPLY TO STOCKS IN PRIVATE HOUSES.

(5)—NO PERSON SHALL ENTER THE AERODROME AT LA VILLIAZE.

(6)—ALL RIFLES, AIRGUNS, PISTOLS, REVOLVERS, DAGGERS, SPORTING GUNS, AND ALL OTHER WEAPONS WHATSOEVER, EXCEPT SOUVENIRS, MUST, TOGETHER WITH ALL AMMUNITION, BE DELIVERED AT THE ROYAL HOTEL BY 12 NOON TO-DAY, JULY 1.

(7)—ALL BRITISH SAILORS, AIRMEN AND SOLDIERS ON LEAVE IN THIS ISLAND MUST REPORT AT THE POLICE STATION AT 9 A.M. TO-DAY, AND MUST THEN REPORT AT THE ROYAL HOTEL.

(8)—NO BOAT OR VESSEL OF ANY DESCRIPTION, INCLUDING ANY FISHING BOAT, SHALL LEAVE THE HARBOURS OR ANY OTHER PLACE WHERE THE SAME IS MOORED, WITHOUT AN ORDER FROM THE MILITARY AUTHORITY, TO BE OBTAINED AT THE ROYAL HOTEL. ALL BOATS ARRIVING FROM JERSEY, FROM SARK OR FROM HERM, OR ELSEWHERE, MUST REMAIN IN HARBOUR UNTIL PERMITTED BY THE MILITARY TO LEAVE.

THE CREWS WILL REMAIN ON BOARD. THE MASTER WILL REPORT TO THE HARBOURMASTER, ST. PETER-PORT, AND WILL OBEY HIS INSTRUCTIONS.

(9)—THE SALE OF MOTOR SPIRIT IS PROHIBITED, EXCEPT FOR USE ON ESSENTIAL SERVICES, SUCH AS DOCTORS' VEHICLES, THE DELIVERY OF FOODSTUFFS, AND SANITARY SERVICES WHERE SUCH VEHICLES ARE IN POSSESSION OF A PERMIT FROM THE MILITARY AUTHORITY TO OBTAIN SUPPLIES.

THESE VEHICLES MUST BE BROUGHT TO THE ROYAL HOTEL BY 12 NOON TO-DAY TO RECEIVE THE NECESSARY PERMISSION.

THE USE OF CARS FOR PRIVATE PURPOSES IS FORBIDDEN.

(10)—THE BLACK-OUT REGULATIONS ALREADY IN FORCE MUST BE OBSERVED AS BEFORE.

(11)—BANKS AND SHOPS WILL BE OPEN AS USUAL.

(Signed) THE GERMAN COMMANDANT OF THE ISLAND OF GUERNSEY

JULY 1, 1940.

Guernseyites watch German troops marching through the streets of Saint Peter Port (left), the island's main town. On the day following the invasion, the Wehrmacht commandant took over the local newspaper and printed and distributed special copies (above), which set down precisely what was to be expected of the conquered. The islanders complied fully, although some of them mocked the arms regulation by buying toy pistols and presenting them to the Germans. Though courteous, the occupiers were deadly serious; subsequent proclamations prescribed the death sentence for anyone possessing pigeons—which the Germans believed could be used to send secret messages to Britain.

A Nazi flag proclaims Jersey's Town Hall to be the German headquarters on the island.

AIR RAID
SHELTER
→

Posted under a portrait of the Führer, billboards on a Guernsey

On the island of Guernsey, a German soldier stands guard at a former British installation

movie theater advertise a Nazi film called Sieg im Westen—Victory in the West—that extolled recent German feats of arms in the Low Countries and France.

Siting a light gun to cover an island inlet, the
crew sets up on a wooden platform overlooking
the water. The soldier at right puts a final
touch on the flooring by nailing a loose plank.

A two-man motorcycle patrol pauses to check
out a rocky section of sea front. One important
job of these German patrols was to guard
against any attempts by the British to land
spies or armed raiding parties on the Islands.

In a Guernsey storage depot, German soldiers wearing thick mittens to protect their hands stack barbed wire for defensive entanglements to be set up in village streets and along beaches. In the background stands an old fort built by the British to defend against French attacks during Napoleonic times. The Germans repaired the aging redoubt and incorporated it into their own island defense system.

A Luftwaffe crew checks out a portable searchlight used to pick up British planes flying over the Islands at night. RAF attacks began almost immediately after the occupation, but were little more than demonstrations designed to encourage the populace without actually risking a hit on the wrong people.

A German lookout, bundled up against damp Channel weather, scans the sea toward England. The map and compass on the table were used to plot the movement of British ships and aircraft in the Channel. Although the islands appeared to be a useful base for an attack against Britain, Hitler overestimated their strategic and political value. As a result, he garrisoned the territory with far more troops than needed for its defense, and the soldiers endured torments of boredom from such duties as this.

1

In the early hours of June 5, 1940, two high officers of Germany's Luftwaffe tramped along the broad, sandy beaches near the northern French port of Dunkirk and scuffed their boots through the debris left behind by a retreating army. It was the morning after the last of an armada of destroyers and small ships had carried off the remnants of the British Expeditionary Force before the relentless pincers of the German Army snapped shut around them.

Across the beaches was littered the matériel that the British had abandoned, the flotsam and jetsam of defeat: thousands of shoes discarded by the soldiers wading out to the rescue boats, hundreds of bicycles on which they had ridden to the beaches, long lines of trucks and heavy guns, piles of rifles, mountains of canned food, and in every direction, blowing about in the chill dawn wind, random bits of clothing and a snowstorm of army papers.

At one point, the two walkers came to a mound of empty wine and whiskey bottles—the leftovers from some officers' mess—no doubt swigged by the troops as they waited their turn to be rescued. One of the Germans, General Hoffmann von Waldau of the Luftwaffe General Staff, prodded a bottle with a toe and waved an arm across the landscape.

"Here is the grave of British hopes in this war!" he said. Then, contemptuously indicating the bottles: "And these are the grave stones!"

The other officer shook his head. He was a squat, fleshy man whose uniformed chest bore campaign ribbons from World War I, and whose small, dark eyes had the look of someone accustomed to command. He was General Erhard Milch, the egocentric but capable administrator of the German air forces—the Inspector-General of the Luftwaffe as well as deputy to its chief, Field Marshal Hermann Göring.

Milch stared through the mist at wrecked British ships in the shallows and at the evidence of the British Army's disarray all around him. But the expression on his face showed none of his companion's elation. "They are not buried yet," he commented. Then, after a slight pause, and almost to himself: "We have no time to waste."

Later that day, General Milch attended a meeting of the Luftwaffe's High Command called by Field Marshal Göring aboard his armored train, which was located some miles distant from Dunkirk. With Milch around the conference table were General Albert Kesselring, General Hugo Sperrle and

BRITAIN AT BAY

General Hans-Jürgen Stumpff, commanders respectively of the Luftwaffe's Air Fleets 2, 3 and 5, and Göring's Chief of Staff, General Hans Jeschonnek.

Göring was in a jubilant mood. Euphoria over Germany's victories in its lightning sweep across Holland, Belgium and northern France seemed to have given the Field Marshal a special glow. He looked unusually fit. His nurse, who was with him aboard the train, had persuaded him to cut down his intake of paracodeine, the mild drug to which he had become addicted, to 30 pills a day. His masseur had pounded off some of his surplus fat. His valet had dressed him in a resplendent new silk uniform.

Beaming, he made his way around the table backslapping and embracing his generals. Then he moved to the head of the table to address them. He began by informing them that there were already feelers out from certain French sources concerning terms for an armistice. He went on to say how overjoyed he and the Führer were that the British Army had been "wiped out" at Dunkirk after suffering such "terrifying blows" from the German forces.

Milch stirred. "The British Army?" he interjected. From what he had seen at Dunkirk, he said, it was far from destroyed. He had counted perhaps 20 or 30 dead soldiers; however, the mass of the British Army had managed to escape unharmed. "I agree that throwing them out of France in the space of three weeks is quite an achievement, and a dreadful blow to English pride," Milch said. "But we have to face the fact that they have gotten practically the whole of their army back across the Channel, and that's worrying."

It was true. Though German bombers had destroyed over 200 ships of the rescue armada, the British had managed to evacuate 224,000 of their troops—fully 85 per cent of the British Expeditionary Force—as well as 114,000 French troops along with a few Belgians. The men were exhausted, their morale was low and they had been forced to jettison all their equipment, but they had ducked the trap the Germans had set for them, and one day soon they would be ready to fight again.

Göring, who had summoned the meeting under the impression that the war was almost over, seemed crestfallen at Milch's comments. He asked his Inspector-General what he thought should be the next move. Milch was emphatic:

"I strongly advise the immediate transfer to the Channel coast of all available Luftwaffe forces. . . . The invasion of Great Britain should begin *without delay. . . . I warn you,* Herr Field Marshal, if you give the English three or four weeks to recoup, it will be too late."

Göring's initial reaction to the proposal was a terse "It can't be done." But as the talk continued, he began to swing round to Milch's point of view, and over the hours a plan eventually took shape—a plan for the Battle of Britain.

The following day, Göring arrived at Hitler's temporary headquarters in the Belgian village of Bruly-le-Pêche, just across the border from France. The Field Marshal exuded confidence as he presented Hitler with the plan the Luftwaffe staff had threshed out. Clearly he had been won over to the notion that the war in the West could be brought to an end soon by the invasion and conquest of Britain.

"Mein Führer," Marshal Göring said, "here is the blueprint for victory!"

The plan was a good one—if it was carried out with the utmost speed, before the bruised and battered British forces had a chance to get their breath. It envisioned an airborne invasion, starting with a massive bomber and dive-bomber attack on the south coast of England. Under cover of the attack, paratroops would drop on English soil and seize an airfield. In their wake would come a shuttle service of Junkers troop transports carrying the five crack divisions that were to be transferred to the Luftwaffe from the German Army; these soldiers would fan out like a brushfire across the English countryside.

Aside from the opposition to be expected on the ground, the plan took account of other formidable obstacles:

To bring the British to their knees, not only would their planes have to be shot out of the sky, but the seaways that brought them their food would have to be closed to their shipping, and their ports put out of action. That meant reckoning with the British Navy, still the most powerful in the world. But Göring foresaw that the invasion would compel the Empire's fighting ships to leave their present positions in the North Sea and the Mediterranean, as well as their heavily protected lairs at Scapa Flow in Scotland, and bring them full steam into the English Channel. The entire Royal Navy would be concentrated in this narrow strip of water; meanwhile, the entire Royal Air Force would appear over the battlefield. Thus, Göring went on, "This will enable me to use the Luftwaffe not only to destroy the enemy's forces in the air but their mighty force of ships at sea."

He conceded that the struggle would be bloody and desperate, and the losses on both sides high. But at the climactic point, he explained, five more divisions transferred from the Army, and held in reserve on the other side of the Channel, would be brought into play. With this "mere handful" of fresh soldiers, Göring predicted, "we will bring about the final decision—and England will be ours."

From the Field Marshal's own private standpoint the plan had added merit in that it was to be a Luftwaffe-controlled operation. Not only would the 10 Army divisions be under his direction, but also the ships and barges that would be required from the German Navy for backup and follow-up purposes. He was confident that the Luftwaffe could stop British naval interference as well as destroy Britain's air force. As overall commander of the Luftwaffe, Hermann Göring was bound to get the lion's share of the glory from the successful outcome of the invasion.

He did not, of course, convey this thought to Hitler. Instead, he concluded by stressing the one prerequisite for the success that would win the War. The operation must be carried out immediately—within days. It must be launched while Britain was still reeling from the heavy defeat it had suffered in Belgium and France, and while the British Ex-

peditionary Force evacuated from Dunkirk was still demoralized and bereft of arms and equipment.

"I await your orders, mein Führer," said Göring, with expectant confidence.

But the order he got stupefied him and put General Milch into a raging fury when he heard about it. For Hitler made it clear that while he appreciated the practical points of the plan, he was against putting it into operation—not for the reason that he did not think it would succeed, but because he did not believe it was or would be necessary.

"Do nothing," he told Göring. He was convinced that the British, being a reasonable people, had by this time realized that their position was hopeless, and he counted on the British government's being ready to accept the peace settlement that he was prepared to offer. At the same time, while this was being arranged, he did not wish "to rub their noses in the mud of defeat" by invading them.

To Milch this was madness, though he dared to say so only in the privacy of his diary. He did not believe that the British would make peace. He was convinced that they were girding themselves for battle, and that the only way of conquering them was to destroy their air force, send their navy to the bottom, blockade their ports, then go in and fight them on English soil. That was what the Battle of Britain meant to the Inspector-General of the Luftwaffe, and every

hour that Germany waited gave the British a vital 60 minutes in which to prepare for resistance.

And, had Hitler chosen to listen, he would have had no doubt as to how stiff the English resistance would be. Winston Churchill himself, only recently installed as Prime Minister, had spelled it out in a speech to Parliament, even as the last British soldiers were escaping from the debacle at Dunkirk: "We shall fight on the beaches, we shall fight on the landing-grounds, we shall fight in the fields and in the streets, we shall fight in the hills; we shall never surrender."

Hitler's professed reluctance to humiliate the British half of the Western Alliance did not extend to the other major partner, the French. Slightly more than two weeks after Dunkirk, France's last-ditch stand against the Nazi blitzkrieg collapsed, and a newly formed government under 84-year-old Marshal Henri Philippe Pétain asked for an armistice. To turn that armistice into an act of national humiliation, Hitler ordered that the talks be held in the forest of Compiègne, in the same railway carriage where emissaries from the Kaiser's Germany had defeat imposed upon them in World War I. As Pétain's representatives listened to the reading of the preamble of the armistice terms, Hitler sat in the chair occupied by the victorious commander of the Allied forces in 1918, Marshal Ferdinand Foch.

The French signed the terms on June 22. The railway carriage was borne off in triumph to Berlin, and the granite monument marking the 1918 ceremony was blown to smithereens by German engineers. On the next day Hitler treated himself to an intensive round of sightseeing in Paris, where swastika flags now were flying from the public buildings.

With the fall of France, the German war machine slipped its gears into neutral. German troops bathed in the waters of the Channel at Deauville and Le Touquet, and patronized restaurants and cafés that bore signs saying *Man Spricht Deutsch* where, a few weeks earlier, the same bistros had said *English Spoken Here*.

But not all was rest and recreation along the northern French coast. To the chiefs of the German armed services, Hitler's order to "do nothing" against Britain meant quite literally that he wished no attack on the island kingdom at present; however, it did not preclude preparing for the eventuality that he might suddenly change his mind.

And so the Luftwaffe engaged itself in moving Air Fleet 2 to the Channel from its base in the Low Countries, and Air Fleet 3 from fields near the recent battlefronts in the north of France. Fighter and dive-bomber squadrons, under the command of the daredevil General Wolfram von Richthofen, cousin of the celebrated Red Baron of World War I, were assembling on French airfields just behind the Channel coast facing England—20 minutes' flight to the cliffs of Dover, and an hour to London.

Behind them bomber squadrons and Junkers troop transports were moving in from their bases in Germany, and soldiers were beginning to spread the smell of liverwurst and beer through French barracks, which had recently reeked of Caporal cigarette smoke and *vin ordinaire*.

The German Navy, too, was busy. Barges and small craft were being rounded up and moved down the Rhine and through the network of canals in Holland and Belgium to assembly points on the Channel and on the North Sea coast.

Though Hitler's shackling orders barred any full-scale attack on England, the Luftwaffe was giving its pilots useful rehearsals by sporadic raids that also served to remind the British that the enemy was still there, waiting to move. Small flights of night bombers picked isolated targets—airdromes and industrial plants beyond the relatively well-defended areas of the south and east—to try out the accuracy and effectiveness of their attacks. By day, fighter pilots zipped across the Channel, attacking convoys, hoping to persuade RAF planes to come up and do battle—and thus get a notion of British skill and mettle.

Occasionally, too, German reconnaissance planes would overfly and photograph the Kent, Sussex and Hampshire countryside. In spite of this activity and surveillance, however, the Wehrmacht was unable to see what was going on in British factories, or, as important, in British minds.

There were some influential Britons who felt that the time had come to make peace with Germany, and not all of them were faint-hearts or traitors. A number of practical statesmen, both in and outside the government, surveyed Britain's situation and quailed not for their own safety but at the thought of the vast loss of life and appalling destruction that a fight to the death would entail—a fight, moreover, that they felt Britain had scant chance of winning.

The alternative, peace with Hitler, would mean recogniz-

A few days after the fall of France, Reich Marshal Hermann Göring (fifth from right) and members of his Luftwaffe staff gaze across a low-lying haze over the English Channel toward the white cliffs of Dover 20 miles away. In a fateful stab at personal glory, Göring was about to launch an air offensive that he—and Hitler—believed could bring Britain to its knees without the last resort of a mass invasion by the German Army.

ing his dominion over the Continent and returning the overseas colonies taken from Germany after World War I. At least so went the rumors emanating from Europe's neutral capitals, encouraged by Nazi diplomats. Hitler, it was reported, genuinely admired the British, their empire and their civilization; as Anglo-Saxons, they measured up to his standards of a master race; he had no wish to destroy them.

By the end of June, German peace-feelers were reaching London through various neutral sources. The Vatican sent an inquiry by way of its Papal nuncio in Switzerland. From Sweden, the King himself urged a settlement with Germany. In Spain, Nazi emissaries were having direct talks with the British Ambassador, Sir Samuel Hoare.

Officially, Prime Minister Churchill stood adamant against these overtures. As he put it in his reply to King Gustav V of Sweden: "Before any such requests or proposals could even be considered, it would be necessary that effective guarantees by deeds, not words, should be forthcoming from Germany which would ensure the restoration of the free and independent life of Czechoslovakia, Poland, Norway, Denmark, Holland, Belgium and above all, France." But some evidence unearthed after the war indicates that, unofficially, Churchill encouraged both appeasers in Parliament and intermediaries in neutral countries in the belief that his government would not be unwilling to come to an arrangement with the Nazis, provided the Führer meant what he said about preserving the British Empire "as a factor in world equilibrium."

The truth was that Churchill was playing for time. Farmhands, retired Army majors from World War I and other local defense volunteers banded together in the Home Guard were patrolling Britain's roads and 5,000 miles of coastline with hunting weapons, obsolete rifles, even pitchforks and golf clubs. Until they could be furnished with proper equipment; until the veterans of Dunkirk and other regular army troops could be rearmed; until fortifications could be strengthened, tank-traps dug, beaches mined; and until the RAF could be beefed up with more planes and pilots, every day gained was precious.

Churchill's real attitude toward peace approaches from Hitler was hardly in doubt. One evening he called a meeting of the Imperial General Staff in a bare chamber in the labyrinthine underground headquarters that was known as the "Hole in the Ground," beneath Whitehall, close to the Houses of Parliament and government offices. As the Prime Minister entered, the assembled generals and cabinet ministers stood and looked at him in a silence that was interrupted only by fans pumping air into the arid room. He stopped, took the cigar out of his mouth, waved it around the spartan dugout, then pointed it at the wooden chair positioned at the head of the conference table.

"This is the room from which I'll direct the war," he declared. "And if the invasion takes place, that's where I'll sit —in that chair." He placed the cigar back in his mouth, puffed and then added: "And I'll sit there until either the Germans are driven back or they carry me out dead."

By early July, Hitler's confident assumption that the British would come to their senses was beginning to fade. Contrary to what he had been led to expect, neither fear nor chaos had beset them in the wake of Dunkirk. Indeed, they had made good use of the surcease since the evacuation, stepping up production of the planes and tanks and other weapons that would turn their island into a fortress. As Churchill was later to recall:

"Men and women toiled at the lathes and machines in the factories till they fell exhausted on the floor and had to be dragged away and ordered home, while their places were occupied by newcomers ahead of time."

To Hitler, Churchill was a brandy-swilling boor; the men who were helping him run Britain, stubborn fools. In the 10 months since the outbreak of war the previous September, the armed forces of the Reich had brought the whole of northern Europe, from Poland's Bug River to France's Channel coast, under German control. Yet the people across the Channel chose to ignore this reality.

Their obstinacy not only baffled the Führer but threatened to throw a monkey wrench into his other plans as well. The next big item on his agenda of conquest was the invasion and destruction of his present ally, the U.S.S.R. That project, which he had scheduled for sometime in 1941, would be made infinitely more complicated if a hostile Britain were still to be opposing him.

If the British persisted in their refusal to make peace —treating him "so shabbily," as he complained in a letter to his Axis partner, Mussolini—they would have to face the consequences. On July 16, a top-secret directive to Germany's military leaders announced the Führer's decision:

"Since England, despite her hopeless military situation, still shows no sign of willingness to come to terms, I have decided to prepare, and if necessary to carry out, a landing operation against her," the directive read. "The aim of this operation is to eliminate the English motherland as a base for carrying on the war against Germany, and, if necessary, to occupy the country completely."

While the directive put the onus on Britain for continuing the war, the key words were "if necessary." Hitler was still hoping that the British would recognize their predicament, and come around to his way of thinking.

The code name selected for the operation was Lion (soon expanded to Sea Lion). The name was not much of a cover up; even the most amateurish sleuth could have figured out that the lion was Britain's national emblem. But General Alfred Jodl, chief of staff of the German armed forces and the man responsible for designating code names, was short on subtlety; around headquarters, one historian has observed,

INGENIOUS DEFENSES FOR A BELEAGUERED ISLAND

"The English territorial defense is nonexistent!" exulted Nazi Foreign Minister Joachim von Ribbentrop to his Italian counterpart during a visit to Rome in September 1940. Such, indeed, had been the case a few months earlier, but by now the British were working night and day on plans to turn their islands into a fortress.

Well they might. The Wehrmacht was reported to be massing for an invasion, and the job of defending Britain's 5,000-mile coastline required both ingenuity and hard work. Beaches were protected by pillboxes, barbed wire, and a curious antitank weapon called the Flame Fougasse: a camouflaged oil drum filled with petroleum, lime and tar that could be ignited and then rolled into the path of an invader.

Extending farther offshore were pipes, laid beneath the surf, through which oil could be pumped to spread over the surface of the water. When ignited by flare pistols, the oil would blaze into a wall of flame (right, below) designed to incinerate troops approaching in landing craft.

Most ambitious of the coastal defense installations were the sea forts. These towering structures, each the size of the Arc de Triomphe and resembling modern offshore oil rigs, were constructed on land, floated out to sea and then sunk into place (right, above), three of them around Liverpool and four more in the Thames estuary. The sea forts bristled with ordnance —Lewis guns, Bofors, and 3.7-inch antiaircraft cannon—and, on the Thames towers, radar antennae. These supplemented the low-level, shore-based radar installations and proved to be highly effective in tracking mine-laying Luftwaffe planes and fixing the locations of the mines that they dropped for later disposal by Royal Navy minesweepers.

As its hollow concrete pontoons fill with sea water, a camouflaged sea fort settles into the Channel.

Moments after being ignited, the oil pumped from underwater pipes blazes along England's coast.

he was in fact famous for choosing names "far too suggestive of the true operation."

Any attempt at secrecy was, in any case, futile. Britain was already girding itself for battle.

Operation *Sea Lion* lacked the melodrama of the abortive Milch-Göring plan for an airborne invasion of England, but it was far more grandiose in concept. It envisioned landing as many as 250,000 German soldiers on the southern shores of the island, over a broad front—about 200 miles long—stretching all the way from Ramsgate, east of the cliffs of Dover, to Lyme Bay, west of the Isle of Wight. Such well-known places as Brighton and Folkestone were to be landing points, along with others more obscure. One was Pevensey, landing site for William the Conqueror's successful invasion in 1066.

Only a few of the invading troops would be airborne; most would cross the Channel in converted river barges, tugs, motorboats and larger transports. Arriving in three waves, they would secure their beachheads, then push inland, their primary goal to cut off London from the rest of the country. Once the capital was occupied, other matters could be attended to: the immediate arrest by the Gestapo of some 2,000 of Hitler's archcritics, from Winston Churchill to writers Aldous Huxley and Virginia Woolf and actor Noel Coward. All able-bodied English males who were between the ages of 17 and 45 were to be interned and eventually transferred to the Continent.

But the success of *Sea Lion* would entirely hinge on a safe Channel crossing. To ensure this, huge mine fields would be sown along the western and eastern flanks of the assaulting forces, thus preventing the Royal Navy from effectively attacking. And, of course, the Luftwaffe would have to have defeated the RAF and gained command of the air.

Among the planners of *Sea Lion* there was one notable doubter: Grand Admiral Erich Raeder, Commander-in-Chief of the German Navy. What worried Raeder—aside from the losses his navy had suffered in Norway—was that his fellow strategists viewed *Sea Lion* as just another river crossing, only wider. They could not seem to grasp that there was all the difference in the world between an attack force storming across the half-mile-wide Vistula River into Poland, or ferrying across three quarters of a mile of the Rhine into France, and an invasion force plowing its way over 25 miles of tidal, frequently rough, Channel waters onto English soil.

As Raeder's colleagues saw it, only two modifications would have to be made in the standard river operation at which the Germans had proven themselves so adept. The Luftwaffe bombers would have to substitute for ground artillery, and the navy would have to assume the transport function, which was normally assigned to army engineers.

Raeder was appalled by this casual attitude. He was well aware that a seaborne landing was the one kind of operation in which the German forces had not been intensively trained. Moreover, he knew that his navy did not possess the craft necessary to protect and supply the 200-mile-long invasion front projected in *Sea Lion*. When he argued for a narrower front, the army chiefs retorted that this would be putting their troops "straight through the sausage machine." Hitler decided, at least tentatively, on a compromise—a somewhat smaller front than originally planned, excluding the area west of the Isle of Wight.

The German Army was confident that *Sea Lion* could succeed. While Raeder continued to air doubts, General Walther von Brauchitsch, the Army's Commander-in-Chief, and General Franz Halder, chief of its general staff, assured Hitler of their total commitment to the operation. But they left themselves a convenient escape hatch. Hitler agreed that before the seaborne invasion could be launched, the Luftwaffe would first have to neutralize the RAF and completely destroy Britain's air defenses.

In thus tossing the ball to Field Marshal Göring, the two generals had Admiral Raeder's ardent support. In later years he was to recall his relief on learning of this move. It would let him and his navy off the hook in a double sense. If the Luftwaffe failed to defeat the RAF, then there would be no invasion from the sea, and Raeder would not have to risk the remainder of his naval forces against the might of the Royal Navy. If, however, the RAF were destroyed and the seaborne landings began, Hitler would be in supreme command and it would be he who got the blame (or the credit, of course) for whatever followed.

The Führer, however, was not quite ready to launch *Sea Lion*. Often inclined to postpone making difficult decisions, he planned to give Britain one last chance to be reasonable. On July 19 he convened the members of the Reichstag at

AN EPIDEMIC OF SUPERPATRIOTISM

In May 1940, with the German Army rolling toward the shore of the English Channel, Britain was swept by a witch-hunting impulse to clear the country of spies and saboteurs—both real and imagined. Any attic or coastal shack might hide an enemy agent sending coded radio messages. Behind any sand dune might lurk a saboteur ready to blow up a gun emplacement or blink visual signals across the few miles of open water.

On May 12, two days after the Nazi invasion of the Low Countries, the British rounded up 2,000 aliens, mostly men of German or Austrian origin living within 20 miles of the Channel coast. During the next five days, several thousand more aliens were seized. And finally, on May 27, as headlines blared "Intern the Lot!" all remaining men and women born in countries hostile to Britain were arrested and then hustled off to makeshift concentration camps set up on racetracks, in old factories and elegant country estates and even at summer resorts such as the Isle of Man. The internees were joined in less than two weeks by 4,000 expatriate Italians, who were rounded up when Italy declared war. By the middle of July, almost 50,000 aliens had been put behind barbed wire.

For a brief time the wave of superpatriotism threatened to engulf anyone or anything that could be even vaguely construed as foreign. English employers fired workers of German ancestry; landlords advertised flats for British only; restaurants that had served foreign dishes now touted British foods. The owner of one fish-and-chips shop in the town of Partick, Scotland, posted a notice, which read: "ALL SCOTS—Fish, Potatoes, Dripping, Proprietor, Assistants and the Cat."

Fortunately, the xenophobia was short-lived. In rounding up alleged enemy aliens, Britain had indeed caught a few outspoken Nazis and potential spies. But trapped in the crowd were tens of thousands of devout anti-Nazis—including many recent refugees from Hitler's storm troops. Public shock at the random imprisonments turned to outrage by summer's end, and a demand for redress. Within months, many internees were released, vouched for by British friends or relatives. And in less than two years, only about 5,000 men and women—one tenth of the original bag—remained in British civilian prison camps.

A restaurant in London's Old Compton Street informs its patrons that its spaghetti is loyally British.

Armed Tommies in a London railway station guard aliens who are entraining for an internment camp.

the Kroll Opera House in Berlin. The boxes were packed with foreign diplomats; they had heard the rumors that a final peace proposal was to be offered.

It came at the end of a long speech extolling Germany's victories to date in the war. "At this hour," Hitler declared, "I feel it is my duty to appeal, in good faith, for reason and wise counsel on the part of Great Britain, as of all other countries. I consider that my position allows me to make this appeal, since I do not speak as a defeated man begging favors but as the victor speaking in the name of reason. I really do not see why this war should continue."

The only obstacle in the way of peace, Hitler charged, was an unscrupulous "criminal warmonger" named Winston Churchill. The megalomaniac Churchill and the ignorant fools who surrounded him were duping the British people and were concealing from them the terrors that might soon be raining down upon their heads if the peace terms were not accepted.

The Führer's voice rose to an angry crescendo: "It almost causes me pain to think that I should have been selected by Fate to deal the final blow to the structure which these men have already set tottering. Mr. Churchill ought, perhaps, for once, to believe me when I prophesy that a great Empire will be destroyed—an Empire which it was never my intention to destroy or even to harm."

German planes flew to Britain that night to drop copies of a leaflet containing the full text of the Führer's speech, "so that you will know the truth that your Government is concealing from you." In fact, the speech received full presentation in Britain, over the radio and immediately thereafter in the newspapers. But it was over the BBC, within an hour

of the moment when Hitler finished speaking, that the reply came—defiant and wholly spontaneous.

The broadcaster, a journalist named Sefton Delmer, spoke without bothering to get any official permission. Speaking in German, he addressed the Führer directly: "Let me tell you what we here in Britain think of this appeal to what you are pleased to call our reason and common sense. Herr Führer and Reich Chancellor, we hurl it right back at you—right back into your evil-smelling teeth."

By now, virtually all of the people of Britain concurred and the nation's adamancy amazed most members of the German General Staff. However, at the same time they were relieved, because now they could release the brakes that Hitler had applied and get the Nazi war machine rolling again.

Hermann Göring, the man on whose shoulders would rest the responsibility for shattering Britain's defenses and thus opening its gates to Germany's invading forces, spent the evening of July 19, after the Opera House speech, celebrating at home. He had good reason to be festive. In one of the passages of the speech, Hitler had announced that he was promoting a dozen of his generals to the rank of field marshal, in recognition of the part they had played in the conquests of Poland and France. Three of them were Luftwaffe generals: Milch, Kesselring and Sperrle.

But for their chief, Hermann Göring, there had been a special reward. The Führer himself read the citation:

"For his mighty contribution to victory, I hereby appoint the creator of the Luftwaffe to the rank of Reich Marshal of the Greater German Reich, and award him the Grand Cross of the Iron Cross."

A helmeted British Air Raid Precautions worker laughs at the contents of Nazi propaganda that was dropped from a German bomber on the night of August 2, 1940. The broadside contains an English translation of a speech Hitler had made in the Reichstag July 19, in which he suggested that Britons lay down their arms.

No soldier in the history of the German armed forces had ever held such rank, and Göring marked the extraordinary occasion by giving a dinner party for a few friends at his Berlin residence, the Leipzieger Palace. Among the guests was a young Swede, Thomas von Kantzow, the son of Göring's dead first wife, Karin.

The dinner, Thomas remembered later, was a Lucullan feast of nonwartime food and drink that had been imported, for the most part, from the European countries the Germans had conquered. "Hermann had brought back *pâté de foie gras* from Paris," he said, "and as we ate it we drank numerous toasts, each one in a different colored vodka from Poland. Then we had roast salmon from Danzig which we accompanied with Moselle from a cellar Hermann had acquired in Trier, a goose from his estate at Veldenstein with Château Haut Brion, and then very light tiny Viennese *torte* with Château d'Yquem."

Afterwards the men drank Napoleon brandy, and the women French liqueurs. The wives were all dressed in the latest fashions from Paris and had dabbed themselves liberally with France's famous perfumes.

"Everyone got quite tipsy," Thomas recalled. "It was a very jolly and sentimental occasion."

But some days later Reich Marshal Göring got back to business. On the 6th of August he summoned his top Luftwaffe chiefs, including the newly elevated field marshals Milch, Kesselring and Sperrle, to a conference at Karin Hall, the lavish country house in East Prussia that Göring had named in honor of his late wife. From now on, he announced, the attacks against Britain's air defenses were to be stepped up in intensity until the RAF was destroyed. The full force of the Luftwaffe was to be unleashed against England. The start of the operation, to be known as Eagle Day, was set for the 10th of August.

"I have told the Führer," Göring announced, "that the RAF will be destroyed in time for Operation *Sea Lion* to be launched by September 15, when our German soldiers will land on British soil."

He added, casually, that he believed he was allowing the Luftwaffe more than ample time to blow the RAF out of the skies, and that he expected Britain to have been rendered helpless and vulnerable well before the promised date of September 15. His tone, when he referred to the RAF's pilots and planes, was scornful and patronizing; the Luftwaffe was in every way superior, he said, in the caliber of its pilots and its machines. Moreover, he went on, numerically the Luftwaffe had the advantage over the RAF of at least two to one, with abundant reserves to fall back on.

In these sanguine calculations the newly created Reich Marshal was to be proven wrong, and his contemptuous estimate of the British capability would cost him and Germany dearly in the weeks and months to come.

Göring spoke to his Luftwaffe commanders on the 6th of August as if the Battle of Britain were still off in the future, and in the sense that he was rallying them in preparation for the supreme effort this was true. But from the British point of view, the battle was already underway. Even while the Luftwaffe's chiefs were having their meeting, a dogfight was in progress over the Straits of Dover as German dive bombers, protected by fighters, sought to sink, split or turn back a British convoy that was attempting to break through to the Thames estuary and the Port of London.

RAF fighter planes were dispatched to drive them off, and in the subsequent clashes, which lasted all afternoon, the British lost six of their planes and the Luftwaffe seven of theirs. The convoy got through.

It was on this day that a fussy RAF control-room commander listened with shocked astonishment to the language coming over the loud-speakers in the room where members of the Women's Auxiliary Air Force were at work plotting aircraft positions on the control-room's operation tables. The loud-speakers were directly connected to the airborne RAF pilots dogfighting over the Channel, and in the heat of battle their language both to the ground and to their comrades was uninhibited and coarse. The control-room commander decided that it was much too rough for "my ladies" to have to listen to, and ordered them to move out of the range of the loud-speakers. A pert squadron officer, speaking on behalf of her staff, refused.

"Good heavens, sir," she said, "most of us have been listening to words like that since we first heard our fathers and brothers cussing around the house." And, the forthright young lady added, "I expect we're going to hear much worse than this before this lot is over."

She was right.

READY FOR JERRY

By way of preparation for air raids by the Germans, bathing-suit-clad vacationers on a Devonshire beach combine gas-mask drill with a stint filling sandbags.

BUTTONING UP FOR THE BATTLE

Road signs, which had been removed to confuse possible invaders, await storage. British drivers turned out to be the only victims of this measure.

As the Germans, victorious in France by the spring of 1940, turned to finish off England, few Britons doubted a bleak prediction by the Imperial Defense Committee: in a German air attack, 600,000 would die, more than a million would be wounded; no one even guessed at what the casualties might be if the Germans invaded. Herbert Morrison, the tough cockney chief of London's city government, admitted he was "a frightened man. Frightened by what's going to happen if we aren't ready."

Morrison needn't have worried. Britons did prepare, with stoicism, enthusiasm and good humor. Not since the days of Napoleon had England had to give serious thought to invasion, and few people had any idea what to do. Zoo officials wondered how to keep animals from escaping if their cages were bombed. The government hastily organized a Home Guard of civilians, recruiting almost anything that moved: one squad consisted of eight highly decorated generals and one inexperienced shop clerk. Some of the women who joined auxiliary services never could seriously believe there was any sense in carrying a gas mask; their masks quickly became jammed or broken from sharing space with cigarettes, powder compacts and gloves.

Ambulance drivers and other motorists faced some irksome hazards. In the daytime, they had to find their way without the aid of road signs, which had all been removed to baffle potential invaders. At night, the blackout compounded that problem by adding the dangers of near-total darkness. One London bus driver, following a long night's work, groused, "If that's what it's going to be like, I'd be better off joining up and driving a tank."

The German soldiers never did arrive, of course. But the bombers did. When the dreaded raids began, the British bore up calmly, ready or not. One matron noted in the wake of her first bombing: "The maids were cool as cucumbers. . . . But we clean forgot to open the front door in case anyone wanted shelter. Also, we forgot to dress, which was silly, and wouldn't have done in winter. However, we shall know not to make these mistakes next time."

A keeper at London's Regent Park Zoo coaxes a boa constrictor into a crate—its home during air raids. The electric light on the crate kept the snake warm.

City of London employees ring a lamppost with white paint to make it visible for drivers and pedestrians during blackouts. Despite such precautions, traffic deaths climbed during the first month after the lights went out; but they dropped when the after-dark speed limit was subsequently reduced to 20 miles per hour.

An aide fits blackout shields over the headlights of a British government car. The cardboard masks the lights' high beams altogether, while the heavy paper projections prevent any glow from the low beams from shining upward.

The windows of a London commuter train get a coat of dark blue paint, which permitted night travelers to use the trains' standard reading lamps instead of the dim blue bulbs that had been installed initially as a blackout measure.

Volunteers on a London street impersonate the victims of imaginary bombs in an air-raid drill. A helmeted air-raid squad man crossing the street at rear had the job of calling for first-aid teams and seeing all four "wounded" off to a nearby hospital. The bravura performance was under the direction of the warden at right, his helmet marked with a "W," and Admiral Sir Edward Evans (wearing homburg), one of London's two civil defense chiefs. Later, the Admiral reviewed the acting ability of the mock casualties as being "most realistic."

Bemused inhabitants of North London inspect some of the first so-called
Anderson Bomb Shelters issued to Britons. Prefabricated sections of
the steel shelters, named after Home Secretary Sir John Anderson, were
given free to householders, along with a bag of nuts and bolts and
sketchy instructions for assembly. The shelters, made of corrugated steel
arches, were supposed to be sunk deep into the ground. Unfortunately,
virtually all the ground in these urban areas of London was thickly paved.

Two Londoners test the fit of the combined side and roof sections of their air-raid shelter. The huts were theoretically designed to hold a family of six.

Housewives line up to salvage scrap, responding to posters like the one above. The official editing on the bottom line was meant to persuade Londoners to abandon the prewar practice of burning rubbish, initiated to cut municipal expenses and hence, to lower taxes (called rates). Instead, the government now wanted to recycle everything possible, from newspapers to brass beds. Some women bought lightweight aluminum cookware and then contributed their heavy old aluminum and iron pots to the war effort. And one peer gave the body of his Rolls-Royce to the recycling drive; the chassis was converted into a mobile canteen.

Members of the Women's Auxiliary Territorial Service, a volunteer group that relieved rear-echelon soldiers for combat, try out courier motorcycles. Critics of such involvement by females protested that Britain's women might soon be at the front. One writer mocked the antifeminist uproar with a poem about the changing roles at home and at military installations like England's Aldershot training center: "Rockabye baby, or Daddy will spank. Mother's at Aldershot driving a tank."

Female letter carriers troop out in uniform to start delivery, with their mailbags slung over their shoulders. The Post Office van seen in the background bears a sign that warns against gossip that might be overheard by spies.

Wearing gas masks and gas-proof coveralls, the two-woman crew of an ambulance, newly converted from a London carpet-cleaner's van, lines up for inspection. A more conventional ambulance is parked behind their vehicle.

Munitions workers, with their hair bound neatly and safely into scarves, check a consignment of artillery shells. Women took on such work at least partly at the instigation of Winston Churchill, who said in January 1940, "Millions of new workers will be needed, and more than a million women must come boldly forward into our war industries."

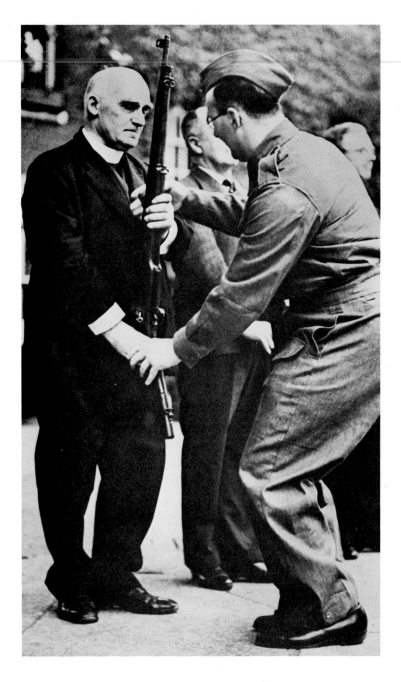

Dr. Jocelyn Henry Temple Perkins, a 70-year-old clergyman recruited for the Home Guard, the auxiliary defense force that had signed up more than a million Britons by August 1940, endures some instruction in the manual of arms. Retired noncoms were the instructors for the recruits, most of whom lacked uniforms for weeks after joining up.

Two Home Guardsmen on roller skates, the better to speed through city streets and attack paratroopers, pin down a comrade playing the role of a German. In combating armored vehicles, the woefully underequipped Home Guard was trained to thrust crowbars into tank track wheels. Recruits were told: "Better to use any form of attack than none at all."

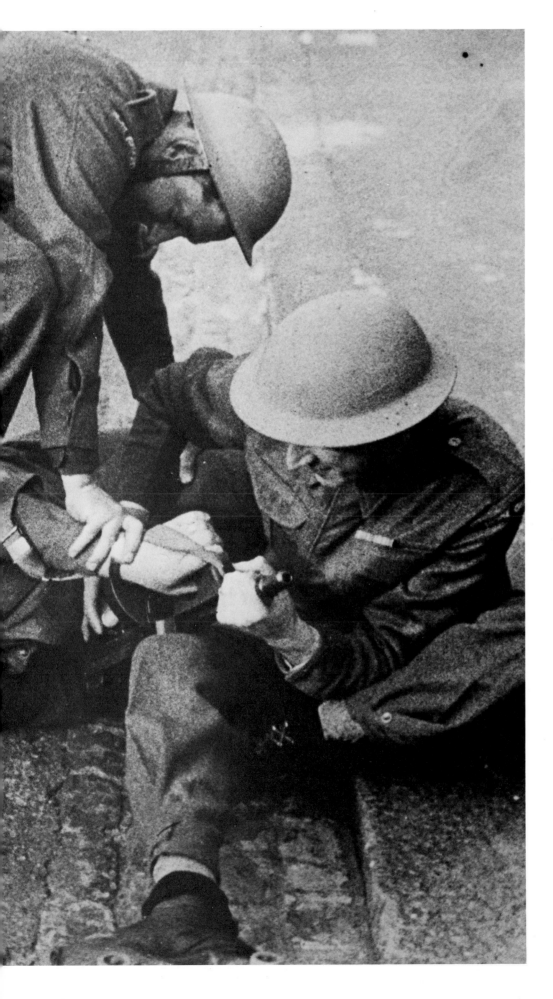

Camouflaged with burlap, soot and leafy branches, a Home Guardsman practices the art of concealment. He and his fellows also learned how to immobilize an automobile by pouring sugar into the gas tank, and how to use kitchen kerosene to make homemade grenades.

A Home Guardsman armed with the British Army's Lee-Enfield rifle mans a roadblock made of barbed wire and a horse-drawn hay rake. This checkpoint also

boasted a World War I light machine gun (foreground), whose crew stands nonchalantly aside while a comrade makes an I.D. check on an auto driver.

2

The legend has grown since the fateful summer of 1940 that the Battle of Britain was a David-and-Goliath confrontation between a brave but weakly defended island kingdom and the mightiest air power the world had yet known. This impression of the Luftwaffe as not only powerful but invincible was, initially, the work of Nazi propagandists, and was skillfully developed in the years before World War II—and with notable success. Terrifying stories of the Luftwaffe's capabilities were fed to every distinguished visitor to Germany during that period. The visitors in turn went back to France or Britain or the United States and petrified their listeners with predictions of the fire and brimstone likely to rain down upon any nation foolish enough to incur German hostility. One of the travelers, Colonel Charles A. Lindbergh, toured German air stations and factories and noted in a memorandum of September 22, 1938, to the United States Ambassador to Britain, Joseph P. Kennedy:

"I feel certain that German air strength is greater than that of all other European countries combined, and that she is constantly increasing her margin of leadership. . . . Germany now has the means of destroying London, Paris and Prague if she wishes to do so. England and France together have not enough modern war planes for effective defense or counterattack."

Although Lindbergh's German hosts had made sure that he saw only what they wanted him to see, he was not far wrong in his estimate of relative strengths—in 1938. Where he was mistaken was in the amount of destruction the Luftwaffe could heap upon large cities. Nevertheless, his message was heard, both by the many air officers in Western nations who believed that bombers alone could win wars, and by their civilian leaders.

The image of the Luftwaffe as unbeatable was enhanced by its performance in Poland in September of 1939. It completely wiped out the Polish Air Force and inflicted severe damage on Warsaw. And when, in May of 1940, much of the city of Rotterdam was reduced to rubble, the might of the Luftwaffe no longer seemed arguable.

How, then, could the Royal Air Force, its morale reportedly low and its numbers depleted as a result of the defeat in western Europe, stay in the sky once the Luftwaffe appeared over Britain? How could it expect to pit its puny strength against the enemy's? The Luftwaffe was estimated

THE PREFIGHT ODDS

to have some 4,500 first-line aircraft, the RAF 2,900—hardly the best of odds for the British to contemplate.

But though the Luftwaffe was stronger than the RAF—indeed the strongest air force then existing—the protagonists in the Battle of Britain were much more closely matched than was generally realized. In the quality if not the quantity of its planes, Britain could compete favorably with the Luftwaffe. Moreover, Britain had far outstripped its foe in developing the all-seeing eye of radar. The British possessed, furthermore, the incalculable advantage of fighting on their own home ground. This meant, among other things, that many RAF pilots shot down in aerial combat over their homeland could be recovered and returned to action, while downed German pilots would be permanently lost to the Luftwaffe. And, finally, each day that Hitler delayed the launching of his projected all-out air attack, Britain's frantically speeded-up aircraft factories gave it the chance to narrow the gap in numbers of planes.

In this endeavor the British got help from the enemy. German industry was still operating on a peacetime footing in mid-1940; speeding up production, Hitler believed, would alarm a population that had been repeatedly told they would see a string of easy successes. (Indeed, the Führer himself thought the war was all but won.) What production there was had been directed elsewhere: in allocating priorities for scarce raw materials, the army's guns came first.

The British also benefited from spotty Luftwaffe management, both in procuring planes and in developing new models. These crucial tasks had been assigned to General Ernst Udet, a hard-drinking, womanizing, happy-go-lucky World War I ace who had served with Luftwaffe chief Göring in the Richthofen Flying Circus. Appointing Udet as the Luftwaffe's technical chief was Hitler's idea; he had decided in early 1938 that Udet was not only an excellent pilot, which he was, but also a technical genius—which he was not.

Nor was he an administrator. Under the pressure of war preparations, his bailiwick ballooned from nine to 28 departments. Department heads often had to wait months for a key decision from Udet; he liked to sit around chinning with aides about the planes of the future. Even his conferences with Reich Marshal Göring, convened to solve the Luftwaffe's immediate problems, often ended as long sessions of reminiscence about their World War I exploits.

But Udet's status as an old comrade of Göring's could not save him when the Luftwaffe's internal troubles began to surface in 1940. Göring and his chief deputy Erhard Milch—the two men who actually had the final say on what planes were to be produced and in what quantities—turned on Udet and made him a scapegoat, driving him to suicide a year later. Over his body was found a scrawled farewell message to the Reich Marshal: "Iron Man, you deserted me."

Trouble of an even more fundamental nature was to dog the Luftwaffe during the Battle of Britain. This problem was created by the very concept on which the German Air Force had been based. The Luftwaffe's creators had envisioned it as an adjunct to the German Army, primarily providing offensive support for ground troops. And so the building program had put great emphasis on dive bombers and medium "level-flight" bombers. As had been proved in Poland and France, both types performed superbly at such tactical tasks as disrupting communications and providing "flying artillery" in support of deep-driving panzer spearheads. But they were not intended to inflict the kind of havoc—the devastation of entire cities and industries—that were going to be required to defeat Britain.

To this end, long-range heavy bombers, capable of carrying massive bomb loads, were needed—and the Luftwaffe had neglected their development. The failure was in part due to the death of General Walther Wever, the Luftwaffe's first Chief of Staff. He had been an advocate of heavy bombers, and had launched a program calling for long-range, four-engine planes capable of "flying right around Britain under combat conditions." But Wever was killed in an air crash in 1936, and the program languished. Subsequently, the Germans developed what was to be the one truly strategic bomber in their arsenal, the Heinkel-177, but it suffered from an unpredictable tendency to catch fire and incinerate its crews, and was not even operational until 1944.

The best of the German medium bombers was the Junkers-88, a fast, rugged machine with a 1,500-mile range, but it was just coming into production at the time of the Battle of Britain. As a result, the work horses of the Luftwaffe's medium-bomber stable were the Dornier-17 and the Heinkel-111. Both had relatively short ranges and were vulnerable to fighters coming in at them from certain angles.

THE LUFTWAFFE'S BELLWETHER BOMBERS

The Luftwaffe's massive attacks during the Battle of Britain were spearheaded by two aging but effective bombers: the Dornier-17 *(right)* and the Heinkel-111H *(far right)*. Developed in the early 1930s, the Dornier could carry a maximum explosive load of 2,200 pounds, and, in the hands of an expert pilot, could destroy its targets with deadly accuracy: on August 15, 1940, a low-flying Dornier pin-point bombed the components store of the Short Brothers aircraft factory in Rochester, causing extensive delays in the production of the bombers the British so desperately needed. The Heinkel, which was also a middle-aged aircraft but which had a 5,500-pound bomb capacity, could deal out proportionately greater destruction—and did.

But neither bomber could outrun or, more importantly, outshoot the RAF's Spitfires and Hurricanes. The Dornier, which was the outgrowth of a 1934 mail-plane design, could manage only 265 mph at full throttle; the Heinkel was 7 mph slower. Moreover, both of the German bombers were inadequately armed to defend themselves from the British fighters. In desperation, Dornier crews took to carrying hand grenades with them, which they tossed out of the windows of their planes at pursuing fighters. And Heinkel airmen were known to throw out tin boxes that were attached to reels of wire, in hopes of fouling the propellers of enemy craft.

What both bombers lacked in speed and fire power was made up in numbers. In June 1940, the Luftwaffe deployed more than 1,000 bombers in the Battle of Britain, while the RAF could count only 565 service-ready fighters. Moreover, when the Germans first shifted to night attacks, these bombers proved to be less vulnerable than they were during the day. British night-spotting techniques were still rudimentary, and the ground defenses, particularly of such large cities as London, were unable to track the attacking planes effectively.

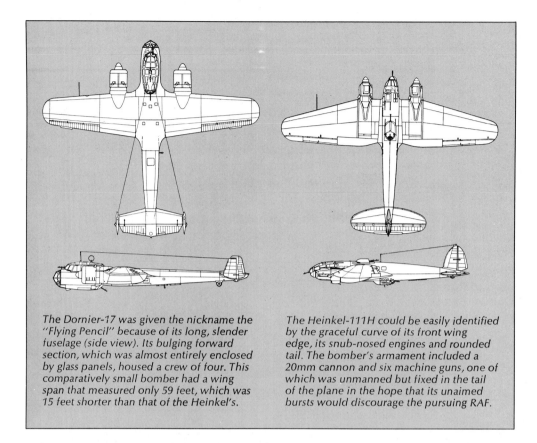

The Dornier-17 was given the nickname the "Flying Pencil" because of its long, slender fuselage (side view). Its bulging forward section, which was almost entirely enclosed by glass panels, housed a crew of four. This comparatively small bomber had a wing span that measured only 59 feet, which was 15 feet shorter than that of the Heinkel's.

The Heinkel-111H could be easily identified by the graceful curve of its front wing edge, its snub-nosed engines and rounded tail. The bomber's armament included a 20mm cannon and six machine guns, one of which was unmanned but fixed in the tail of the plane in the hope that its unaimed bursts would discourage the pursuing RAF.

The crew of a Heinkel-111H, back from a July 1940 mission over the English Channel, removes its gear after landing. An early version of this bomber had scored substantial successes in the Spanish civil war, where it could easily outrun opposing fighters, but by World War II the lumbering Heinkel was obsolescent.

Ironically, the Luftwaffe's worst failure in the skies over Britain was to come from its most reliable plane during the Continental campaign: the Junkers-87 dive bomber, otherwise known as the Stuka. The Stuka was Ernst Udet's brain child. On a visit to the United States before the War, he had seen a Curtiss Hell Diver in action, and on his return home promptly went to work on an adaptation.

The Stuka proved highly effective against Polish warships in the Baltic, Polish troops on the Vistula plain, British troop transports off Norway, and Allied infantry in Belgium and France. For one thing, its bomb drop was extremely accurate; the plane could be held perfectly straight as it swooped down, thus becoming, in effect, a kind of huge gun pointed at the target. And it was capable of creating panic in its prospective victims; instead of producing the usual whine of a plunging plane, the Stuka was fitted with vanes that emitted an unearthly scream.

Over Britain, however, the Stuka turned out to be decidedly vulnerable to a fighter plane with a good operational speed. Once a Stuka peeled off into its dive, it attracted enemy fighters "as honey attracts flies," in the words of one RAF pilot. There was no effective armament to beat off a fighter attacking from the rear; and since the Stuka carried its bomb load beneath the fuselage, air resistance generated by the load made its dive comparatively slow, a maximum of only 150 miles an hour. Thus a fast-attacking fighter had plenty of time to go in for the kill. The result was to be a daily massacre of Stukas by RAF fighters.

The Luftwaffe's basic fighter plane was the formidable Messerschmitt-109, whose maximum speed, 354 miles an hour, made it one of the fastest planes in active service in any air force. But because Luftwaffe strategy had called for a preponderance of ground-support bombers, the Germans had not built enough Me-109s. When the Battle of Britain began, Germany was desperately short of fighters needed to fulfill the various tasks demanded of them. Moreover, thanks to organizational shortcomings, the Luftwaffe lacked sufficient replacements for downed fighters.

That was not all. The Me-109 was a splendid plane for free-flying combat against other fighters, or for shooting down enemy bombers. But Göring insisted that it should also serve as escort to the fleets of bombers slated to drop their lethal loads on Britain. When its pilots were forced to fly as body-guards to bombers, they felt as frustrated as polo ponies acting as outriders on a herd of slaughterhouse steers.

But the Me-109's worst fault as a combatant in the Battle of Britain was its lack of range. Even the fact that it flew from bases in France that were close to Britain did not really solve the problem. A single-engine plane, the Me-109 carried enough fuel for 80 minutes' flying. However, it took 30 minutes to attain sufficient height over France and reach the English coast, and 30 minutes to get back to base—which left only 20 minutes for operations over England. Large numbers of Me-109s failed to make it back not because they were shot down, but because they ran out of fuel.

In an attempt to make up for the Me-109's deficiencies, the Luftwaffe had produced the Messerschmitt-110, a twin-engine plane with a range that was almost twice that of the Me-109. Göring announced that the Me-110s would be assembled into "destroyer units" that would become "the strategic fighter elite of the Luftwaffe." This prophecy was not destined to be fulfilled. With a maximum speed of 340 miles per hour, the Me-110 was about 30 miles per hour slower than the British Supermarine Spitfire with which it was to clash. It was big, hence easy to recognize and hit; it was clumsy and lacked good acceleration. Thus, it did little to relieve the Me-109 of its battle chores.

Despite these weaknesses, the German air armada that assembled in occupied territory for the final assault on Britain was a fearsome force. Göring and the men under his direction who put it together had many reasons to believe that it would soon cause the British to buckle. Its past successes had imbued its crews with high morale. Confidence was further heightened by intelligence reports seeming to confirm that the RAF had been perilously weakened by the French campaign, and that only a feeble air defense stood between the Luftwaffe and a victory opening Britain to invasion.

This was a fatal miscalculation.

The British fighter force had indeed suffered heavy losses during the German blitzkrieg in France. In the first three days alone, 232 RAF fighters had been shot down, destroyed on the ground or captured, and these numbers rose as the campaign reached its crescendo. In response to frantic appeals from British and French military and civilian leaders for more fighters to be sent from Britain, Prime Minister

Churchill had promised that, if necessary, he would "cut our defense to the bone" in order to get the added planes across the Channel and stave off the Allied defeat. And indeed, if he had kept his promise the RAF's fighter strength —then chiefly consisting of the older Rolls-Royce-powered Hawker Hurricane—might have been nearly wiped out.

Air Chief Marshal Sir Hugh Dowding, Commander-in-Chief of RAF Fighter Command, had warned Churchill that if he sent more planes to France at this late juncture "we shall not have a single Hurricane left in France *or in this country.*" Dowding had described as "wastage" the policy of attempting to go to the aid of an already defeated France, and demanded that the RAF's fighters be kept at home in preparation for Britain's own impending travail.

Hugh Caswall Tremenheere Dowding was 58 years old in 1940, and was known in the RAF as "Stuffy." The nickname referred to his way of life—he was a vegetarian, a nondrinker, a bird watcher and a spiritualist—rather than to his views on air warfare. Though a veteran of the Royal Flying Corps on the Western Front in World War I, he could in no sense be derided as a holdover from "the joystick generation." More than many of his younger colleagues, he had actively crusaded for modernization of the RAF.

It was Dowding who had fought for speedy, up-to-date fighters for Britain's air defense force. Once he got them —though never as many as he wanted—he had forced the Air Ministry to fit them with bulletproof windshields, which the bureaucrats in Whitehall considered an unnecessary expense. He had won this argument by saying: "I do not see why the gangsters of Chicago should be able to have bulletproof glass when our pilots cannot." Dowding had also encouraged a recruiting campaign to attract Britain's brightest young men into the cockpits of the new planes.

Against Churchill's emotional promise to send the beleaguered French every plane they asked for, Dowding had opposed cold statistics. On May 16, he had brought to a meeting of the British Cabinet a graph of the RAF's losses in the war to date. If fighters continued to be risked on French airfields, Dowding warned, the line on the graph would soon plunge to zero, and "defeat in France will involve the complete and irremediable defeat of this country."

However, if an adequate fighter force were retained at

An RAF bomber crew ambles back to base after a night mission over Germany, dropping propaganda leaflets (inset) that claim the German High Command is lying about Luftwaffe plane losses and urge: "German People! Demand the truth!" Though British politicians and some high brass cherished such leaflet drops for their assumed psychological impact, pilots were scornful of them. One officer claimed "the only thing achieved was . . . to supply the Continent's requirements for toilet paper."

home, if the Royal Navy did not suffer too many losses and if ground forces were suitably organized to resist invasion, Dowding said, "we should be able to carry on the war singlehanded for some time, if not indefinitely."

The planes were never sent. They did, however, provide some air cover for the evacuation of the British Expeditionary Force from Dunkirk. In attempting to keep the Luftwaffe away from the rescue ships shuttling to and fro across the Channel, the RAF fought some savage and costly battles, losing 106 fighters and 75 pilots. Even so, returned soldiers were bitter about the RAF's failure to give them greater protection. With other losses since the start of the blitzkrieg in the Low Countries and France, the total RAF fighter force had now been reduced by one fourth. On June 5, by the time the last ships from Dunkirk were back in British ports, Britain counted only 466 serviceable fighters, with just 36 more in reserve. The Germans, encouraged by their own propaganda, considered the RAF a spent force, and the Luftwaffe pilots chafed to give it the *coup de grâce*.

For the British, two factors changed what could have been a hopeless situation. First, Hitler's failure to attack Britain immediately after Dunkirk provided a period of respite. Second, a 61-year-old dynamo of a man, the Canadian-born newspaper publisher Lord Beaverbrook, was placed in charge of Britain's aircraft building program. He proceeded to galvanize the industry, requiring a seven-day week and "work without stopping." No potential source of supply escaped Beaverbrook's eye. To collect the aluminum essential for building planes, he appealed to the women of Britain to empty their households of all items containing the metal. The response was a flood of pots, pans, kettles, vacuum cleaners and bathroom fittings.

In the month that followed the evacuation at Dunkirk, British workers built 446 new fighters for the RAF—at least 100 more than the Germans were turning out for the Luftwaffe. British production was to exceed Germany's for the rest of the war. All over Britain, fighter planes or their components were being produced not only in factories but also in small garages and workshops. Other planes were beginning to flow in from Canada and the United States.

The fighter planes of the Royal Air Force were of three types: the older, reliable Hurricane, the Supermarine Spitfire and the Boulton-Paul Defiant. The Hurricane had been the mainstay of the RAF since the war's outset. Sturdy and dependable, it was, in effect, a flying gun-platform. Early models were equipped with eight machine guns. Later, four more machine guns were added, and by 1940 some were fitted with four 20mm cannons. However, it had two fairly serious faults. It was slightly slower than the Messerschmitt-109, and the highest altitude at which it could efficiently fly was 1,000 feet lower than the Me-109's 35,000-foot service ceiling. Also, the Hurricane had a blind spot that allowed an enemy plane to sneak in from above.

The Hurricane was gradually being replaced by the Spitfire, a far superior plane. Somewhat faster than the Me-109, the Spitfire was much more maneuverable: it could turn inside its opponent in combat—a vital advantage, since it enabled the Spitfire to get behind an Me-109 in a dogfight. This was a plane the Germans learned to respect.

However, the Spitfire, like the Hurricane, also had a serious weakness. The engine had no fuel-injection mechanism, so that when the Spitfire went into a steep dive it was apt to conk out, often with fatal results to plane and pilot.

Britain's lack of a fuel-injection device resulted from one of the war's dramatic bungles. One day in early 1940 a British aircraft engineer who had done intelligence work for his country was sitting in a café in Belgrade when a stranger unaccountably handed him a paper parcel. When he looked inside he found it contained an Me-109 fuel-injector pump, which he immediately recognized. The engineer passed the pump on to officials at the British Embassy in the Yugoslav capital. But they failed to appreciate its significance. They sent it on to the Air Ministry in London by mail, via Italy. It never reached its destination.

The third RAF fighter, the Defiant, was a two-seater about the size of a Hurricane but without the Hurricane's blind spot behind the cockpit; moreover, the Defiant was fitted with an armored turret with four machine guns in the rear and a wide field of fire. So long as German pilots mistook this aircraft for a Hurricane and tried to take it from behind, it could deal them a deadly lesson. But once they learned to recognize the Defiant, it proved to be highly vulnerable. Low speed and rate of climb, as well as a general lack of agility, made the Defiant as ineffectual during daylight operations as the Me-110 was to prove for the Germans.

THE FIGHTERS THAT STAVED OFF THE LUFTWAFFE

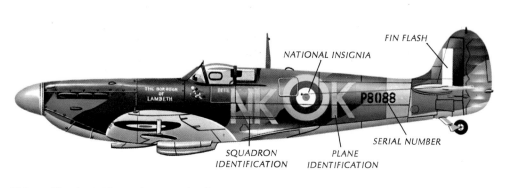

FIN FLASH

NATIONAL INSIGNIA

P8088

SQUADRON
IDENTIFICATION

PLANE
IDENTIFICATION

SERIAL NUMBER

This profile of a Spitfire II shows its slender nose with straight upper line and upward curving chin, bubble cockpit hood and small, rounded tail fin. The large NK identifies its squadron, placing it in 118 Squadron; the single K farther aft identifies the specific plane. Between the two sets of letters is the RAF bull's-eye. The serial number, P8088, is in front of the tail, which has a tricolor rudder marking, or fin flash, bearing the colors of the British flag.

Seen from above, the Spitfire is distinguished by its thin fuselage, and elliptical wings carrying eight recessed .303 caliber machine guns.

The survival of Britain in the great air battle of the summer and fall of 1940 was made possible in large measure by a superb pair of fighter planes: the Spitfire *(above)* and the Hurricane *(below)*. Of the two, the Spitfire was the superior in most respects. It had the edge in speed, 370 mph versus 325 mph for the Hurricane. Although it could not match the climbing rate of its chief adversary, the Messerschmitt-109, the Spitfire was swift enough to outrun the German plane—a feat that the Hurricane was not able to match.

Adapted from the design of a racing sea-plane, the first Spitfire fighter plane rolled off the assembly line at the Supermarine Division of Vickers-Armstrong before the outbreak of World War II, in 1938. Its streamlined design enabled it to carry a pilot, a 1,175-hp Rolls-Royce engine and eight machine guns, yet it still managed to achieve such a high degree of maneuverability that it could turn in a tighter radius than any other front-line fighter. The quickness and agility of the Spitfire prompted one aircraft expert to describe this airplane as "the best conventional defense fighter of the war."

A rugged defender

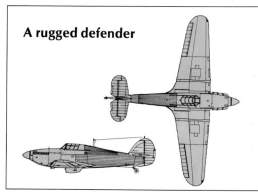

Although it lacked the beauty, speed and quick-turning ability of the Spitfire, the slightly larger Hawker Hurricane was a key weapon in Britain's air defense during the summer of 1940. The Hurricane fighter first saw service in 1937—almost a year after the first Spitfire got off the ground—and in September 1940, when the Battle of Britain was well under way, nearly half of Britain's 61 fighter squadrons were equipped with Hurricanes, while only 20 of them had Spitfires.

Although the Hurricane's top speed, a re-spectable 325 mph, was almost 30 mph less than that of the Messerschmitt, its superior range—600 miles—enabled it to remain in the air longer than the German fighter. Because the heavily armored Hurricanes were slower and less maneuverable than the Spitfires, the British developed the tactic of letting them take on the vulnerable German bombers while the Spitfires went after the fighters. As a result, the Hurricanes shot down more planes in the Battle of Britain than any other plane.

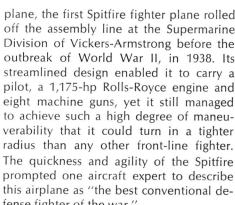

Britain had its bombers, too; they were sent out to attack targets in Germany's industrial heartland, the Ruhr, and in German-controlled Channel ports, where increasing numbers of German ships were assembling for Operation *Sea Lion,* the projected seaborne invasion of Britain. But at this stage of the war, British bombing raids—though they did succeed in diverting some of the Germans' air units—were essentially a sideshow. What was at stake in the summer of 1940 was the defense of the British Isles, and that task would mainly devolve upon the RAF's fighters.

The Germans would also have to cope with Britain's ground defenses—most notably, radar. In 1940 this remarkable device was still relatively new, but it had already proved its ability to detect distant objects, and to determine their location and their speed, by analyzing the ultra-high-frequency radio waves reflected from their surfaces.

As early as 1936, the British had begun to build a chain of radar stations around the United Kingdom from the Orkney Islands at Scotland's northern tip to the Isle of Wight in the Channel. The heaviest concentration lay along the south and east coasts of England—an "invisible bastion," as British officials liked to call it, against whatever air power the Germans might hurl across the Channel.

The Germans knew about radar—they called their own system Freya, after the Teutonic goddess who protects those slain in battle—and in some ways they were ahead of the British in radar technology. They had been concerned enough about Britain's progress by the late spring of 1939 to send their great dirigible, the *Graf Zeppelin,* across the North Sea to cruise near the English coast and record the range and frequency of the radar beams that were encountered. As it happened, something went wrong—probably with the receivers installed in the gondola beneath the airship—and the crew heard nothing. British radar plotters, following the giant blip the *Graf Zeppelin* formed on their screens, were overjoyed when the airship's repeated signals back to its base revealed the mission was fruitless.

Unfortunately for the Germans, the programing of their own radar had been put into the hands of their navy. Though Hitler's admirals saw the device as useful in ocean reconnaissance, they failed to appreciate its importance in air combat. On the other hand, radar's proponents in Britain had always seen it as an invaluable handmaiden of the RAF and antiaircraft defenses. Its two leading advocates were Robert Watson-Watt, a Scots physicist who was head of radio research for the National Physics Laboratory, and Sir Henry Tizard, scientific adviser to the Air Ministry. Watson-Watt and his team of experts, some of them refugees from the Nazis, worked all through 1939 and the spring of 1940 to improve the already-established radar chain around Britain, deepening its range and improving its clarity.

Well before the Battle of Britain began, Watson-Watt was able to tell a Cabinet scientific advisory committee that his radar stations could now pinpoint aircraft rising into the sky up to 150 miles away. At this statement, another member of the committee snorted in disbelief. The skeptic was Professor Frederick Lindemann, long an intimate of Churchill's and now his most influential scientific adviser. Since Churchill's arrival at 10 Downing Street, all scientific decisions made by the government first had to be approved by Lindemann. The professor took little stock in any scientific project favored by Sir Henry Tizard—his onetime friend but now his detested rival—and he opposed giving radar the top priority its sponsors wanted. Lindemann preferred his own pet projects for preventing enemy bombers from breaking through, such as the detection of incoming aircraft by infrared devices and the aerial bombing of such formations after they were detected.

Had Churchill become Prime Minister earlier, before the outbreak of World War II, Lindemann's opposition to radar might have come in time to prevent it from playing its crucial role in the Battle of Britain. But by the summer of 1940 it was too late for Lindemann to block progress. Plotters were already on the alert at radar stations from Land's End, at the western tip of the Channel coast, all the way to the North Sea. These stations monitored enemy air activity in occupied France and reported plane movements back to the central plotting room at RAF Fighter Command headquarters at Bentley Priory, just outside London.

Named for the ancient religious retreat that once occupied the grounds, Bentley Priory was an oddly romantic choice for its new purposes. An 18th Century mansion that had harbored such guests as the Duke of Wellington and Lord Nelson, the Priory had metamorphosed from a private estate to a hotel to a girls' school to an abandoned near-

A DEADLY RIVAL FOR THE RAF'S FIGHTERS

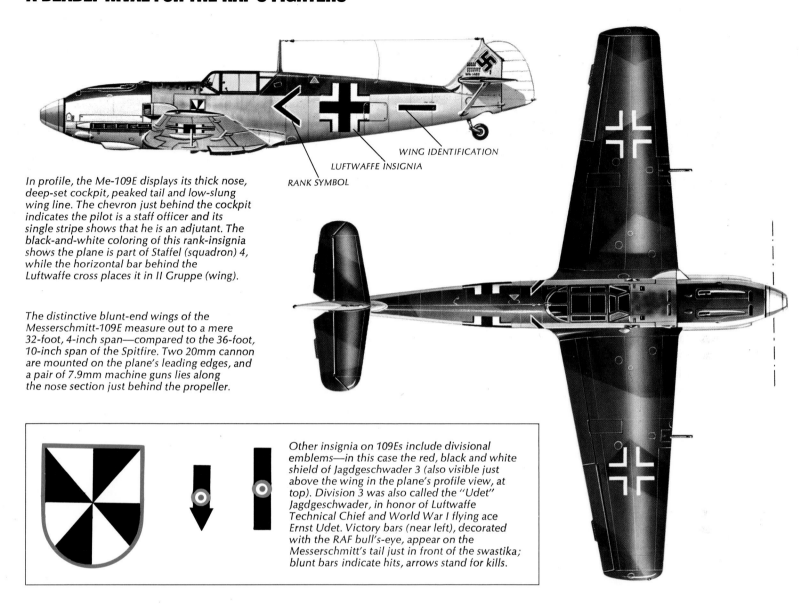

WING IDENTIFICATION

LUFTWAFFE INSIGNIA

RANK SYMBOL

In profile, the Me-109E displays its thick nose, deep-set cockpit, peaked tail and low-slung wing line. The chevron just behind the cockpit indicates the pilot is a staff officer and its single stripe shows that he is an adjutant. The black-and-white coloring of this rank-insignia shows the plane is part of Staffel (squadron) 4, while the horizontal bar behind the Luftwaffe cross places it in II Gruppe (wing).

The distinctive blunt-end wings of the Messerschmitt-109E measure out to a mere 32-foot, 4-inch span—compared to the 36-foot, 10-inch span of the Spitfire. Two 20mm cannon are mounted on the plane's leading edges, and a pair of 7.9mm machine guns lies along the nose section just behind the propeller.

Other insignia on 109Es include divisional emblems—in this case the red, black and white shield of Jagdgeschwader 3 (also visible just above the wing in the plane's profile view, at top). Division 3 was also called the "Udet" Jagdgeschwader, in honor of Luftwaffe Technical Chief and World War I flying ace Ernst Udet. Victory bars (near left), decorated with the RAF bull's-eye, appear on the Messerschmitt's tail just in front of the swastika; blunt bars indicate hits, arrows stand for kills.

Perhaps the deadliest weapon in the Luftwaffe's arsenal during the Battle of Britain was the stub-winged Messerschmitt Bf-109E fighter. Called the "Emil" by German airmen (and often referred to simply as the Me-109), the plane had an initial climbing rate of 3,100 feet per minute—against the Spitfire's 2,530. Though its top speed of 354 mph was 16 mph slower than the Spitfire's maximum, the 109's ceiling of 36,000 feet gave it a 2,000-foot advantage over the British plane. These factors, plus a fuel-injection system, which kept its 1,150-hp Daimler-Benz engine going in the pressure of steep, sudden dives, made it possible for skilled Luftwaffe pilots to maneuver

their 109s above and behind opponents, and then dive down on them for the kill.

Although some German fliers candidly considered the Spitfire more maneuverable, British pilots who had a chance to handle captured 109s tended to disagree, rating the two a close match on this critical score. And all pilots agreed that only an expert could successfully operate the very tricky 109. Extremely sensitive to the pilot's touch, it was hard to hold steady and was cursed with a barely controllable tendency to veer to the left on takeoff and to the right or left on landing. Moreover, to achieve maximum speed and maneuverability, its designers had sacrificed

a certain amount of structural strength, which sometimes caused its wings or landing gear to collapse under stress. For the Battle of Britain, however, in which the 109's principal function was to fly escort, its most serious defect was its very modest 410-mile maximum cruising distance, which allowed only 20 minutes of fighting time over enemy terrain. On at least one occasion this range limitation proved costly. On a two-hour bomber escort mission to Britain, twelve 109s from Luftwaffe ace Adolf Galland's wing headed home. Five of them barely managed to pancake down on the French shore, but the seven others went down in the Channel.

ruin. Now it had a new lease on life as the top-secret hub of Britain's defensive air operations.

In the plotting room, members of the Women's Auxiliary Air Force (WAAFs) moved aircraft symbols across a giant chart of the area under radar surveillance, according to reports coming in from the coastal stations. Supplementing these reports were others telephoned in by members of the Observer Corps, watching the skies from hilltops, church towers and other vantage points. Aside from radar and RAF spotters, these observers were the chief source of information on enemy activity in the air over Britain.

From a balcony in the plotting room, Air Chief Marshal Dowding and his air-controllers would watch the great chart below them. The moment a flight of German planes took to the skies over France and began to climb, the WAAFs would begin to move the symbols across the chart, and RAF battle dispositions would be made.

In deciding how to allocate these dispositions, Dowding had another invaluable aid besides radar—an aid so secret that not even his subordinate commanders knew about it. The British had acquired a machine that enabled them to break the complex German code; thus they could estimate the Luftwaffe's intended targets and the numbers of aircraft that were involved even before the planes left the ground. Transcripts of the Germans' radio traffic were available to Dowding when he sent his own planes aloft.

By mid-July, 1940, both sides were primed for the great test that was coming. The main thrust of the Luftwaffe's attack was to be carried out by its two strongest air fleets. One was Luftflotte 3, under Field Marshal Hugo Sperrle, with forward headquarters near the once fashionable French resort of Deauville. Sperrle's forces faced the Isle of Wight, the port of Southampton, and the great British naval bases at Portsmouth and Plymouth. Luftflotte 2, under Field Marshal Albert Kesselring, had its forward headquarters on the cliffs near Boulogne in northeastern France, looking across the Strait of Dover and round the southeastern corner of England into the Thames and the Port of London. A third air fleet, Luftflotte 5, operated out of Norway and Denmark; it was to play only a minor role in the battle.

Göring and his advisers had divided the operation against Britain into three main phases. First would come the campaign over the Channel to sink all British merchant shipping, to attack Royal Navy ships, bases and installations, and to destroy or drive out of the sky any RAF fighters that sought to prevent these maneuvers. Second would come a massive onslaught to paralyze Britain's air arm once and for all by obliterating all RAF fields, defenses and aircraft factories in a gigantic combined bomber and fighter blitz. This operation initially was dubbed the "grand slam," by Göring's bridge-playing deputy, Field Marshal Milch, but it soon received the more warlike code name of *Eagle Attack*. In the third and final phase, the Luftwaffe would cover and help implement Operation *Sea Lion*, the invasion of the British Isles by the combined forces of the Reich.

For Phase One, the neutralization of the English Channel, neither Göring nor his aides anticipated much difficulty, and nothing like the whole strength of Air Fleets 2 and 3 was assigned to it. Instead, the task was given to just two flying corps, one under General Bruno Lörzer, based at the Pas de Calais, and the other under General Wolfram von Richthofen, based at Le Havre. Richthofen was Germany's leading expert on the use of dive bombers.

Luftwaffe strategists thought that the easiest part of Phase One would be the closing of the 21-mile wide Straits of Dover, through which all British convoys steaming in from the Atlantic had to pass to get to the Port of London. This task was handed over to one of General Lörzer's subordinates, Colonel Johannes Fink.

The RAF Fighter Command, under the overall direction of Air Chief Marshal Dowding, had two main groups waiting to do battle. One of them, so-called 11 Group, under a New Zealander, Air Vice Marshal Keith Rodney Park, had its headquarters at Northholt, an outer suburb of London. Its job was to defend the south coast of England from just west of the Isle of Wight, through the Straits of Dover and along the banks of the Thames River to London itself. The other, 12 Group, under the feisty Air Vice Marshal Trafford Leigh-Mallory, was headquartered near Nottingham, in the English Midlands. Leigh-Mallory was to control the area from north of the Thames estuary through the industrial heart of England up the North Sea coast to Yorkshire.

Between them 11 and 12 Groups had by this time built their strength up to 640 combat-ready front-line fighters, most of them Hurricanes and Spitfires, with a backing of Defiants. Luftwaffe Air Fleets 2 and 3, between them, counted 824 fighters—656 Me-109s and 168 Me-110s. Thus, in a contest of fighter versus fighter, the odds were actually not so long. However, the chief target of the RAF's fighter planes would be the Luftwaffe's bombers; the total number the Germans had available was 1,191—including 316 Stukas. To clean the skies of such a swarm of enemies, Air Marshal Dowding said grimly, "Our young men will have to shoot down their young men at the rate of five to one."

Even during the lull ordered by Hitler after Dunkirk, the Luftwaffe's fighters had been out over the south coast of England, trying to coax up the RAF. When the British fighters refused to respond to fighter-plane provocation—they were under orders to husband their strength—the Germans sent over a few bombers with the fighters. Because the bombers were easier prey, some Spitfires were persuaded to come up and tangle with the enemy.

It was in this way that German pilots learned something more of the skill and mettle of the Spitfires and their pilots. Once, over the Hampshire downs, German ace Adolf Galland spotted a Spitfire and dived on it, a sitting duck cruising 1,000 feet below. But the RAF pilot had seen Galland and put his machine into a tight turn. Galland tried to follow him but found that his Me-109 would not take the stress. By the time he straightened out, his adversary had vanished.

When Galland got back to base, he compared notes with his friend, Werner Mölders. He, too, had sighted an easy target, only to discover that the Briton had slithered out of his line of fire "like an eel doubling up on itself to escape a shark," as he put it.

"We were no longer in doubt," Galland recalled, "that the RAF would prove a most formidable opponent."

The first big test of the two sides came on July 10, over a stretch of water in the Dover area soon to be known to the world as Hellfire Corner. On that day, in the neutral capitals of Europe, Hitler's agents were still spreading the word of his deep desire for peace with the British. But Göring thirsted to get on with Phase One of his Luftwaffe operation: to lure the RAF into the skies by attacking British convoys in the Channel, and thus to achieve two knockouts at once —smashing the RAF's first-line fighters while ending the Channel's usefulness as a British lifeline.

A gusting wind fell on southeast England on July 10, and gray clouds hung low over the Straits of Dover. But early in the afternoon, through a patch of clear sky, a reconnoitering German pilot spotted a convoy steaming westward from the Thames estuary with a guard escort of six Hurricanes. A German radio-monitoring unit on the French coast picked up the pilot's alert and flashed the news to Luftwaffe headquarters. Back to Colonel Fink—Commander of the Luftwaffe fighter force based on the cliffs of Cap Blanc-Nez overlooking the Straits—went a single word message: "Vernichten!" ("Destroy!"). Fink newly charged by his superiors with waging what they had dubbed "the battle of the Channel," reached for the field telephone in the ancient French bus that was serving as his command post.

At 1:30 p.m., British radar plotters on the cliffs of Dover, 21 miles across the water, saw a crowd of blips appearing on their screens, indicating that a concentration of planes was building up behind Calais. A few minutes later they confirmed that at least 70 enemy planes were on their way—a far greater number than in the German probes of the previous weeks. From headquarters of Fighter Command at Bentley Priory, an order was immediately given to reinforce the six Hurricanes escorting the convoy: elements of four RAF squadrons from neighboring sectors were to scramble and rendezvous over the Straits of Dover.

With the understatement typical of his countrymen, a British chronicler later summed up what followed as a "lively action." The German pilot who had given the first alert was more lyrical. Looking around him in the sky, he saw "a magnificent dogfight . . . from a distance the aircraft looked like bunches of grapes." The battle went on for less than 30 minutes. When it was over the attackers recorded their losses at four fighters; the outnumbered defenders recorded theirs at three fighters, plus one small ship of the convoy sunk. But both sides found reason for self-satisfaction with the engagement—the British in the way squadrons from different sectors had coordinated their efforts, the Germans in their success in flushing out so many of the enemy's planes. The more aircraft that they could entice up into the skies, the sooner the RAF would be destroyed.

In the small garden outside his command post, Colonel Fink and a dozen of his pilots toasted one another in champagne and looked forward to pursuing their new strategy.

THE INTREPID MR. CHURCHILL

His bowler momentarily set aside for a steel helmet, a confident, smiling Churchill relaxes in a shelter during an RAF-Luftwaffe air battle over Dover.

A GILDED LADDER TO THE LEADERSHIP OF BRITAIN

In 1889 Harrow student Winston Churchill, 15, is photographed proudly wearing the obligatory formal school turnout: topper, cutaway and cane.

In the grim summer of 1940, Britain was blessed as few nations have been in times of trouble. In the new Prime Minister, Winston Leonard Spencer Churchill, the country had a leader whose style, temperament and background made him the ideal wartime leader—just the man to take hold of a battered country as Reich Marshal Hermann Göring's Luftwaffe set out to bomb Britain into surrender.

Churchill loved power and command, and he loved a good fight, too. He was enormously energetic and competitive, striving to excel not only in his career, but also in a range of avocations that included painting, writing, polo and hunting. As a boy he fought his unorthodox way through Harrow, stubbornly refusing to learn the required Latin and mathematics. He then went to the military academy at Sandhurst, served enthusiastically as an officer in India, and was elected to Parliament at 26. In 1911, when he was only 37, he became head of the Royal Navy, inaugurating its then revolutionary air arm and learning to fly in the process.

Churchill was also a shrewd opportunist who, in his political career, was not above changing parties when he thought it advantageous. Finally, he was a devout and flamboyant egoist who loved elegant clothes and conspicuous hats, and who was known to observe that "megalomania is the only form of sanity."

Partly because he loved to show off, Churchill as Prime Minister frequently and deliberately ran terrible personal risks. But the people admired him for it, and loved his offhand disregard for danger. Once, when a German bomb landed near his car and nearly tipped it over, he joked, "It must have been my beef that kept the car down"—a reference to his pudginess.

Normally, Churchill's reaction to German bombing was far more bellicose and vengeful. After an inspection of bomb damage in London, he noted that "when we got back into the car, a harsher mood swept over this haggard crowd. 'Give it 'em back,' they cried, and, 'let *them* have it, too.' I undertook forthwith to see that their wishes were carried out; and this promise was certainly kept."

An imperturbable Lieutenant Churchill sits astride a favorite mount while serving in India in 1896 with the Fourth Queen's Own Hussars.

A cabinet member at the age of 35, a white-capped Churchill shakes hands with his host, Kaiser Wilhelm, during military maneuvers in Germany in 1909.

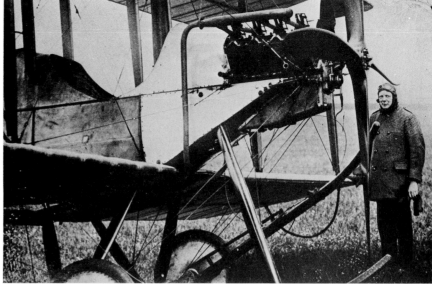

Churchill stands next to a biplane after completing a 126-mile flight in 1914. An impetuous and extremely lucky pilot, he was once in a plane crack-up, but escaped unharmed.

Standing with Allied officers in France in 1915, infantry battalion commander Churchill wears a French helmet—which he regarded as more comfortable than the British model.

Churchill, with wife Clementine at his side, doffs his hat during an unsuccessful run for Parliament, as an independent candidate in 1924. Unabashed, he ran again that year with Conservative backing, and won. During his career, he changed his political parties with the same aplomb as he changed his hats, a special trademark for him. One observer noted that Churchill was the only male extant who owned more hats than his wife. For Churchill, the correct hat for an occasion was as important as the correct word. "A hat was not a hat to him," said one biographer. "It was a discovery, a challenge, a fresh expression of his personality."

On a hunting vacation to France in 1927, Churchill, then Chancellor of the Exchequer, sips some brandy from a flask before mounting up to chase wild boar.

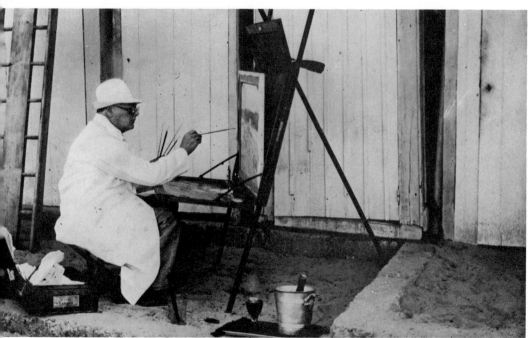

Churchill canters ahead of the Prince of Wales during a polo match in 1924. While serving as a cavalryman in India he led his regimental team to an all-India victory, and he continued to be an excellent polo player well into his 50s.

In his white hat and artist's smock, Churchill paints on the French Riviera in 1935. A deft and ardent painter, he remarked that "when I get to Heaven I mean to spend a considerable portion of my five million years in painting, and so get to the bottom of the subject."

Churchill emerges from a blockhouse, with an escort

In the early part of World War II, First Lord of the Admiralty, but old soldier, Churchill chats with army officers attached to the British Expeditionary Force, which was stationed in France in 1939.

Recently installed as Prime Minister, Churchill huddles over war maps with Admiral Bertram Ramsay in September 1940, while on a tour of the defense network along England's southern coast.

of helmeted Tommies, in a coastal area of southern England, where it was expected that the brunt of the Germans' seaborne invasion was going to fall.

Officers and enlisted men on a battle cruiser in a northern British port give three rousing cheers for their Prime Minister. Churchill, who had proudly served for two terms as First Lord of the Admiralty, maintained a love affair with the Navy. As Prime Minister, he delightedly signed off as "Former Naval Person" during his official communication with his ally, President Franklin D. Roosevelt—who himself had once been U.S. Assistant Secretary of the Navy.

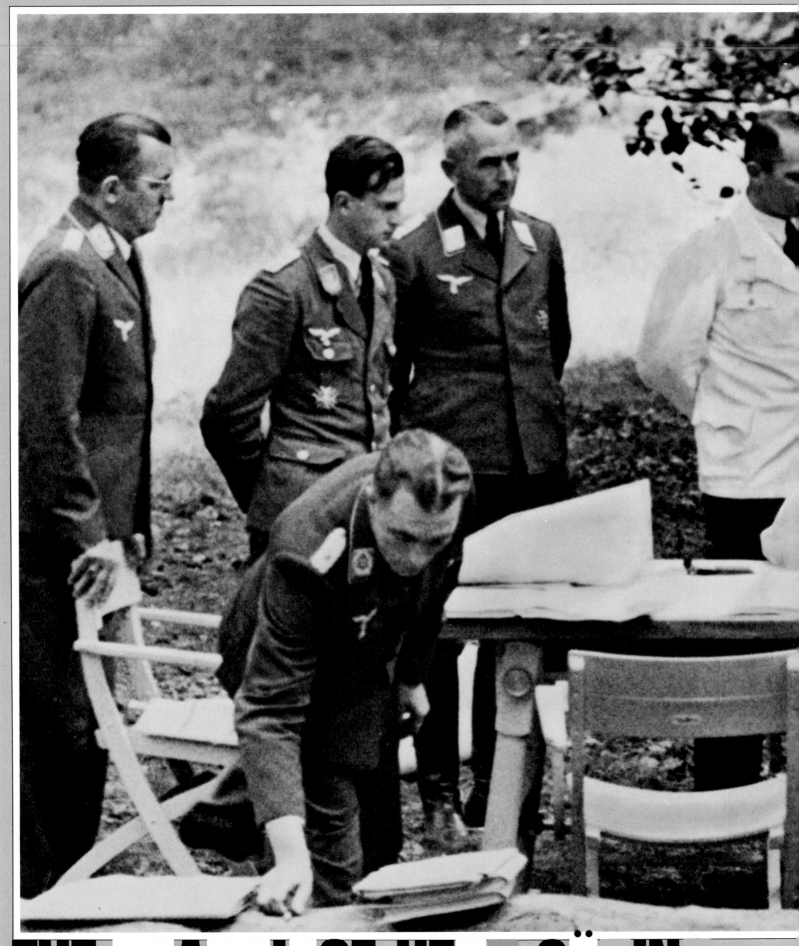

THE MADHOUSE HERR GÖRING

Coatless and in civilian clothes, German air commander Hermann Göring discusses the air assault on England with aides summoned to his estate near Berlin.

A DAREDEVIL CLIMB BY A SWASHBUCKLING ACE

When in mid-1940 Hermann Wilhelm Göring dispatched against England the German Air Force that he had built over two decades, he reached the pinnacle of a career seldom matched in German history. The 3,000 planes of his Luftwaffe made it the most powerful in the world. In addition to leading the air force, Göring, as Reich Marshal of Germany, ranked second only to Hitler in the Nazi hierarchy.

Indeed, Göring regarded himself as the very model of a modern German prince. Bold and vain, he began as a boy to test his strength and daring by climbing mountains. "I have no fear of heights," he once remarked. "They stimulate me." As a pilot in World War I—swashbuckling to the point of recklessness—he shot down 22 Allied planes and earned Germany's highest decoration for valor. After the war, the princely mask slipped a bit. The veteran pilot had to earn money barnstorming, and he gained notoriety by eloping in 1922 with the wife of a Swedish nobleman.

An early recruit of Hitler's, Göring was wounded at the Munich beer hall putsch. While recovering, he developed an addiction to morphine—a tendency he never completely shook. But his devotion to Hitler was unabated: "If the Führer wants it," he proclaimed, "two and two make five!"

In return for such loyalty, Hitler showered Göring with more and more power—plus titles, medals and other perquisites the vainglorious Göring loved. Göring became President of the Reichstag, titular head of the state of Prussia, Reich Master of the Hunt and Master of the Forest. He built a sumptuous palace in the country, where he lived with an actress he married when his first wife died. There he avidly pursued hobbies ranging from hunting to model trains.

Inevitably, such self-indulgences—which also included overeating—led to jokes. Bolder wags publicly called Göring *Der Dicke* (fatty); one Berlin comedian cracked that the Reich Marshal had rubber facsimiles of his medals made so he could wear them in the tub. But Göring, secure in his self-image, was unruffled, even ordering the release of an actress arrested for mocking him. "Fools!" he fumed. "If people make jokes about me, it only proves how popular I am."

In 1908, daring 15-year-old Hermann Göring scales the Gross Glockner, a 12,000-foot Tyrolean peak that he climbed by its most hazardous route.

An air hero in his first year of combat, Göring had been awarded the Iron Cross First Class in 1915 when this picture was taken.

Fledgling pilot Göring (far right) joins fellow World War I aviators for a round of beer at a German café.

In 1915, 21-year-old Göring sits in the rear seat of an Albatros observation aircraft, the first warplane that he saw combat action in, as a photographer-observer, before becoming a pilot.

A swashbuckling flying ace by 1918, Göring proudly displays the late Baron Manfred von Richthofen's walking stick, a symbol of leadership over the Flying Circus fighter squadron.

At a rally on October 11, 1931, a bemedaled Göring (third from right), by now head of the National Socialist Party in the Reichstag, lines up with Nazi officials in Bad Harzburg in Brunswick. In the front row are SS Commander Heinrich Himmler (second from left) and Storm Trooper chief Ernst Röhm (third from left).

Göring flashes a politician's grin to Franz von Papen (second from left), a sure-footed diplomat who opposed Hitler in the beginning but subsequently became the Führer's Vice Chancellor.

A tense and angry Göring argues with his bitter rival, Nazi Propaganda Minister Joseph Goebbels, at a rally in Berlin.

Strolling with Hitler at Berlin's Tempelhof Airport, Göring wears a black mourning band to commemorate the death of his first wife, Karin (overleaf).

At the reception for Göring's second wedding, the beaming groom and bride, actress Emmy Sonneman, sit next to honored guest Adolf Hitler. The ceremony was the social event of 1935 in Germany. Some 30,000 SA men lined the streets and 200 airplanes flew by in salute as the couple walked to Berlin's Town Hall for a civil ceremony. Göring's first wife, a Swedish noblewoman named Karin von Kantzow (below), had died four years previously. Göring had her body brought to Germany in 1934; with a final theatrical flourish suggesting a pagan funeral rite her coffin was wheeled in an open cart past flaming obelisks for burial near Karin Hall—the country house that he had constructed in her memory.

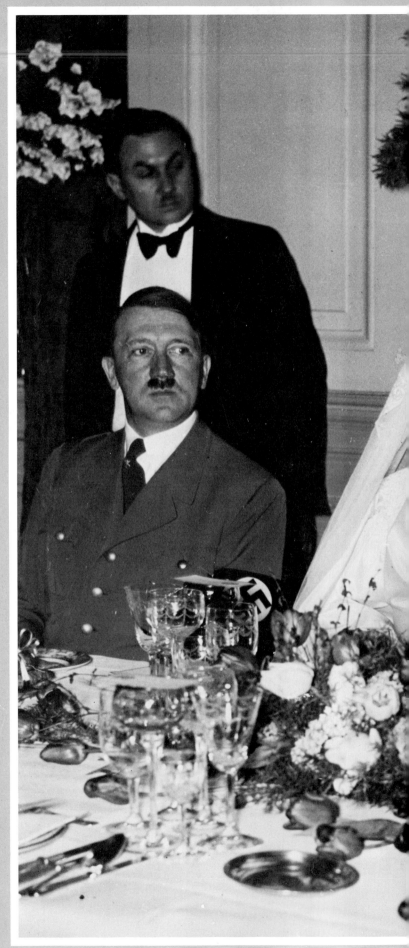

A sweatbanded Göring, grown portly since the early 1930s, swats a forehand.

Hobbyist Göring proudly shows a visitor his elaborate model railroad, whose

At the Berlin zoo, a playful Reich Marshal frolics with Mucki, a lion cub.

Seated in a dinghy, Göring prepares to send off a model of a square-rigger.

ins, tracks and houses sprawl across the floor in the spacious attic of Karin Hall.

A photograph of Göring, wearing the official uniform of Reich Master of the Hunt, hangs in an honored place amid the trophies at Karin Hall. At right, the Master himself recapitulates the shooting of two boar that he bagged while hunting in a forest near Hanover. An avid hunter, he was also an ardent conservationist; as Reich Chief Forester, he permitted shooting only under very stringent seasonal limits, and sought to preserve several endangered species such as the eagle and the falcon.

3

In the intensifying clashes between the RAF and the Luftwaffe over the Channel in mid-July 1940, there was no doubt which side at first had the preponderance of expert fliers. The Germans had been honing their skills as air warriors ever since the Spanish Civil War. Their killer capabilities had been sharpened not in exercises or war games but in the arena of real combat, where a man was either quick or dead. Scores of pilots who flew out to tangle with the RAF over the Straits of Dover had flown with the Condor Legion, the German air force unit that had contributed to Generalissimo Franco's victory in Spain. They were trained to make the best use of sky, sun, their enemy's weaknesses and their own superb sense of discipline and coordination. As technicians they could not be matched—not yet, anyway—and this the British swiftly learned.

"They come down on you out of the sun like ruddy thunderbolts," RAF Flight Lieutenant Alan Deere reported. Flying a Spitfire with No. 54 Squadron, Deere saw one of his companions jumped by an Me-109 and shot down in flames. He himself survived only by flying straight at a 109, forcing a glancing midair collision, and then limping back to a crash landing in Kent with a dead engine and bent propeller blades. "It was a miracle I got away with it," he said.

Deere and his fellows were soon aware that something was badly wrong with their tactics in the air, and it was taking its toll in planes and lives. Adolf Galland, a Condor Legion veteran who commanded a wing of Me-109s over the Channel, put his finger on the nub of the British problem:

"The first rule of all air combat," he said, "is to see the opponent first. Like the hunter who stalks his prey and maneuvers himself unnoticed into the most favorable position for the kill, the fighter in the opening of a dogfight must detect the opponent as early as possible in order to attain a superior position for the attack."

This the British were sometimes fatally late in doing because the RAF fighters' method of flying while on patrol restricted their ability to see and maneuver. They flew in tight formations, wingtip to wingtip; this made a spectacular sight at air shows but was not much good in a fight. It is not easy to fly airplanes in close and meticulous order. The British pilots were so busy keeping in formation—and staying out of one another's way—that they had little time to look around for the enemy, and no room to move when he came at them.

DAY OF THE EAGLE

The German fighters, on the other hand, had learned over Spain to fly in loose formations. Units patrolled and stalked the enemy at different heights, with plenty of room between individual planes. Each pilot could keep a sharp lookout for attackers or quarry instead of worrying about the proximity of his flying neighbor's wingtip. He had freedom to initiate maneuvers and attacks of his own, and he had a much greater range of vision. Yet his friends were close enough so that he retained the protection of his unit.

So in their opening encounters with the Germans, the Royal Air Force got hurt. In 10 days of clashes, starting with the first big engagement over "Hellfire Corner," near Dover, on July 10, the RAF lost 50 fighters—a critical drain in view of the pace at which the action was mounting. True, the RAF had shot down 92 Luftwaffe planes during the same period, but only 28 of these were the precious—and dangerous—Messerschmitt fighters.

Six RAF pilots died on July 20, the largest toll yet, but others managed to struggle out of the cockpits of their damaged planes and parachute into the Channel. A number of German pilots also ended up in the water, and a race to recover the downed men developed between the two sides. To the RAF, pilots were more valuable than planes, for they were in even shorter supply. Pilots were also valuable to the Luftwaffe; besides, letting one drown if he could possibly be saved was dangerous for morale.

To rescue their fliers—and to snatch British pilots away from the RAF—the Germans used seaplanes painted white and marked with the symbol of the International Red Cross. These planes often flew daringly through dogfights to land on the water and pick up fliers, and it was only a question of time before one of them got shot at by the British. When a rescue plane did indeed get hit by a Spitfire, the Air Ministry in London issued a warning: all "ambulance aircraft," Red Cross symbols or not, would be shot down if they ventured into the combat zone. The British claimed they were taking this step because the enemy was violating the Red Cross Convention by using the rescue planes to report movements of British convoys. Actually, they feared that the planes would not only rescue too many Luftwaffe pilots but would also make prisoners of war of downed RAF pilots.

At the time, the RAF had only motor launches to pick up their men. The official launches were augmented by other small boats, mostly fishing vessels from Channel ports, which proved willing to take considerable risks to rescue British fliers but were known to leave Germans to drown.

One Spitfire pilot, Geoffrey Page, who was badly burned when his plane was hit and set afire by an Me-109, managed to open his parachute though his hands were fried to the bone. The flames had destroyed his uniform and scorched his face and body, and he wallowed in the water half-naked and in great pain, dimly sensing that a boat was circling him. Finally, through the agony that racked him, Page heard a voice calling out:

"Who are you—a Jerry or one of ours?"

It took Page some time to spit out the sea water and cry back through his cracked lips:

"Stupid f------ bastards, pull me out!"

The boat immediately pulled up alongside him and strong arms reached out to lift him aboard.

"The minute you swore, mate," one of the crew said, "we knew you was from the RAF."

At the outset, the battle of the Channel seemed to be going just the way the Germans wanted. At Luftwaffe headquarters hands were rubbed in glee and orders were given to step up the attacks, while the British were still learning the facts of life and death in air combat.

But they learned quickly. Geoffrey Page was by no means the only pilot to be sent to a plastic-surgery ward with dreadful burns. As RAF commanders studied the gaps in their ranks, they did some urgent rethinking. Within days, they had abandoned tight formations and were trying out new tactics, taking over many of the Luftwaffe's methods. Finally the RAF began flying the so-called Finger Four formation—each plane at the tip of a finger of an imaginary outstretched hand. This procedure, which broke up the rigidity of the old formations, improved the odds on survival when the British now met the Germans in the sky.

For the rest of July, what took place over the Channel and southern England was a kind of war of modern gladiators, professional fighters struggling for mastery. The British ships trying to sail through the Straits of Dover with food and supplies, and the Stukas trying to bomb and sink them before they got out of range and under antiaircraft cover were, in a way, only pawns in the game.

As the ships brought out the Stukas, British Spitfires and Hurricanes swooped down on the lumbering dive bombers. But this was what Colonel Johannes Fink's Me-109s were waiting for, thousands of feet higher up. They would dive to the attack, surprising the RAF fighters while they were busy with the Stukas. Thus began the clashes between fighters that were the heavy pieces in the struggle; on the outcome of their dogfights would depend the next phase of the war.

In these spectacular contests, which painted wildly swirling vapor trails all over the sky, the vulnerable and the unwary were quickly eliminated. To gain extra fighting time over the Channel, the Luftwaffe threw in twin-engine Me-110s, but their unwieldiness made them easy prey. After suffering some savage losses at the hands of the RAF, the 110s tried to give themselves greater protection by flying in ring formations that reminded some combatants of the circles the Boers had formed to ward off Zulu attacks in South Africa or that wagon trains used against Indian raids in the American West. The tactic failed. In seeking mutual protection, the 110s not only had to abandon their primary task of guarding the Luftwaffe's bombers, but they also became easier targets; RAF pilots often hit two or three 110s at once.

The RAF, too, had troubles, especially with its twin-seater Defiant fighter. The Germans quickly came to realize that, unlike the Hurricane it resembled, the Defiant carried no forward-firing armament; its only guns pointed rearward. After that, the Defiant's effectiveness was largely at an end. On July 19, nine Defiants flying out of Hawkinge, a frontline airfield overlooking the Channel, met 20 Me-109s that came at them out of the sun. Almost at once five Defiants spun into the sea. A sixth managed to reach Dover where it crashed in flames. The remaining three planes of the squadron were rescued by Hurricane Squadron No. 111, which shot down one of the Me-109s and managed to hold off the rest until finally the German machines had to turn back to France because they had run out of fuel.

At this stage of the battle over the Channel, most pilots in both air forces were now on alert for more than 12 hours each day, awaiting orders to scramble. RAF squadrons in the combat zones bordering the Channel in Kent, Sussex and Hampshire were flying as many as four sorties a day, patrolling for an hour and a half at a time. The Luftwaffe's fighter and bomber squadrons were not being worked quite so

hard for the moment, but three sorties a day for fighter pilots, and two for Stuka pilots, was not unusual.

The most dangerous part of the sorties, the dogfights, rarely lasted more than 10 or 15 minutes. Often they were clearly visible from both sides of the Channel. German soldiers followed the encounters from the bluffs between Calais and Boulogne; British civilians watched from the cliffs outside Dover, and those who could not be there could listen to running commentaries from BBC reporters.

The weather for much of the summer of 1940 was warm, soft and sunny; but from time to time scuds of rain swept over the sea, early or late mists blotted out the coastlines, and cold winds drove across the Channel, herding thick thunderclouds before them. Frequently the storms surprised the Germans and forced them to cancel operations. In this regard the British had the advantage; changes of weather usually came in from the Atlantic and moved eastward, so the RAF knew what the elements were going to be before the Germans did. But the Luftwaffe operated in all but the wickedest weather, because Göring wanted quick results.

"There was a distinctive difference between the objectives of the opposing sides," Air Marshal Dowding recalled. "The Germans were out to facilitate a transfer of ground troops across the Channel, to invade the country and so finish the war. Now, I wasn't trying with Fighter Command to finish the war. I was trying desperately to prevent the Germans succeeding in their preparations for an invasion. . . . I had to do that by denying them control of the air."

Dowding had every reason to believe the Germans were in a hurry to begin a landing. By late July, RAF intelligence had informed him that the German Army had moved 15 divisions of assault troops to ports facing England in northern Germany, Belgium and northern France. The reports were fairly accurate; actually, the invasion force contained 13 divisions with two in reserve, and Field Marshal von Brauchitsch, the Commander-in-Chief of the Army, had told his Navy opposite number, Grand Admiral Erich Raeder, that they would meet each other on British soil within a month.

German expectations were high because Göring's strategy seemed to be succeeding. The Luftwaffe chief's own intelligence experts kept assuring him that RAF commanders were now throwing all the fighter planes they possessed into the battle of the Channel in a desperate effort to sweep back the harbingers of invasion. But just in case the British still had reserves tucked away, Göring urged Field Marshals Kesselring and Sperrle to do all they could to inveigle more and more RAF planes into the air. Thus, in addition to routine operations, so-called decoy-duck tactics were used to tempt RAF fighters into chasing German planes back to the French coast, where Me-109s waited to pounce.

Adolf Galland had a favorite ploy for luring even the most experienced RAF pilots into foolhardy maneuvers—a trick that incidentally had training value for his own men.

"I had quite a few new pilots coming into the wing at that time," Galland later remarked, "and I wanted to give them speedy battle baptism and instill them with self-confidence by setting up a kill for them."

Galland would fly out across the Channel alone in his 109; when he saw an RAF patrol, he would meander around in its vicinity, but just out of range, until one of them broke away to take him on. He would then immediately turn back for France, always keeping just ahead of his pursuers, and meanwhile radioing two of his neophyte pilots who were airborne and waiting over the French coast.

"In many cases the Englishman couldn't resist the temptation," Galland said. "It was obvious he believed I hadn't seen him, and that was why I didn't try to shake him off. So he hung on, hoping for an easy kill, and ran into my boys."

It was in this fashion that one of Dowding's most brilliant pilots lost his Spitfire—and almost lost his life—for the second time. Alan Deere chased a 109 back across the Channel and realized he had been tricked only when he saw the enemy pilot "stand his aircraft practically on its nose and dive vertically towards the airfield, which I now recognized as Calais/Marck," a main Luftwaffe fighter base. Two other 109s immediately turned to cut Deere off "as, with throttle wide open, I headed for home at sea level, muttering to myself: 'You bloody fool.' "

Only total concentration and combat experience saved Deere. As he fled back to England, the two 109s formed up on either side of him and alternately attacked him. He forced them to break off by making a vicious turn in the direction of first one attacker, then the other, resuming his retreat for home as they re-formed. He was in sight of the Dover cliffs when one of the 109s shot up his instrument panel, canopy and gas tank. His watch was also shot off his wrist, though he didn't realize it at the moment.

By the time RAF planes had come up to protect him, driving off the 109s, Deere's Spitfire was in flames. But he turned it over and parachuted out. In the process he broke his wrist, but with his usual good luck fell into a field 50 yards from an RAF ambulance that happened to have halted on a nearby road while its driver and orderly ate lunch.

Though Deere lived to fight again, many others didn't. Dowding, alarmed at the steady drain on his manpower, instructed his group commanders never to scramble their planes just for the sake of a dogfight, and not to allow their pilots to take on the foe beyond gliding distance of the English shore. "I want live fliers, not dead heroes," he told them.

Dowding, of course, had radar's help in using his fighter

strength to best advantage. It monitored the enemy movements during all 24 hours of the day.

Radar was not always infallible, however. RAF pilots found that though it pinpointed the enemy's distance from them, it often underestimated the plane's height, sometimes by as much as 5,000 feet. After a time, pilots began to add at least 5,000 feet to the altitude the radar operators gave them over the radio, to avoid being ambushed from above.

The Luftwaffe envied the British their technical aids. One German area commander said ruefully: "Sometimes when our boys get into battle their briefings are two hours old. The British are getting theirs through their earphones all the time, even while they are fighting."

In an attempt to neutralize radar's advantages, Luftwaffe tacticians took to tricking the RAF by sending masses of planes aloft on false maneuvers. These movements, they knew, would be seen as blips on British radar screens, and RAF squadrons would be ordered to scramble. As the Spitfires and Hurricanes circled the sky and waited to pounce on what they believed were approaching enemy fliers, all the while eating up their flying time, the first batch of Luftwaffe planes would be ordered to return to base, and fresh formations of 109s would sweep out to take on the RAF fighters as they were running low on fuel.

To counter this tactic RAF tacticians worked out a routine designed to make sure their planes never scrambled unless a genuine target was in view. Relays of Spitfires and Hurricanes would shuttle between bases well inland, where they were out of easy range of enemy fighters, and forward airfields near the Channel, where they could wait until the last possible moment before getting airborne.

In July, Dowding noted in his journal that he had a feeling time was on the side of the RAF and Britain "if we can only hold on." What he did not know was that Luftwaffe intelligence officers were on his side, too. The figures of RAF casualties that they produced for Göring toward the end of the month convinced the Reich Marshal that Phase One of the Battle of Britain had already been won—that the Channel had been closed and the RAF crippled in the air. The truth was that small coastal convoys still sailed through the Straits of Dover and would continue to do so. As to the RAF it had more front-line fighters at the end of July than at the beginning; in this one month alone, British aircraft workers had produced 496 fighters—four times the number turned out in a typical month before Dunkirk.

Göring triumphantly presented his own set of statistics to Hitler and asked permission to ready his forces for Phase Two of the battle. He was jubilant at Hitler's response. On August 1 the Führer gave the go signal for the all-out attack on Britain's air defenses. The order he issued, War Directive No. 17, decreed that from now on, "to produce the necessary conditions for the final conquest of England," the following actions would be taken:

• The Luftwaffe would destroy the RAF and Britain's air defenses, once and for all, by attacks not only against flying formations, but also against airfields and other landing grounds, supply organizations, the aircraft industry and the factories that produced antiaircraft equipment.

• Once this had been achieved, all ports along Britain's south coast were to be destroyed except those selected for use by German invasion forces.

• The Luftwaffe was to carry out its task with speed, ruthlessness, enterprise and daring, but was to take care to preserve sufficient strength to be battle-worthy for the actual invasion—Operation Sea Lion.

Hitler added one proviso. The Luftwaffe must in no circumstances execute any "terror raids" against British civilian populations, not even in retaliation for RAF raids on Germany, unless and until he gave personal orders. "Bombing with the object of causing a mass panic," he declared, "must be left to the last." He told Göring that this ban particularly applied to London; the British capital was to be off limits to the Luftwaffe's bombers.

As a code name for the all-out air assault on Britain, the German High Command chose Adlerangriff, or Eagle Attack. No date for the opening day—Eagle Day—was specified by Hitler, except that it was to begin "from the 5th of August." However, he left a general impression that he expected it to be launched approximately 48 hours from that date, and British intelligence so reported to Winston Churchill. The Prime Minister in turn informed the RAF that the Luftwaffe's supreme effort was imminent.

And so on August 8, Air Marshal Dowding issued an Order of the Day to members of Fighter Command:

"The Battle of Britain is about to begin. Members of the

This midair photograph, made from the cockpit of a Luftwaffe fighter, shows a British Hurricane losing a wing (spinning off at upper right) after a burst of fire from the German plane. The Hurricane's pilot (top) has already bailed out and is parachuting to safety. Visible at the bottom are the chalk cliffs of Dover along England's southern coastline, the major arena of aerial combat during the opening phase of the Battle of Britain.

Royal Air Force, the fate of generations lies in your hands."

That day there was a noticeable boost in the pressure of Luftwaffe attacks, and everyone in the RAF presumed that the decisive battle had begun. From early morning, Stukas made continuous onslaughts upon a large convoy in the Channel, while other bombers laid mines outside almost every port along England's south coast.

Dogfights raged over Hampshire, Sussex, Kent and the Channel, and by dusk the two sides, between them, had flown over 1,000 sorties. When they totaled up their victories, the RAF pilots exultantly claimed to have shot down 24 of the Luftwaffe's bombers and 36 of its fighters, while the Germans no less triumphantly announced that they had bagged 49 RAF fighters. Both sides were exaggerating; the Luftwaffe had lost 31 planes and the RAF 19. In any case, it had been the heaviest day of air combat thus far, with both sides suffering the highest casualties of the battle.

But it was not yet Eagle Day. In a series of conferences the preceding week at Karin Hall, Göring's palatial estate in Prussia, sharp differences over operational plans had emerged between Field Marshals Kesselring and Sperrle, whose Air Fleets 2 and 3 would bear the brunt of the action once the knockout round began. The two men were not mutual admirers and had been uneasy collaborators from the start. Almost at once they began to bicker.

Kesselring proposed that all the attacks should be concentrated on one target—London. "By the time we have killed a few thousand Cockneys," he said, "the British will be screaming for peace."

Sperrle sourly retorted that by putting all the thrust on attacking London without first having destroyed the RAF they would be playing into the hands of the British, because the RAF would be able to assemble its fighter forces on the perimeter of the capital and cause havoc with the massed Luftwaffe bomber attacks. This would be especially risky, as Sperrle's Chief of Staff, Paul Deichmann, crisply pointed out, since the bombers would be flying beyond the range of their escort of Me-109s.

Göring disposed of this part of the quarrel by reminding the conferees that the Führer had specifically declared the city of London off limits.

Kesselring then proposed that the Luftwaffe's attacks be concentrated on some other big city instead of being dissipated over a wide number of targets, as Sperrle wanted, and that the RAF's bases and supply factories be bombed later. But Sperrle's ideas were more in line with Göring's thinking and Hitler's orders; the conference got down to such matters as which targets would be allocated to which air fleet and how flight plans would be coordinated.

While their staffs were working out the details, the two air fleet chiefs retired to Göring's indoor pool for a relaxing swim, only to have the argument break out again at poolside. Finally Kesselring said hotly:

"I have never believed in this war against England! I have always believed the way to win is to take over Gibraltar and bottle up the English in the Mediterranean. That will bring them to their knees!" This unpopular advice was ignored.

Not until August 6 was a date finally set for Eagle Day. It would be just four days hence—if the weather was right.

It wasn't. On August 10, squalls ripped across southern England and thunderclouds hung low over the Channel and northern France. For the next two days the skies were cloudy or misty. The Luftwaffe's waiting bomber crews, who had heard rumors that the big push was coming, were beginning to fret. Aware of the dangers of a psychological letdown, Göring announced Eagle Day as August 13.

This time the date was kept—but only just. As the Luftwaffe's weather forecasters had predicted, the morning proved stormy; Göring immediately ordered the cancellation of the planned operations until the afternoon, when the weather was expected to clear. However, Göring's recall order came too late to stop a flight of 74 Dornier bombers and 50 escorting Me-110s, which had already taken off against RAF fields and installations in Kent.

Field Marshal Kesselring then sent urgent radio messages calling the raiders back. The 110s promptly turned for home, but the Dorniers were under the personal leadership of Colonel Johannes Fink himself, and this was a day the commander of the battle of the Channel had been waiting for. He decided to carry on, relying on heavy cloud cover to give him the protection he had lost with the withdrawal of his fighter escort. He was lucky. An RAF radar team miscalculated the number of bombers that were on the way and fed the wrong information to Fighter Command, which scrambled an insufficient number of fighters to deal with so

THE EARLY WARNING NETWORK

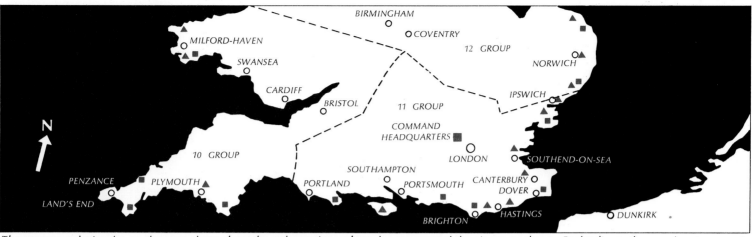

The squares and triangles on the map above show the radar stations whose beams covered the air approaches to England's southern and eastern coasts.

The radar network that helped Britain survive the air blitz was the world's first, and, for a long time, remained the most extensive and most sophisticated. Begun during 1936, it was concentrated mainly along England's eastern and southern coasts, as indicated above. Initially, the system was built around 240-foot-high long-range antennae *(squares on map)* that could pick up planes as far as 150 miles away at altitudes of up to 30,000 feet. But low-flying aircraft could sneak under the beams from these towers, so in 1939 low-level antennae *(triangles)* were added to the network to detect planes flying barely above the waves as they came in from offshore.

As the Battle of Britain began, the instant a coastal radar station spotted enemy planes, technicians monitoring screens determined their number, distance and approximate altitude and phoned these data to RAF Fighter Command headquarters. There the information was collated with reports of visual sightings, plotted on a map and flashed to the operations rooms of Command Headquarters and to fighter groups. As RAF squadrons engaged the foe, Women's Auxiliary Air Force (WAAF) personnel matched the moves of friendly and enemy aircraft with symbols on a map while staff officers from a balcony above directed the course of battle.

At Fighter Command Headquarters near London, headphoned WAAFs wielding long magnetic rods manipulate markers, which represent RAF and German squadrons, as staff officers watch intently from above.

formidable a force of bombers. As a result, Fink's Dorniers got through and dropped their bombs on Eastchurch airfield, losing only four planes shot down and four damaged in the clashes that followed.

The rest made it back to France, reporting that they had put a main RAF fighter station out of action and destroyed 10 Spitfires on the ground. Actually, Eastchurch was manned by second-line fighters and light bombers, and, though heavily hit, was ready for use again within 10 hours.

The real unleashing of the Eagle Day offensive began at 3:45 p.m. with an attack by bomber squadrons and fighter escorts against targets in southern England from Southampton to the Thames estuary—a distance of 150 miles. Against Southampton, Britain's largest port, the Germans threw 150 bombers, escorted by a force of Me-109s. Four squadrons of RAF fighters were sent up to meet them.

The attacking bomber force included both Stukas and twin-engine Junkers-88s, the Luftwaffe's fastest and most up-to-date medium bomber. The flight path along which the Ju-88s approached Southampton was guarded only by Blenheim fighters, a modified version of the Blenheim Mark IV bomber. Usually used for night fighting—they were pioneers in the use of airborne radar—the Blenheim fighters, 10 miles an hour slower than a fully loaded Ju-88, were not fast enough for daytime combat. The Junkers took on the Blenheims, damaged several, and blasted their way through to bomb the port, destroying or setting afire a large area of docks and warehouses.

The Stukas were less lucky; they fell among Spitfires. Thirteen Spits patrolling high in the sky over the Channel dived through the Stukas' escorting Me-109s, shooting one down on the way, and went to work on a flock of 40 Stukas. The Spits had the sun in their favor and the Stukas did not have a chance. Nine were shot down, several others were damaged, and the rest jettisoned their bombs and scattered.

This massacre was the work of members of 609 RAF Squadron, one of whom made a comment about it that later found its way into RAF records. The previous day, August 12, had marked the official opening of Britain's grouse-shooting season, known as the Glorious Twelfth. The jubilant Spitfire pilot declared, "I couldn't get away for the Glorious Twelfth this year—but the Glorious Thirteenth was the best day's shooting I ever had!"

The Germans were boasting too. Although Eagle Day had not begun until the middle of the afternoon, they had flown an unprecedented number of sorties—1,485 compared to 700 by the RAF. Luftwaffe crews came back with reports of successful attacks on six RAF airfields and other installations, the destruction of dozens of planes on the ground, the wiping out of several small factories, and the paralysis of the port of Southampton.

But what pleased Göring most was the number of RAF planes his pilots claimed they had shot down. That night the German High Command's communiqué announced that 88 RAF fighters had been destroyed—70 Spitfires and Hurricanes and 18 Blenheims. Luftwaffe losses were put at 12 planes. An overjoyed Reich Marshal ordered champagne to be served in all pilot messes in the combat area. Because of the overoptimism of his intelligence reports, he did not know Eagle Day's real losses: 13 RAF fighters had been shot

In a cartoon by David Low deriding Hitler's boast that he would receive Britain's surrender on August 15, 1940, a reception committee toting bouquets and submachine guns waits at the water's edge. By an odd coincidence, on the day the acerbic cartoon appeared, the Luftwaffe conducted one of its heaviest raids against Britain; the shattered German planes in the cartoon proved to be prophetic when the raid cost the Luftwaffe over twice as many aircraft as the RAF lost in defensive action.

down as against 23 Luftwaffe bombers and 11 Luftwaffe fighters. These losses were grievous to both sides—but there was an important point in the RAF's favor: the Luftwaffe had miscalculated the balance of its profits and losses.

In interrogating pilots and crews to try to evaluate the lessons of Eagle Day, the Luftwaffe's intelligence officers learned that one fact about the day's combat had made a particularly painful impression on the bomber forces: the British always seemed to know where the enemy was. More than ever, Britain's radar system was coming into its own. Though the Germans had known of its efficacy for more than a month, the radar's improving accuracy was now being reported from every Luftwaffe base in the war zone.

Fortunately for the British, who had more than their share of luck at this period, the reports do not appear to have convinced Göring and his High Command that radar was by far the most dangerous threat to their enterprise. Though dealing with radar had been one of the subjects discussed by the Karin Hall conferees, none of them had suggested assigning top priority to its destruction. All they had done was to agree that preliminary attacks upon the radar system should be made before Eagle Day proper began.

The first of these assaults had taken place one day earlier, on the 12th of August. Bombing raids were made on six RAF radar stations along the south coast of England; one station, at Ventnor on the Isle of Wight, was completely destroyed. Since Ventnor was the station that screened the approaches to the port of Southampton, its leveling was a great triumph for the Germans.

But they did not know it. Evidently they were unaware that the Ventnor station had gone off the air; that a 10-mile gap had been blown in the coastal radar chain. Through this hole their bombers could have struck without warning, en masse, to sow death and panic.

Radar stations were attacked again a few days later, but not with sufficient strength to put any of them out of action for more than a few hours. Yet the British radar system, had the Germans known it, was vulnerable in a special way: its personnel was largely unprotected. The operators of this invaluable defensive cordon were members of the Women's Auxiliary Air Force, who worked near the radar towers in flimsy wooden huts, built aboveground and so hastily camouflaged that they were easily visible. Well-placed bombs —or cannon shells from fighter planes—could have reduced the huts to splinters.

But this happened on only two occasions, and then, it seems, by accident. What the Luftwaffe dive bombers set out to destroy were the narrow radar towers themselves, and direct hits on them were as difficult as dropping peas on pinheads. Not only that, the towers were easily replaceable, whereas the trained WAAF operators were not. While the attacks on the towers went on, the WAAFs went on working, steadfastly feeding Fighter Command the information that would help in the raiders' own destruction.

Had Göring realized the extent of the crisis created for the RAF by the extinction of the Ventnor station, he might have ordered his bombers to press their attacks on Britain's radar chain. But the apparently fruitless raids on the stations convinced him that they were invulnerable. He issued a memorandum to his field commanders saying:

"It is doubtful whether there is any point in continuing attacks on radar sites, in view of the fact that not one of those attacked has been put out of action."

Reich Marshal Göring made many mistakes during World War II—and this was certainly one of his worst—but he can be forgiven for being totally ignorant of another asset possessed by the British in addition to radar: the ability to read encoded German radio messages. If the RAF radar network had been destroyed, the Germans probably would soon have been able to deduce that the British were continuing to get information from another source—over German radio —and, accordingly, would have changed their codes.

Two days after Eagle Day, on the morning of August 15, the Luftwaffe was ready to get back into all-out action. The weather was sunny and warm, with a light cloud cover over the Channel and crystal clarity over the North Sea. Göring ordered the commanders of Air Fleets 2 and 3 to put every available fighter into the air, together with 75 per cent of their dive bombers and 50 per cent of their bombers. Counting the new planes that had been sent on to replace those damaged or lost, that amounted to 975 fighters, 190 dive bombers and 432 bombers—the largest number of planes yet used in the war for a single operation. The remaining bombers were held back for a second-wave attack.

General Hans-Jürgen Stumpff, who commanded Luftwaffe

PLUCKED FROM THE SEA TO FIGHT ANOTHER DAY

A downed British pilot who destroyed an enemy bomber before parachuting from his plane comes ashore in a battered rowboat, still in his life jacket.

In the summer skies above the English Channel, battling German and British airmen often found themselves in a special kind of double jeopardy. If they had to bail out of a plane crippled by enemy gunfire, they stood a fair chance of parachuting down into the cold, choppy waters of the English Channel. Both sides lost scores of men to the Channel. But at the outset of the battle, the Germans, with characteristic thoroughness, were far better prepared to salvage their fliers.

The Germans had a fleet of rescue floats anchored a mile or two off the French coast (*right*). Each float was equipped with blankets, rations and medical supplies to keep a flier warm and reasonably well until he could be picked up by friendly craft. For men who ditched farther out, standard gear on every Luftwaffe fighter included inflatable dinghies. And each flier carried a container of fluorescine, a brilliant green dye, which, in the water, spread out into

A curious Briton peers out of an empty German rescue float that has drifted across the Channel to land on the coast of England.

a patch of color easily spotted by one of the Luftwaffe's rescue fleet of medically equipped Heinkel-59 seaplanes.

The British at first were more offhand in their rescue efforts. They relied on passing ships, planes that just happened to overfly downed men, and on a fleet of small craft that patrolled the coastal waters (*above*). Otherwise, British fliers had only their Mae West life jackets—and the hope that one of their squadron mates would sight them and radio their location to shore.

So many British fliers were lost in June and July that special observation planes were finally assigned to locate men and relay their positions to offshore craft. The task of spotting grew perceptibly easier when the RAF issued flares and—emulating the Germans—fluorescine dye. Results were good: though air casualties rose on both sides as the fighting intensified in August and September, fewer British airmen were lost to the sea.

Air Fleet 5 out of Norway and Denmark, finally received orders putting his men in action, but he lived to regret them. Completely forgetting about radar, and in the dark about the breaking of the German code, Stumpff decided to launch a surprise attack across the North Sea against airfields and aircraft factories in northeast England, between Tynemouth and northern Yorkshire.

His planes were tracked on radar for at least an hour before they arrived, and the RAF's fighters had ample time to position themselves, up-sun, to descend on the two main waves of bombers. One attacking force of 65 Heinkels, escorted by Me-110s, was almost immediately scattered and forced to drop its bombs far from its scheduled targets. Fifty Junkers-88s, also escorted by 110s, managed to hit an ammunition dump on an airfield near Bridlington and to destroy 10 Whitley bombers at an RAF bomber station at Driffield before being routed. Stumpff's planes limped back to Norway minus 16 Heinkels and six Ju-88s, a loss representing 20 per cent of Stumpff's total bomber force. Seven 110s were also shot down.

Not a single RAF plane was lost in the air. Considering that the fighter defenses in northeast England had been drastically pruned to reinforce the Channel coast, it was an impressive victory for the British. Stumpff's forces were judged to be so badly mauled that his fleet was retired from the Battle of Britain after one more sortie.

In southern England on August 15, however, the going was rougher for the British, both in the air and on the ground. Stukas, Heinkels and Ju-88s methodically shuttled back and forth across the Channel, bombing RAF airfields. Hangars were set afire and runways were pocked with bomb holes all the way from Portsmouth to the Thames estuary, and inland as far as Biggin Hill, in the outer suburbs of London. There was hardly a patch of sky over 200 miles of coastline where air duels were not in progress.

Not only were vapor trails visible but the watchers below could also see the smoke from damaged planes or the sudden red flash of flame as one of them exploded. Though the dogfights were being fought thousands of feet up, the noise of battle reached the ground—racing motors pushed to their limit; the scream of propellers and engines as planes went into impossible dives and turns; the rattle of machine guns and the thud of cannon; and the thunderclap of a Spit, or a Hurricane or a 109 as it blew up in the air.

There had never been a day like it. So far as dogfights were concerned, there would never be one like it again. By the end of the fighting that night, when the exhausted pilots turned in, the Luftwaffe had flown 1,780 sorties—520 of them bomber raids—against the RAF and its installations. The Germans claimed 12 RAF stations put out of action and 99 RAF planes destroyed in the air. The British in turn reported huge damage inflicted on the enemy—182 Luftwaffe planes destroyed in the course of 974 RAF sorties.

As in previous encounters, both claims were overblown. The Luftwaffe's real toll of the RAF was 34 planes, not 99. The RAF's bag was 75 Luftwaffe planes, not 182. But both sides were shaken by the extent of their losses, both of planes and pilots. Many of the German planes that were shot down had crews of three or four, while the British, many of whose planes were single-seaters, suffered a total of only 17 dead and 16 hurt.

By the third week of August, true summer weather prevailed; the sun was bright, the sky unclouded. Conditions for daily combat—for killing or getting killed in the air —were ideal. The pilots on both sides were now living a strange life. From dawn onwards they hung around the airfield, listening for the bell that would signal them to scramble. After hastily relieving themselves beside their planes, they were off for an encounter with the enemy that rarely lasted more than 15 minutes. But these were 15 minutes in which a man lived or died, got his skin burned off or his arm blown away, ended up in the drink, walked home from a wreck, or swooped down in triumph to report a victory.

RAF pilots considered it bad form to mourn lost comrades or to reveal that they were frightened, and on the surface they tended to take things lightly. The moment darkness fell and the fighting was finished, they were on their way to London and a show or a nightclub, a pretty WAAF or a girl in one of the revues.

Luftwaffe pilots who were based in northern France found the inhabitants aloof if not hostile; the airmen kept to themselves. In contrast to the British, they ceremoniously grieved over lost comrades by leaving an empty place at the table and drinking a toast of farewell. But they lived well—plenty of excellent French wine, the best *cuisine française*. And they were able to find at least some women for companionship when things got lonely.

As the air war raged on, both sides were bleeding badly, and heroes were beginning to emerge. So fierce and frequent were the battles that it was something of an achievement for a man to end a day of dogfights with himself and his plane still in one piece. But certain pilots achieved even more. Some showed great qualities as inspirational leaders of their fellow fliers, others proved to be specialists in the kill, and still others combined these talents.

One of the most ruthlessly efficient of the killer-leaders was British; another, German. R. R. Stanford Tuck was a lean, ruddy-faced Briton who joined the RAF in 1935 but first learned the art of the chase as a boy, going after stags in Scotland and ducks in his native Sussex marshes. During the retreat from Dunkirk, Tuck had shot down eight German planes in four days. His successes continued to mount through July and August. "He always seems to be around when the Nazis show up," said a fellow pilot, after Tuck had downed two enemy planes while out on what he called a "pleasure spin." By November he had bagged 25.

Besides his uncanny skill at outshooting the enemy, Tuck knew how to command a flight, how to protect his weaklings, how to nurture fledgling pilots, and how to get his formation safely home again after battle.

On the German side was the equally formidable Werner Mölders, a superb airman and innovator. It was Mölders who had taught his comrades over Spain how to fly the loose-winged formations that had first wreaked so much havoc on Spanish Republican pilots in 1937, and subsequently proved to be equally devastating against RAF neophytes in the early clashes of 1940. Mölders was an implacable enemy of the British—and anyone else who stood in the way of Hitler's plans—and he gave no quarter in battle. His November score was 45 enemy planes, making him Germany's ace of aces —and most decorated soldier.

Another of the great hunters who prowled the skies over the Channel was the RAF's Douglas Bader, commander of a wing of Spitfires. Bader showed the Germans no mercy and cut into his opponents with cool, savage expertise each time he found them. "I am not one of those," he observed, "who regard war as a game of cricket—first to shoot each other and then to shake hands."

Bader had joined the RAF as a cadet in 1930, and 18 months later lost both his legs in a flying accident. Invalided out of the service, he had learned to manage on artificial legs, even playing golf. When war came in 1939, he persuaded the RAF to take him back, and amazed his juniors by his agility. His hard-driving determination and skill as a pilot and dogfighter won him such esteem from enemy fliers that when he was shot down over France in 1941—after accounting for 23 German planes—his captors arranged for the delivery of a spare leg, dropped to him by the RAF to replace one smashed when he crash landed.

DOUGLAS BADER

ADOLF GALLAND

These two aces, deadly enemies in the English skies, met through a chivalrous encounter in France. When Bader, who flew his Spitfire despite two artificial legs, was shot down and captured, he was mortified by the chance that his conqueror might be a noncommissioned officer. Galland, who commanded the squadron that bagged Bader, later recounted that his men were not sure who had downed the British ace, but to mollify him, a top officer was chosen as the victor—to Bader's relief.

An unlikely friendship eventually developed between Bader and Germany's deadly but gentlemanly Adolf Galland, who had joined the Luftwaffe in the early 1930s when German rearmament was still a secret. Galland learned to fly in gliders. Later he developed his fighting skills in powered aircraft over Spain. Good-looking, with a Groucho Marx moustache and a flair for showy uniforms, cigars, champagne and girls, Galland was second only to Mölders as a Luftwaffe ace, with 40 planes to his credit by the autumn of 1940. More a patriotic German than an admirer of the Nazis, he blamed Göring's inefficiency for the mistakes Germany was making as the Battle of Britain was nearing its crescendo.

Galland did not hesitate to say as much when the Reich Marshal visited the front. Göring asked him what he and his comrades most needed to help them win the battle. "A squadron of Spitfires," said Galland.

Galland curtly refused to accept a Luftwaffe directive ordering that RAF pilots who bailed out after losing their planes be machine-gunned, and he instructed the pilots of the Me-109 wing he commanded to leave them alone. The order had been in reprisal to the British decision to destroy the Red Cross rescue seaplanes that the Luftwaffe was sending out to search for downed German pilots. Galland felt that this was barbarous of the British, but did not allow it to affect his own sense of honor toward the enemy. He was unfailingly gallant with his opponents—including Bader himself. When Bader was recuperating in Saint-Omer Hospital after being shot down, Galland sent his own staff car to bring the British flier to Group Staff Headquarters for tea and a tour of the German air base. Indeed it was Galland who interceded with Göring to have Bader's spare leg dropped, and he criticized as "not very friendly" the RAF's use of the occasion to unleash a heavy load of bombs on the air base and other targets near Saint-Omer.

At the end of the War in 1945, when Galland, by then a general, was brought to Britain for questioning, one of the men before whom he stood as prisoner was Douglas Bader. The Englishman, much mellowed by War's end, showed great concern for Galland's well-being and plied him with cigars. In later years the two became fast friends, exchanging frequent visits and attending air meets together.

Such an outcome would have seemed preposterous indeed during the increasingly ferocious encounters over the Channel after Eagle Day. In the four days starting August 15, the RAF shot down 194 Luftwaffe planes—actual, not merely claimed—and these were heavier losses than even Göring was prepared to bear. He ordered the Stukas and Me-110s that had taken most of the punishment withdrawn from the battle, and insisted that the Me-109s give his bomber squadrons closer protection.

Meanwhile he comforted himself with intelligence reports that claimed the Luftwaffe's losses were light compared with those of the foe. Their statistics indicated that the RAF was no longer a serious defensive force. By August 16, Göring's experts calculated, RAF front-line fighter strength was down to 300 planes; four days later, with 160 RAF fighters reported destroyed in the interim, the British were believed to have fewer than 150 left.

The truth was that the RAF still had 750 fighters. Nevertheless, Fighter Command was now reaching the point of exhaustion, and Dowding was worried about the ability of its personnel to keep up with the demands now being made of them. Far too many pilots had been killed or wounded. East Grinstead Hospital in Sussex was filling up with horribly burned fliers, their faces, hands, hair, skin scorched away. They were the first wave of a group of young men who came to be called the Guinea Pigs, because cosmetic surgeons had to experiment on them to give them back some semblance of human appearance.

Their surviving comrades, though still physically intact, were bone-tired. And their morale was wilting, because the Germans never seemed to let up. On the ground, labor squads worked night and day to get bombed bases repaired and fit again for action. Often this proved to be an exercise in futility, because each time that the squads got a runway back into use, down would come the Luftwaffe's bombers to wreck it again.

The weariness and near despair of the over-strained RAF pilots were felt by Squadron Leader E. M. Donaldson of 151 Fighter Squadron as he went on leave in August. "I was convinced that we were beaten, that we had lost the battle," he later wrote. "I was fantastically tired and utterly depressed. My squadron had been in heavy fighting since May without a break. I left it, I thought, a very depleted and thoroughly beaten fighting unit." And the real test was yet to come.

EXODUS FROM THE CITIES

Parents and tykes left behind in the city wave goodbye to a trainload of children being evacuated to safer temporary homes in the country.

SEND-OFF FOR A LILLIPUTIAN ARMY

During 1939 and 1940, a stream of reluctant recruits assembled on railway platforms and at highway pickup points in England's major cities and marched resolutely onto waiting transport. The marchers were city children, off to new foster homes in rural and suburban areas. Herded along by schoolteachers, each was carefully tagged with an identification card and armed with a gas mask, a toothbrush, a towel and a change of underwear. Like many a real soldier, these youngsters did not know where they were going. Some looked scared; some cried; but many managed the appearance of good spirits before setting off into the unknown.

The journey started well for most of the children, but problems began to arise almost as soon as they arrived at their new homes. In some reception areas hosts—who were paid a modest allowance by the government—snatched up the most presentable-looking evacuees like so many slaves at market, leaving the fate of scruffier ones to billeting officers. And in the eyes of British country and suburban families, a few of the children, particularly the slum dwellers, were appallingly scruffy: some had lice, others relieved themselves in any convenient corner.

Despite some of the shocks and even hostility of first meetings, the child-lift was generally successful. Many families came to love their small evacuees, and maintained close contact with them for years afterward. Most of the children enjoyed their holiday in the country where they romped on real grass, and discovered that apples grew on trees and that milk came from a wondrous animal called a cow, which one child described as having "six sides . . . and a head for the purpose of growing horns."

In two years about two million children were removed to the countryside. Some mothers of small children, as well as many pregnant women, invalids and old people were also evacuated. Some of the children went home after a few weeks, while others remained in their foster homes throughout the War. Back in the cities, their parents, as one father put it, were "better able to stand up to the Nazis without worrying what will happen to our tots."

Two passengers at London's Charing Cross Station read a notice that says regular trains have been commandeered for the evacuation of children.

A soldier gives a farewell kiss to his son, who is equipped with an identification tag, a parcel of belongings and a gas mask in a box slung over his shoulder.

Children assemble in their London schoolyard for the trip. While one teacher checks a girl's identification, a king-sized Boy Scout, who has been pressed into service for the child-lift, prepares to lead the youngsters to their trains.

In Plymouth, departing children scurry to catch a lorry. When rail lines became overloaded or bombed out, trucks, buses and automobiles helped carry children out of the cities.

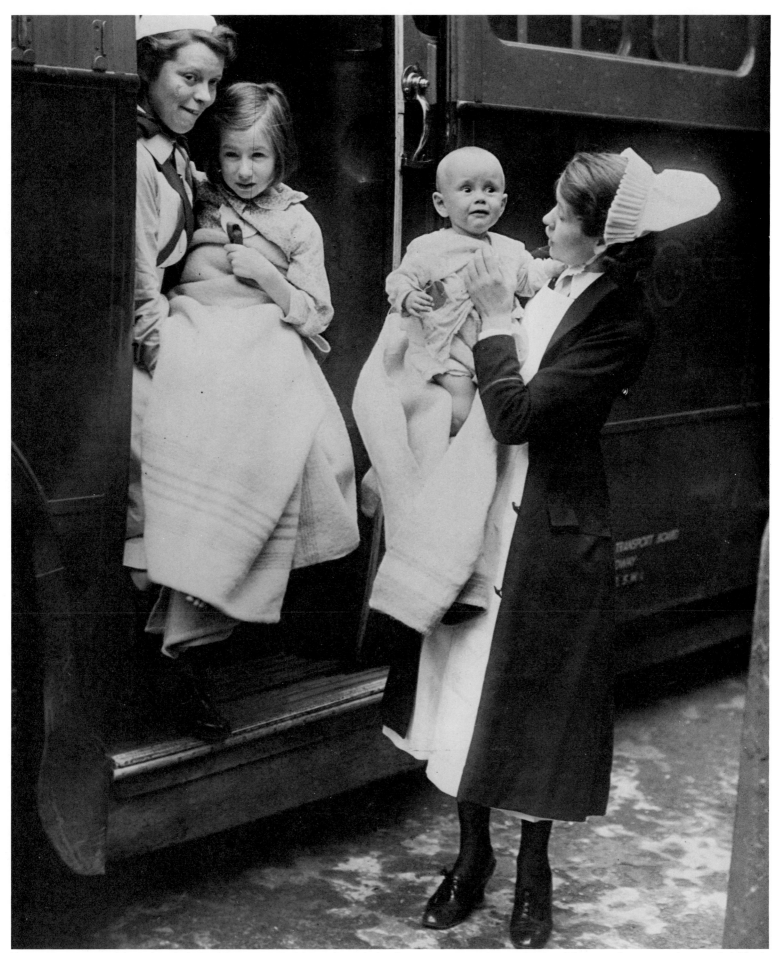

Youngsters evacuated from hospitals in cities are carried from the train by their nurses; sometimes adult invalids were also removed to rural sickbeds.

Evacuees in a Devonshire cottage dutifully line up for a bath in a tin tub on the kitchen floor. The homeowners who adopted this small mob originally signed up for just two, but liked them so well they increased the number to nine.

To help alleviate the housing crush that was brought on by visiting children, the citizens of some towns loaned out trailers like this one in Cambridge—which evacuees promptly adorned with a homemade coat of camouflage.

Youngsters and their mothers, who have been evacuated from their bombed-out homes in the tinder-box slums of London's East End, gather for communal tea of bread, margarine and jam.

A group of tots lines up to receive an issue of new shoes that were donated by a local factory at Bletchley, near Northampton. Other manufacturers and private citizens all over Britain donated blankets, clothing, toys, fresh fruits and vegetables for the evacuees.

Toddlers from London grab smock-tails to play "caterpillar" at their new home on an estate in Buckingham. Though many owners of English mansions gladly took in children, some refused to accept them, or did so only grudgingly. One wit described such reluctant saviors thus: "Inspired by Britain's glorious cause/With seven maids to do the chores/Gather round at country teas/And grouse about evacuees."

Under the watchful eye of their teacher, city-bred tots discover the unfamiliar and fascinating world of beetles, leaves and mud along a peaceful country lane.

Two boys from the East End acquaint themselves with a pair of rural kids on a farm in Worksop, Notts.

At a party given by policemen in Kent, guests try to pin the mustache on the man who started it all.

111

A temporary reunion of evacuated children and their parents takes place in a joyous rush on the platform of a rural station. To ease the strain of separation,

the government arranged for special "cheap days" on the railroads so that parents could travel to evacuation areas for periodic get-togethers like this one.

4

Reich Marshal Hermann Göring was a firm believer in the strategy of the carrot and the stick, and when he made an inspection tour of the Luftwaffe's bomber and fighter units in northern France on August 21, 1940, he brought the stick with him. So far the Reich Marshal had had little but the highest of praise for his pilots; now at Cap Blanc-Nez he had only withering words for them.

Behind Göring's wrath lay the fact that the timetable for the destruction of Britain's war-making potential was breaking down, and the date for the launching of Operation *Sea Lion*—the invasion of the island kingdom—would have to be postponed. Each time his intelligence officers reported the near annihilation of the RAF, squadrons of Spitfires and Hurricanes subsequently rose into the sky and proceeded to knock down his bombers. The Luftwaffe's reverses raised a flock of questions. Where did the RAF's fighters come from? Why were they not being sought out in their hiding places? And why were the RAF's supply factories and repair shops not being bombed out of existence?

Göring railed at his weary pilots. The bolder ones, like Adolf Galland, defended themselves. They deeply resented his criticism, and they were cut to the quick when he called some of them cowards. But Göring's rough tactics worked. His taunts provoked a rage that drove the tiredness out of the men, and their fighting instincts were further rekindled as he outlined the next move to be made against the enemy.

It would begin in just three days—August 24—and its objective would be no less than the total erasure of Britain's air power. The days of mere dogfighting over the Channel were past. Phase Two of the Luftwaffe's grand plan was at hand: Massive numbers of bombers, amply escorted by fighters, would level not only the RAF's ground installations, but also the oil tanks that supplied its fuel and the factories that produced its parts and replacements. The assault on these targets would go on "by night and day," Göring declared, and thus would be bound to bring out the RAF's damnably elusive fighters. The Reich Marshal instructed his pilots: "The enemy is to be forced to use his fighters by means of ceaseless attacks."

Before returning to Germany, Göring went to a forward observation post on Cap Gris-Nez, overlooking the Channel, and spent some time staring through high-powered binoculars at the cliffs of Dover. The towers of the Dover radar

THE ATTACK ON LONDON

station were in his sights, but he made no comment about them. To one member of the party accompanying him, "It was as if he was trying to look beyond those white cliffs into the minds of his British adversaries."

Had he been able to do so, he would undoubtedly have been pleased, because the RAF Fighter Command was in serious trouble. The problem was not so much airplanes as the pilots to fly them. Thanks largely to the stepped-up production of new planes, the RAF could still put some 700 fighters into the air in spite of a total of 270 aircraft that had been shot down, damaged beyond immediate repair or destroyed on the ground since August 8. However, Fighter Command had also lost 94 pilots killed or missing since that same date, and another 60 fliers had been hospitalized with wounds or burns.

To fill the gap, Air Chief Marshal Dowding and his Group Commanders had at their disposal a number of volunteers newly arrived from other lands. There was one squadron made up entirely of Canadians, and other squadrons were buttressed by Polish and Czech pilots. The Canadians tended to be a swashbuckling lot. And the exiled pilots, with their lands conquered and occupied and their families far away and unreachable, flew with the fierce determination of men with scores to settle. But the skills of these new pilots were not yet up to the special demands of the battle of the Channel; in addition, they tended to take too many risks with themselves and their machines.

What Dowding needed was a flock of veterans who could shoot down bombers, dodge the enemy's fighters, and come back whole and ready to fight again. One pilot with battle experience was worth two or even three novices, and the growing scarcity of seasoned men was affecting Fighter Command's strength.

Another trial besetting Dowding was the steadily worsening friction between his two top Group Commanders, Air Vice Marshals Park and Leigh-Mallory, commanders of 11 Group and 12 Group respectively. As Dowding's personal assistant, Pilot Officer Robert Wright, put it later: "While Dowding and Park shared a complete understanding of the tactics best suited to the needs of Fighter Command, the same cannot be said of the 12 Group Commander. Leigh-Mallory appeared to believe that he knew more even than Dowding about how the fighters should be used."

More bluntly put, Leigh-Mallory wanted Dowding's post. At the age of 57, the Fighter Command chief was regarded by younger members of the Air Ministry as too old for his job; he had been retained until now only at Prime Minister Churchill's insistence. Leigh-Mallory believed that his chances of being named successor depended upon his achieving the glory of a great victory over the Germans in the Battle of Britain. And that, he was convinced, would not come his way if 12 Group did not get enough of the action.

As Leigh-Mallory saw it, this infuriating state of affairs was due to what he called "the whims and fancies" of Dowding and Park. Although 12 Group's primary function was to protect England's industrial midlands from attack, the Luftwaffe had not yet appeared over the area in any strength; it was continuing to concentrate on southern Britain, the defense of which was the responsibility of Park's 11 Group. Park —with Dowding in full accord—felt that Leigh-Mallory's less harassed pilots might well be used to cover 11 Group's bases while Park's squadrons were off tangling with the Germans. Leigh-Mallory disdained the notion. Instead, egged on by his most effective, impatient and persuasive pilot, Douglas Bader, he took to sending his 12 Group planes into Park's territory in search of independent, offensive action against the enemy. Thus they were usually someplace else when Park needed their defensive help.

What this meant to 11 Group was swiftly demonstrated when Phase Two of the Luftwaffe operation began on the morning of August 24.

It was a fine day, a Saturday, and by 9 a.m. more than 100 Luftwaffe bombers and fighters were swarming over 11 Group's bases. The first airfield to be hit was at Manston, near Ramsgate. Its runways were quickly blanketed with bomb craters, while virtually all of its buildings were completely destroyed, and its telephone and teleprinter lines cut. Manston itself was also badly hit, and there were a large number of civilian casualties. So great was the havoc that the town had to be permanently abandoned. Not far away from London, two other fighter bases, North Weald and Hornchurch, also suffered heavy damage. Hitting these targets was a special triumph for the German raiders, for they were Fighter Command sector stations—the nerve centers that controlled and directed the British pilots once they went aloft. An appeal to 12 Group to protect the bases brought two squadrons from Duxford but they arrived too late to be of any use.

In the days that followed, Britain's defenders were made increasingly and more painfully aware of the soundness of the enemy's new strategy in the air—and the ingenuity of his new tactics. To confuse British radar plotters, formations of Luftwaffe planes were flying all day long up and down the French coast, just within range of the RAF's radar screens. The plotters had no way of predicting when one of the formations would suddenly turn north and whip across the Channel on a genuine raid.

By this time the Germans had withdrawn the ineffectual Stukas from the battle, but their Junkers-88s and Dorniers were penetrating well inland, right to the outskirts of London, dropping their deadly cargoes on Fighter Command sector stations, aircraft factories and repair shops.

The German bombers were protected by long-range Messerschmitt-110s, some of which had been equipped for double duty: loaded with bombs, they would nip in for remarkably effective strikes of their own. All too often, RAF fighter pilots flying back to base from an encounter in the sky would find that, in their absence, the Luftwaffe had made a shambles of the airfield; a number of 11 Group's planes were wrecked, and the pilots killed, in attempts to land where no safe landing surface remained.

Before very long Air Vice Marshal Park was not merely asking for help from Leigh-Mallory's 12 Group; he was demanding it. Dowding therefore issued a direct order to Leigh-Mallory requiring that his 12 Group provide protective patrols over 11 Group's bases.

Leigh-Mallory reluctantly assented; however, more often than not his fighters did not get there until after the Luftwaffe had already done its damage. The main energies of 12 Group were still being employed elsewhere. With Leigh-Mallory's blessing, Douglas Bader was experimenting with putting five or more squadrons into the air as a group, their aim being to destroy the attacking Luftwaffe fleets en masse. These so-called Big Wings were enjoying a certain measure of success in the interception and cutting up of enemy concentrations of bombers and fighters as they were returning from their missions. But Big Wings took

so long to assemble that by the time they reached operational height the enemy was likely to be gone. Furthermore, the bombs had already been dropped.

One day, at a hurriedly called conference at Bentley Priory, Dowding brought his contending commanders face to face. The bitterness was unconcealed; the two men immediately launched into a shouting match over the efficiency of the Big Wings. It became abundantly clear that Commanders Park and Leigh-Mallory harbored fundamentally different views of the nature of the battle in which their country was engaged. Leigh-Mallory didn't care *when* he fought the enemy's bombers so long as he knocked them down. Park wanted the bombers knocked down *before* they hit his fields or vital neighboring factories.

Dowding, who agreed with Park, finally saw no point in continuing the discussion. He ended it by grimly reminding his commanders that they were arguing about tactics—and that in the meantime the strategic situation was rapidly deteriorating. Fighter Command was now 200 pilots short, and those who were still able to fly were on the verge of exhaustion. Thus far, since August 24, they had managed to inflict more losses each day on the Luftwaffe than the enemy had inflicted on the RAF. But the balance of this scale might shift at any moment.

Dowding's fear proved well-founded. On August 31, the RAF Fighter Command had its worst day. Wave after wave of German bombers roared in to put most of the bases in southeastern England out of action. Landing grounds became bomb-pocked moonscapes, airfield hangars and operational buildings were razed, power cables were cut, planes were blown up and ground personnel killed. In all, the attackers dropped more than 4,400 tons of bombs.

By the time darkness came, Fighter Command's combat losses totaled 39 planes and 14 pilots—its heaviest casualties ever for a single day. For the first time since the Battle of Britain had begun, fewer German planes had been destroyed during the course of the day than the RAF had lost. After only one week, Phase Two of the Luftwaffe's operation seemed to be succeeding beyond Reich Marshal Göring's wildest expectations.

Next day, September 1, American correspondents in Berlin reported sheer joy everywhere around them. German military men were predicting that Operation *Sea Lion* would

be launched in "the next four days," and that the swastika would soon be flying over London. Two days later, Hitler scheduled the start of the operation for September 21.

For Dowding the picture was one of unrelieved gloom. The damage the Germans had inflicted on aircraft plants had caused a slowdown not only in the production of new planes but also in the repair of old ones. Losses of planes were now exceeding replacements. But far more unbearable to Dowding were the losses in pilots. Moreover, there was a distinct danger that the survivors, nearing the limits of their endurance, would soon lose efficiency and cohesion as a fighting force.

Dowding was a religious man who had never faltered in his belief that God was on the side of the British. At this point, however, the Air Chief Marshal wanted some sort of sign from the Almighty. "What we need now," he confessed, "is a miracle."

What he did not realize was that he already had been handed one: a navigational error by two night-flying Luftwaffe pilots whose blunder was to be a major factor in changing the whole course of the Battle of Britain.

In launching Phase Two of the Luftwaffe operation, Reich Marshal Göring had given his men free rein in every respect except one. They had carte blanche to bomb by day and by night, and in any area where Britain's air power could be hit —including its cities. But Göring had put one city strictly off-limits: England's capital. He had drawn a line around the outer perimeter of the metropolitan area of London and, on Hitler's specific instructions, had banned any bombing attacks inside that line.

Hitler's reasons for ordering the absolution of London have never been adequately explained. He may have wished, once he had conquered Britain, to ride in triumph down an undamaged Pall Mall from an undamaged Buckingham Palace to the undamaged Houses of Parliament. It may have been because he feared the adverse propaganda effect on the neutral world of the destruction of London's ancient monuments. Or he may just have shrewdly calculated that smashing the capital would give him no tactical or strategic advantage whatsoever.

Among the Luftwaffe's commanders, there were some who believed that continuous terror raids upon London

An RAF fighter pilot whose plane was shot down in the Battle of Britain tells smock-clad workers at a parachute factory how one of their chutes saved his life. Flight Lieutenant Peter Townsend (left), one of the RAF's leading aces, and another pilot await their turn to thank the workers. Such visits were arranged by the Air Ministry and the Ministry of Supply, who shrewdly deemed that in-person thanks from grateful hero pilots like these would boost both morale and productivity at the factories where planes and lifesaving equipment were being produced.

would shatter civilian morale, as they had done in Warsaw; that relentless bombing would bring the demoralized British to the negotiating table. Göring did not agree. "Would the people of Berlin capitulate under terror bombing?" he asked. "I do not believe it. I cannot see the people of London pleading for mercy either." For the moment, therefore, neither Göring nor Hitler wanted to see London destroyed.

In Britain, on the other hand, there were those in high places who were actually hoping for the Luftwaffe to turn its attention on the capital. A story current at the time recounted how Churchill went into the garden of 10 Downing Street each night during this phase of the battle and, as he listened to the drone of bombers and the thud of bombs on the outer suburbs, raised his hands to the sky and cried: "Why don't you come here? Bomb us, bomb us!" Whether the story was true or not, certainly this was a moment when Britain needed all the support it could get from the United States, and Churchill believed that nothing would be more likely to gain American sympathy—and aid—than the spectacle of London laid waste.

Dowding, too, wanted to see the Luftwaffe over London —for more practical and immediate reasons. If the enemy's attacks on Fighter Command and its bases went on at the present rate, London would be wide open anyway, because the air-defense system protecting it would have been wiped out. But if the Germans began bombing the capital, that diversion of striking power would take the pressure off Dowding's sector stations and supply bases and would provide Fighter Command with some time to breathe, recoup and gain the strength to fight again.

Too wily to fall into the trap, Hitler maintained his standing order that the Luftwaffe's bombers were to avoid metropolitan London; he showed no sign of changing his mind.

But the error already committed by two of his pilots was to change Hitler's mind for him. On the night of August 24, some 170 Luftwaffe bombers had swept in to raid targets from Kent all the way north to the Scottish border. A number of the planes were assigned to bomb the aircraft factories of the Thames-side towns of Rochester and Kingston and the huge oil-tank storage installations at Thameshaven, some 15 miles downriver from London. The lead planes, which were flying on radio beams, were followed by others that were not so equipped. On the run-in to the targets, two of these planes lost visual touch with their radio-equipped pathfinders and strayed on beyond the main attack pattern. A fountain of flak rose to meet them and the antiaircraft barrage became thicker as they flew on, clinging together. At last, realizing they were lost, the two pilots decided that there was only one thing to do. They jettisoned their bombs, turned east, and raced for home.

As it happened, they were over London itself when they unloaded their bombs. Two of them fell on the heart of the city, razing the ancient church of St. Giles in Cripplegate and ripping John Milton's statue off its pedestal in a nearby square. The rest of the bombs crashed down in the northern and eastern London boroughs of Islington, Finchley, Stepney, Tottenham and Bethnal Green among others, killing customers as they came out of the pubs at closing time and audiences on their way home from movie houses.

There was little doubt, even at the time, that the bombing was unintentional. And later analyses indeed proved that the attack programs of the Luftwaffe over the next few nights called for no raids on London; instead, they were focusing their attention on such vital industrial centers as Liverpool and Birmingham. But Churchill was delighted to believe otherwise—and to act accordingly.

He convened the Chiefs of Staff Committee and got a unanimous decision from its members. An order went to RAF Bomber Command and through it to a wing of Hampden bombers stationed in Norfolk, on England's east coast. During the previous week, this wing had been restricted to scattering propaganda leaflets over Germany, warning that "the war which Hitler started will go on, and it will last as long as Hitler does."

Now the commander of the wing, John Oxley, was told to load up with bombs for a reprisal raid on Berlin. Göring had always assured Hitler and the German people that enemy bombers would never reach the German capital ("if they do, you can call me Meier," he had joked).

The Reich Marshal was, to say the least, discomfited on August 25 when the RAF's Hampdens made a night raid on the Berlin suburb of Ruhleben. Though they did little material damage, they created considerable panic among civilians and they hurt Göring's prestige. The bombs had hardly stopped falling when he promised Hitler that there would be no more such attacks. But there were. Churchill immediately gave instructions that the RAF keep hitting Berlin until the Germans reacted.

After three more quick strikes by the British, Hitler was aroused sufficiently to call in Göring and order him to prepare his bomber forces for a major riposte. On September 4, just after the fourth RAF raid—again at night—the Führer addressed a mass meeting in the Sportspalast in Berlin, and he was in a belligerent mood.

"Mr. Churchill is demonstrating his new brain child, the night air raid," he shouted. "He is carrying out these raids not because they promise to be highly effective, but because his air force cannot fly over German soil in daylight."

But, the Führer went on to assure his audience, he planned to do something about this new effrontery by the British: "When they declare that they will increase their attacks on our cities, then we will *raze* their cities to the ground. We will stop the handiwork of these night air pirates, so help us God! When the British air force drops 3,000 or 4,000 kilograms of bombs, then we will, in one raid, drop 300,000 or 400,000 kilograms. . . . In England they are filled with curiosity and keep asking: 'Why doesn't he come?' Be calm.

Echoing the ancient Roman gesture signifying "kill," a 1940 Italian poster urges thumbs down on the city of London. Tower Bridge (right), the Tower of London (four spires, center) and church spires are all depicted as flaming ruins. Posters like this one were designed to encourage Italians in the belief that their German ally's air power was invincible and that the cities of their enemies were being inexorably destroyed.

Be calm. He is coming! He is coming! . . . The hour will come when one of us will break, and it will not be National Socialist Germany!"

Göring needed no further word. The Reich Marshal left for northern France in his special train the next morning; the following night, on a railroad siding between the ports of Calais and Boulogne, he gave a banquet for his air fleet commanders at which some of his choicest French wines and food were served. From now on, Göring told his guests, he would be taking personal command of the battle. A toast was drunk to "Victory!"

Twelve hours later, on the afternoon of Saturday, September 7, the Luftwaffe chief stood at the forward observation post on Cap Gris-Nez in France, his round red face aglow. Over his head, wave upon wave of Luftwaffe bombers roared across the narrow strip of the English Channel. Their destination: London. At long last, Hitler had been goaded into changing the basic strategy of the Battle of Britain, and Reich Marshal Göring was as excited as a small boy at a country fair waiting for the fireworks to begin.

As for the British, although the air war was about to go generally in the way that they had expected it would, the intensity of the attack took them by surprise and they came perilously close to total disaster before they could recoup.

At 4 p.m. that Saturday afternoon, Air Chief Marshal Dowding was at his desk in Bentley Priory when there was a knock at the door, and his aide, Pilot Officer Wright, came in. Outside, the day was lovely and soft, but Dowding's office was chill with the air of impending disaster. The Luftwaffe's ceaseless attacks had forced him to move his fighter squadrons inland, abandoning those bases nearer the Channel and the North Sea. Now, it seemed, the move had been made at the worst possible time.

That same morning the Air Ministry had issued a curt warning to all RAF commands: *Invasion Alert No. 1.* This was the top priority alarm, signaling the expectation that the German Army itself would be launched in a seaborne infantry attack against England sometime within the next 24 hours. In order to throw back the German troop transports, landing barges and protective screen of fighters as they approached the Channel beaches, Dowding needed the forward airfields—which he now no longer had.

He glanced up as Wright approached the desk. "It looks like a big one, sir," the aide reported. "Ops say several formations of 20-plus are boiling up over Calais."

The two men went to the balcony of the Operations Room and looked down at the great map of the Channel and England spread out over the table below them. Blue-shirted girls of the WAAF, wearing headphones, were pushing blocks across the chart with long rods. Each block represented a flight of planes, either enemy or RAF according to its color. The positions of the blocks were being changed as quickly as new information was received from outlying stations. From the way the blocks were being raked across the table —and from the increasing numbers of them that were being introduced onto the board—it was as if a giant roulette game was in progress.

Dowding could see that the raid being charted was indeed a big one, with all indications that it might be the biggest yet. Already, some 250 bombers and 500 fighters were moving across the Channel, while even more were still assembling behind Calais.

The chief of Fighter Command scrutinized the chart to see what Commander Park of 11 Group was doing to prepare for the onslaught. He was relieved to see that Park's Spitfires and Hurricanes were already airborne. Dowding knew they would follow the system that had proved most effective in the air clashes of the past two weeks. The RAF fighters, fed minute-to-minute information by Fighter Command through an air-ground telephone system, would hover at around 20,000 feet until they were told that the Luftwaffe's big groups were splitting up. That was the customary procedure that the enemy planes had followed once they reached the English coast—heading for aircraft factories, for oil storage tanks and refineries along the Thames, and for airfields and industrial complexes around London. Once the raiding formations were known to have split up, the RAF squadron leader would sound the call for action —the traditional "Tally ho!" of the huntsman on first sighting the fox. Then his pilots would zoom down to take on the foe, section by section, aiming to down as many of the Germans as possible before they could reach their targets.

As Dowding watched the great chart to see how the RAF's defensive maneuvers were developing, he had a sudden premonition, as he recalled later, "like a stab to the heart."

What if, this time, the raiders did not split up, but came on instead en masse? No preparations had been made for that contingency. And the city of London was wide open. Dowding was still contemplating this prospect when his aide spoke up. "That's funny," he said, "they don't seem to be splitting up, do they, sir?"

Some 300 Dornier and Heinkel medium bombers, escorted by 600 Me-109s and 110s, were now on their way. The first wave came in from the east and made directly for the Thames. Sweeping upriver, a few of the planes unloaded bombs on the oil tanks at Thameshaven, still burning from a raid the previous day. But about 150 others went on toward London. The bombers were flying much higher than usual, around 16,000 feet, closely escorted by Me-110s; above them patrolled steplike formations of weaving 109s, ready to take on any RAF fighters.

Watchers far below could see the occasional glint of a wing in the sun as the enemy raiders swept in. But there were no British fighters to intercept them, except on the fringes of their flight path, where a few dogfights developed. As news of the developing massive attack was flashed to Britain's ground defenses, antiaircraft fire opened up along the banks of the Thames and steadily increased in intensity. But the planes were too high, and the white puffballs of smoke as the ack-ack shells burst proved to be more of a salute to the raiders than a threat. The German airplanes came in like a neat and inexorable procession; at fixed points on their flight path, a signal would be given by the leaders and the bombs would be released.

The first target to be hit was Woolwich Arsenal, on the south bank of the Thames, where shells were produced for the army and bombs for the RAF. The hits were direct, sending a hellish mass of smoke and flame soaring into the afternoon sky like great rockets. The next target was the complex of wharves and warehouses of the London docks area, into which most of the city's supplies arrived from the outside world. Then came the Victoria and Albert Docks, the West India Dock, and the Commercial Docks. As they were plastered with bombs, ships were sunk, bridges and catwalks mangled, cranes toppled into the water, and spilled oil set aflame on its surface.

New waves of bombers that were coming in now needed

PORTRAIT OF THE PRIME MINISTER AS A GUN-TOTING GANGSTER

In this original newspaper photograph of a 1940 troop inspection, old soldier Churchill fingers the mechanism of a soldier's tommy gun with interest.

Propagandists on both sides of the Battle of Britain were almost as busy as the pilots, though to less effect. One notable Nazi misfire was the leaflet at right, inspired by a newspaper photograph (above) of Prime Minister Winston Churchill examining a sub-machine gun during a July 1940 inspection of British troops. The Germans got hold of the picture and removed all but a lone, gun-toting Churchill in the pose of a gangster.

Soon thousands of leaflets poured down on England showing the P.M. as another Al Capone, along with some shrill assertions about Churchill's crimes against humanity. But within a fortnight the Führer's astute propaganda chief, Joseph Goebbels, stopped the drops, rightly assuming that the gun-toting image would only enhance Churchill's immense popularity.

Isolated by a propagandist's doctoring, a threatening Winston Churchill looms from the Nazi leaflet contrived from the news picture.

WANTED

FOR INCITEMENT TO
MURDER

This gangster, who you see in his element in the picture, incites you by his example to participate in a form of warfare in which women, children and ordinary civilians shall take leading parts.

This absolutely criminal form of warfare which is forbidden by the

HAGUE CONVENTION

will be punished

according to military law

Save at least your families from the horrors of war!

no signals to tell them where to drop their bombs. The crews pulled the releases wherever they saw smoke and fires beneath them. The repeated drops soon took their toll in the mean streets and overcrowded houses of London's East End. The districts of Silvertown, Canning Town, Limehouse, Barking, Tower Bridge, Poplar and Millwall were pulverized. Residents who escaped being buried in the rubble packed bags, slung them into baby carriages or carts and began making their way out of the city, figuring—rightly, as it turned out—that there would be more bombs coming when night fell.

The RAF, caught off balance, was desperately trying to recover. Park summoned every plane in 11 Group into the air. Dowding ordered Leigh-Mallory to come to Park's aid. Soon fighters from both groups were slicing through the protective layers of Me-109s and 110s and pouncing on the bomber formations, attacking with savage determination. Londoners, staring apprehensively at the sky, took some consolation from seeing the smoke of burning Dorniers and Heinkels, and the carcasses of shattered bombers hurtling earthward to join the debris in the wrecked streets.

But so far as London was concerned, the RAF's effort had come too late. The damage had been done. Some 400 people were already dead, thousands injured. London's docks were badly damaged. And the razing of areas of the East End left a great mass of the city's population homeless. The average Cockney derived cold comfort from the fact that the RAF had shot down 47 of the raiders as they made their way back to base.

The Luftwaffe had good reason to be pleased with itself. Its tactics had made a mockery of London's antiaircraft defenses. Göring telephoned his wife, Emmy, to tell her that the British capital was in flames; he then addressed the German people by radio. His tone was exultant as he told them that he was now in charge of the battle, that London was the target, and that he had already delivered "a stroke straight to the enemy's heart."

There would be more, he promised.

As the afternoon of September 7 gave way to evening, a strange thing happened. Watchers on high ground around London all remarked on the glorious red glow of the setting sun. Then they slowly realized that it was setting in the wrong place. The glow was, in fact, the reflection in the sky of the East End in flames.

The fires served as beacons for waves of night bombers, come to punish the city some more. And as they rolled in, like lines of airborne trucks loaded with disaster, Winston Churchill and his Chiefs of Staff compounded the mess that Fighter Command had made of the day.

At 8 that evening, Britain's war leaders emerged from a daylong meeting in the Hole in the Ground—the government's underground headquarters in Whitehall—and sent an urgent message to all Home Forces in the United Kingdom. The message was a single code word: *Cromwell.*

There has been some argument ever since as to whether the signal *Cromwell* meant "Invasion Begun" or "Invasion Imminent." In any event, on September 7, 1940, there was no doubt about the way it was interpreted: "The German invasion of Britain has begun."

In fact, the invasion had not begun, nor was there any sign in the North Sea or the Channel that barges of German troops were on their way. Because the Germans were sending so many bombers over London, Churchill may have concluded that some of them were serving as transports for paratroopers and airborne units.

The code word *Cromwell* was meant for Army eyes only, but so many Home Guard units of civilians were by now attached to the Army that keeping the secret was impossible. Soon everybody knew about it. Church bells were rung to sound the alarm. Road blocks were set up. Bridges were blown. Mines were sown on roads and in fields.

In London's battered East End, firemen and air-raid wardens—dodging new German bombs raining down on them, fighting raging fires, rescuing the buried and the injured, and directing bombed-out refugees—had their job made even more difficult by orders to keep a careful lookout for parachutists and infiltrators.

"'Ow the 'ell d'you tell friend from foe," asked one Cockney fireman, "when we're all covered in the same s---?"

In round-the-clock raids over the next seven days, 2,000 more Londoners died and more than 10,000 were wounded or entombed in rubble. Scars spread across the face of the city, bringing, in the wake of death, a despairing ache to the hearts of all those who loved London's streets, churches, proud buildings and historic monuments.

But if people and ancient edifices were suffering, there

were compensations for the strategists who were trying to stave off a British defeat. The Germans' concentration on the capital had the immediate effect of taking the pressure off Fighter Command's airfields and supply factories. It also enabled the RAF to hit back at the enemy hard enough to hurt, because now the British knew where the Luftwaffe was focusing its attacks and could be ready and waiting.

On September 15, Göring decided to give London a larger dose of the medicine he had begun to hand out, and ordered a maximum effort from his bomber and fighter units.

The Reich Marshal had spent the previous week oscillating between euphoria and doubt. On the one hand, he was exhilarated by reports of the damage being done to the British capital; he had become convinced that the more Londoners were killed, the more eager would the rest of the nation be to sue for peace. Several times he assured his staff that the Luftwaffe was now so clearly the master of the skies over Britain that Operation *Sea Lion* would not be necessary; he would be able to pound Britain into surrender without a single German soldier having to fight his way up the British beaches.

On the other hand, Göring would plunge into a trough of dejection when Luftwaffe losses over England were reported to him. And when he paid a visit to his units in northern France, he was depressed because he heard nothing but complaints—from the bomber squadrons because they were not being adequately protected, from the fighter squadrons because London was at the far edge of their flying range and consequently they had only 10 or 20 minutes in which to fight before turning for home.

Both fighter and bomber squadron leaders were concerned about mounting losses. Bombers were being hit by certain RAF fighter squadrons which, Luftwaffe intelligence reports had asserted, no longer existed. Fighters were being shot down because they lacked the fuel to help them maneuver in a dogfight; others had to crash land on the Calais beaches with empty tanks.

Göring tried to placate the complainers. One last big daylight raid, he assured them, and it would all be over; the RAF would be eliminated by the *coup de grâce,* and London hit so hard that all it would be able to do would be to scream for mercy.

Sunday, September 15—henceforward to be known in RAF annals as Battle of Britain Day—was again sunny, with only a faint haze blurring an otherwise clear autumnal sky. At about mid-morning, masses of blips began to appear on British radar screens, and soon waves of Luftwaffe bombers were on their way. About 400 bombers, as well as 700 fighters, were involved, sweeping in thickening numbers toward the British capital.

But this time the raiders were attacked from the moment they hit the English coast, and from then on were never let alone. Fighter Command sent up its own maximum force —24 squadrons—and 22 of them, nearly 300 planes, were soon dogfighting with Me-109s or inflicting mayhem on the Dorniers and Heinkels.

The clashes continued all day, until the sky was crisscrossed in every direction with vapor trails. In the last engagement of the day, a pilot in a Hurricane, Sergeant R. T. Holmes, turned his machine guns on two Dorniers over the West End of London. He knocked part of a wing off one and hit the other so hard that it exploded in midair, simultaneously damaging the Hurricane severely. The crew of the first Dornier parachuted onto the Surrey cricket ground at Kennington Oval, and their plane crashed in the train yard of Victoria Station in central London. Holmes himself parachuted down into a garbage can on the King's Road in Chelsea.

The next day a London newspaper triumphantly headlined "185 ALL OUT." That figure was the score of German planes officially announced by the Air Ministry as having been destroyed by RAF and antiaircraft action.

Actually, the true figures were rather more modest: 56 German aircraft had been shot down by Fighter Command, 26 RAF planes had been lost. But several dozen more Luftwaffe bombers limped back to base with some crew members dead, engines ablaze and undercarriages shot away. At least 20 Me-109s, their tanks dry, had come down in the water in the 10-mile stretch between Le Touquet and Boulogne off France.

Göring was chastened. He had told Hitler to expect a turning point in the battle as a result of the September 15 onslaught. The turning point had certainly been reached, but not in the direction the Germans had anticipated.

On September 17, the Führer decided to postpone Operation *Sea Lion* indefinitely, and instructed his generals to bring about the subjugation of the British by other means.

WAITING FOR THE SCRAMBLE

RAF fighter pilots, outfitted for action in flight gear and Mae West life jackets, read, chat and doze in a ready room.

YOUNG WARRIORS ON A NEVER-ENDING ALERT

England was plagued with wasps during the summer of 1940. But one RAF fighter pilot, waiting to fly against the Luftwaffe, found he could dull the edge of his fear by killing the pesky insects—flinging blobs of strawberry jam at them. "They're the ground targets—the jam's the bomb load," he explained to his comrades.

He had just wiped out his 11th wasp, when the loudspeaker in the ready room where the strawberry bomber sat with fellow pilots suddenly rasped: "All sections scramble! Seventy-plus bandits approaching, angels one-five!" More than 70 German Dorniers and Heinkels with their Messerschmitt fighter escorts were coming at 15,000 feet over the Channel, and had to be intercepted. The fighter pilots grabbed their flying helmets, and dashed for Hurricanes and Spitfires lovingly made ready by ground crews and mechanics. Within a matter of seconds, the squadron was racketing away from the airfield in hazardous cross-wind take offs, virtually jumping into the skies.

These hard-pressed men, more than 1,000 of them under the command of Air Marshal Hugh Dowding, were astonishingly young—some were 19 or 20, and not many older than 23. Winston Churchill called them "Dowding's chicks," and said of them in ringing tribute: "Never was so much owed by so many to so few." To which one irreverent pilot responded, "He must have been thinking of our liquor bills."

Indeed, in their fleeting moments of respite from battle, these young men tended to drink and play as hard as they fought. But these moments were all too few. The German attacks in the summer and fall of 1940 were so incessant that many British fighter pilots felt lucky to grab a snack of cold beans and tepid tea between scrambles. Trying to maintain some amenities, the men of one squadron once sat down to roast beef at noon, but they had to break off so frequently that they didn't reach dessert until 3:30. At another base mess, pilots ordered a midday drink when they thought the pressure was off, only to hear their senior officer say, "Don't take too long over that sherry. I've only sounded the all-clear so that we can get some lunch."

Alerted by a telephoned alarm from Fighter Command, an airman sounds an improvised scramble bell to send pilots scampering toward their planes.

Back at home base after battling Luftwaffe bombers and fighters, tired RAF fliers recount the day's action—including the tally of enemy kills and their own losses.

Between engagements three armorers—called plumbers in RAF slang—load fresh belts of ammunition for the eight forward-firing machine guns of a Hurricane. Each fighter plane at an RAF base was assigned a ground crew of 12 skilled airmen to keep it combat-ready.

Propped up into firing position, a Spitfire has its gun sights ground-tested. Two crewmen, perched on the tail, check the sighting of the guns aimed at targets inside the hangar in the background; two other men, on the ground, double-check the accuracy of the guns.

Ground crewmen trundle an ailing Spitfire—its engine cowling removed—into the hangar for repairs. At all other times, planes not in the air were parked at dispersal points around the field to minimize damage from enemy raids.

An intelligence officer at a forward base lectures new arrivals on recognition of enemy aircraft, aided by models of Luftwaffe planes. In poor visibility or in the heat of battle, quick and positive identification could mean the difference between life and death.

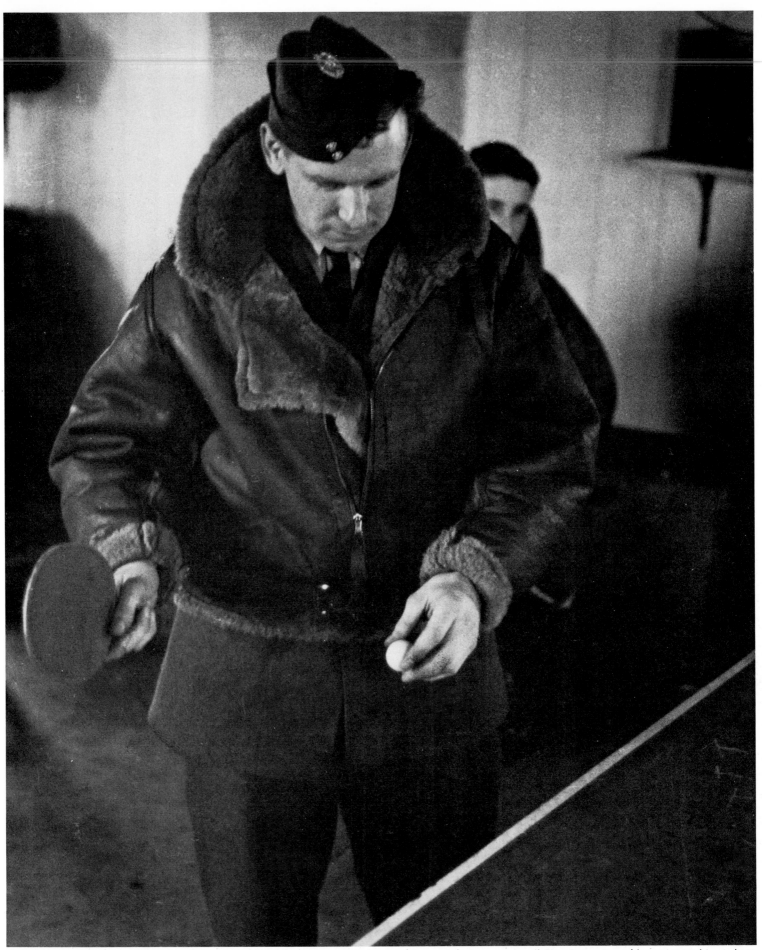

A flight sergeant, although hampered by his fur-lined jacket, concentrates on his serve during a game of Ping-Pong at a table set up at his air base.

Off-duty airmen gather round their airfield's canteen for some conversation and a hot cup of tea, provided by NAAFI, the British equivalent of the USO.

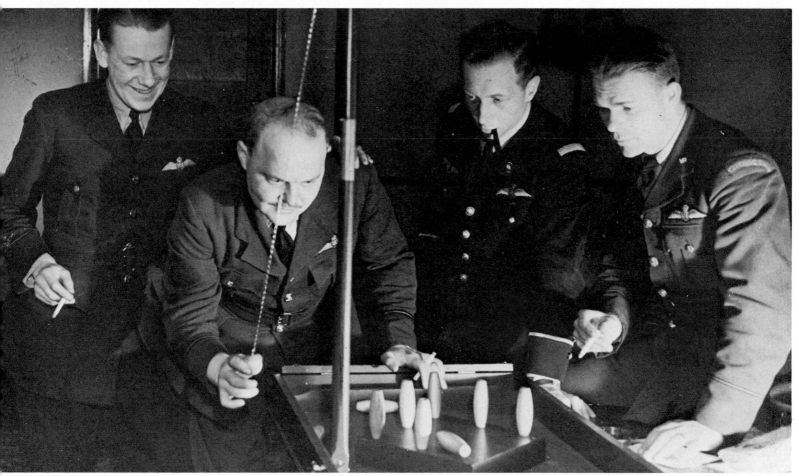

Four fliers enjoy a round of skittles. Other pastimes engaged in while on standby ranged from sedentary to active to hearty—dominoes to quoits to rugby.

Adjusting their gear while on the run, members of a fighter squadron pile out the door of their ready room, or dispersal hut, in answer to an alarm. At the very height of the Battle of Britain, pilots got the signal to scramble from huts like these as frequently as six times a day.

As the Battle of Britain roars to a climax, Hurricanes of Squadron 615 take off from an airstrip in south England to intercept Luftwaffe raiders. The Hurricane,

the workhorse of the RAF at the outset, was later joined by the swifter Spitfire. The Hurricanes of this squadron shot down nearly 100 enemy aircraft.

5

A second legend about the Battle of Britain—almost as widespread as the myth of the outmanned RAF—had Britons unfailingly united and staunch amid the terror and the hardships. They shook their fists at the sky and never wavered in their determination to see the war through. Winston Churchill, with understandable pride and habitual flair, contributed to this oversimplified view of his fellow citizens, describing, in some of his choicest prose, their intrepid conduct under fire. Those were the times, he said after the war, "when the English, and particularly Londoners, who had the place of honor, were seen at their best. Grim and gay, dogged and serviceable, with the confidence of an unconquered people in their bones, they adapted to this strange new life, with all its terrors, with all its jolts and jars."

The truth was that the behavior of the British people under fire was more complex, more varied and more human than that. Many of them indeed showed great courage, while others were terrified; some were excited by the bombings and some were depressed. Not surprisingly, their mood and their resolution tended to escalate or descend with the fortunes of the war in the air. While the balance of the battle swayed to and fro, British attitudes were also fluctuating because of splits caused by class feelings and bitter resentments that the burdens of the war were not being fairly and equally shared. And at one point, these resentments almost flared into outright revolt.

The most restive and disaffected were the Cockneys of London's East End, by tradition the most cheerful people in Britain. Nazi bombs they had to accept; what they could not tolerate was what they felt to be the callousness of British officialdom, which was displaying heartless efficiency in its preparations for the Luftwaffe's big offensive: for example, the London County Council stored thousands of papier maché coffins in warehouses, municipal baths and other depositories; and on the city's outskirts, great pits were dug and supplies of lime assembled nearby, ready for the mass burials of the countless victims who were expected to die under the rain of German bombs.

East Enders, like most people, were more concerned with surviving than with being properly buried. And they were furiously aware that their government, which might now be stockpiling last resting places for the dead, had, historically, failed to provide adequate shelters for the living.

THE CRUCIBLE OF THE BLITZ

Behind their plight was a simple fact of geography. Their squalid houses in Stepney, Wapping, Canning Town, West Ham and other East End communities were next door to some of the most important targets in England, places the Luftwaffe had to destroy if it was to bring London to a standstill. In the East End, for instance, were London's docks, serving more ships than any other port in Britain. There also were armament works; ironworks; car, tank and truck assembly plants; miles of warehouses packed with food and matériel; mills and textile factories.

Many of the factories dated back to the early 19th Century. Around these "dark satanic mills," as the poet William Blake called them, had been built flimsy, leaking, cramped dwellings for the semiskilled (and semislave) labor that had been brought in to man the machines. Descendants of the original labor force were still there, some working at the same benches, in only slightly better conditions.

When the bombs began falling on Wapping's waterfront and Canning Town's dingy factories, the houses near them caught fire like matchwood. Many of the occupants were trapped and incinerated. Far too few street shelters had been built, and these were so fragile that bomb blasts flattened them. There were no deep underground shelters—none, at any rate, that were officially sanctioned.

One of the most badly battered waterside slum areas was Silvertown, where a company named S. W. Silver operated a rubber goods factory. Fertilizer and soap were also Silvertown products; when bombs hit, the result was a noxious nightmare scene in which thousands of gasping people groped through stinking smoke, fire and wreckage in a desperate search for shelter.

Some of the victims took refuge in a local school—where a direct hit killed 450 of them. Silvertown was under the control of the West Ham Borough Council, most of whose members were Socialist and pacifist and had refused to build any shelters at all. So, as the raids continued, a spontaneous evacuation began. Whole families, dragging what was left of their belongings on wheelbarrows or bicycles, set out to find a place to hide.

They and other East Enders eventually settled into an abandoned railway tunnel that ran out of the Stratford Broadway Underground station. Soon it was a cesspit, according to the police chief for the area, Superintendent Reg-inald Smith, who was taken there by one of his sergeants.

"The first thing I heard," Smith reported, "was a great hollow hubbub, a sort of soughing and wailing, as if there were animals down there moaning and crying. And then, as we went on, this terrible stench hit me. It was worse than dead bodies, hot and thick and so fetid that I gagged and then vomited. About 50 yards in I stopped. Ahead of me I could see faces peering towards me lit by candles and lanterns. It was like a painting of hell."

The sergeant added: "There's all sorts in there, all colors, but they're so filthy you can't tell the difference. A lot of the old folks are dying and others are dead, but we won't know how many until they bring the bodies out. You can't tell from the smell. They do everything in there. No sanitation and no shame, I can tell you."

Every night the keening of the sirens sounded, but for the time being only the East End felt the weight of the bombs. In the better parts of town—Chelsea, Knightsbridge, Mayfair, Westminster—it was possible to stand in the blacked-out streets, see the glow in the sky and hear the thud of explosions across the city. But it all seemed a world away.

The Cockneys did not even have the satisfaction of being able to read about their selective ordeal. Strict government censorship was in force. All reports of where bombs had dropped, how many people had been killed and what buildings had been destroyed were deleted not only from local newspapers but also from foreign correspondents' cables. Inevitably, of course, rumors arose, spread and reached the army. Men in London units who were stationed in other parts of the country began to fret about the fate of their homes, their wives, children and parents.

"We queued constantly in our spare time to telephone to London, only to be told of infinite delay," one soldier from Bethnal Green said later. "Almost no letters arrived, morale sank very low, we heard that no ships floated in the port of London, bridges were down. Each day there was no news, and when news came it was a telegram to say F's mother was dead, C's wife; H's house blown to bits, J's wife had been blown on top of her baby by bomb blast."

The commanding officer of this particular man's unit had the kindness—and the sense—to send an aide and a sergeant to London to gather some accurate information and report back. But in other units many soldiers became restive, and desertion rates rose alarmingly.

In the East End itself, most Cockneys uncharacteristically gave vent to anger and bitterness. They felt abandoned and isolated. So long as it was they who were taking a beating, they told one another, the folks up West in Mayfair and Knightsbridge weren't worrying.

"We feel as if we've been put in bloody quarantine," snapped one docker.

The ground was fertile for agitators, and two of the most effective were local Communists. Phil Piratin was a member of the Stepney Council. George "Tubby" Rosen was chairman of the Stepney Tenants' Defense League. In keeping with the current Party line—Russia was not yet at war with Hitler—they regarded the conflict as "the bosses' war" and their constituents as victims of a capitalist plot. As the bombings were intensified in September 1940, Tubby Rosen addressed a large meeting in the Commercial Road.

"Our people are dying like rats here in Stepney," he shouted. "And why? Because the Tory bosses refused us the money that was needed to build deep shelters for our protection. So while we crawl into the surplus hen houses they call street shelters, which wouldn't even protect a rooster from the rain, up West the government's rich friends and their girl friends sleep cozy in double beds, two to a compartment, in their own private, deep shelters. Comrades, it's about time we took them over!"

Many of London's West End hotels had turned their cellars into snug shelters, with bunks for patrons who had come to dine or dance and were forced to stay the night when the sirens sounded. One of the most popular hotels was the Savoy, a favorite rendezvous of government ministers, members of Parliament, Fleet Street reporters and American correspondents. The Duke and Duchess of Kent and such fashionable pacesetters as Margot Asquith and Lady Diana Cooper all had bunks reserved for them in case they happened to be there when the alert came.

So it was to the Savoy that Phil Piratin and Tubby Rosen led a militant procession from East London "to show you buggers how the other half is living," as one of them put it. Headed by a half dozen pregnant women and others with babes in arms, they swarmed into the posh lobby, shoving Hansen, the head porter, before them. The hotel's restaurant was quickly closed and barricaded; although some of the women managed to get inside and demand food, they were refused service. Other protesters tied themselves to pillars. Still others ran down to the shelters, led by Tubby Rosen shouting: "Let's surprise the Archbishop of Canterbury and his girl friend in flagrante bloody delicto!"

One panicky employee of the hotel called in the police and asked them to drive the demonstrators back where they belonged. The police refused. "You're an hotel, you see, sir," a sergeant said, politely. "You come under the Innkeepers' Act. If a bona fide traveler comes in and asks for a meal—and these people look like bona fide travelers to me —then they've a right to be served. Now if they're making a row, or breaking things, or doing a mischief, we'll be willing to escort them out. Otherwise, they're clients of the hotel, and should be treated as such."

Hugh Wontner, the Savoy's managing director, immediately saw the light and ordered that tea be served to the East Enders. But before the cups could be brought out Rosen called a retreat; belatedly he realized he had made a tactical blunder by invading the hotel during the daytime when its

From an overstuffed pouch labeled "Violence, not Victory," Reich Marshal Hermann Göring drops a load of bombs that glance harmlessly off the tough, Cockney heart of London in this cartoon by master satirist David Low. The drawing appeared in the Evening Standard of September 11, 1940, and reflected the response of the English to the Luftwaffe's first all-out raid on central London on September 7.

IMPREGNABLE TARGET

underground shelters were not in use. The marchers retreated, but not without a clamor of antigovernment slogans.

On the following day, newspapers played down the Savoy affair on orders from the censors. But another story the censors had wanted to suppress that same week got front-page treatment; in this case, the anonymous arbiters of what the public should or should not be told were overruled by Prime Minister Churchill himself.

Through a fault in navigation, a group of German bombers, on their way to hit the dock areas as usual, instead veered off and dropped their loads on Chelsea and on Victoria Station, on the fashionable side of London. One of the bombs hit Buckingham Palace. King George VI, the Queen and the two little Princesses were in residence at the time; the Royal Family had a narrow escape when the bomb exploded in the courtyard. The censors promptly banned the story. Then Churchill heard about the order and erupted.

"Dolts, idiots, stupid fools!" he shouted. "Spread the news at once! Let the humble people of London know that they are not alone, and that the King and Queen are sharing their perils with them!"

To a government in trouble with its citizens, the bombing of Buckingham Palace proved to be a godsend. Churchill had been warned that if better measures were not taken to care for the blitz victims in the slums he would have a revolt on his hands—and London was not the only problem. In Liverpool, where civil defense had completely broken down during recent German raids, inhabitants of the city's dock areas had rioted, stormed and looted food stores, and wrecked government offices. Indeed, in all the big target cities the population had divided itself into Them and Us: the rich, comfortable, well-fed middle and upper classes living on the fringes of the battle, and the battered, hungry and homeless in the vulnerable zones.

The harrowing experience to which the Royal Family had been subjected—and which Churchill shrewdly insisted on publicizing—provided a sharp reminder that the peril was universal. The improvement in popular morale did not come overnight; the unrest continued as a plodding bureaucracy strove to meet demands for solid shelters, food-distribution centers, evacuation schemes. But signs of a new, nationwide and classless unity began to emerge, further to be strengthened as the Germans widened their attacks.

An American broadcaster stationed in London, Edward R. Murrow, sensed something of the new spirit as he looked out over the city from a rooftop on a late September afternoon. That night he reported his observations to his transatlantic radio audience. "I saw many flags flying from staffs," he said. "No one told these people to put out the flag. They simply feel like flying the Union Jack above their roof." And, he added, "no flag up there was white."

Another factor that turned British morale upward was the performance of the RAF, which had begun to gain the upper hand in the air. Two days after the bombing of Buckingham Palace, the Luftwaffe was turned back with heavy losses in the great raid of September 15. Immediately after came a new series of reverses for the Germans, bringing great consternation to Reich Marshal Göring.

On September 27, with combined determination and apprehension, Göring ordered his Air Fleets 2 and 3 sent off on one of their most massive attacks on London to date. While he was waiting for the results, he went hunting in his 10,000-acre forest preserve in East Prussia. He invited Adolf Galland as a hunting companion. The young Luftwaffe ace had destroyed his 40th enemy plane over the English Channel the previous week, and Göring wanted to show him some special mark of favor.

As the two men were tramping through the woods, they glimpsed a magnificent king stag in a clearing. Göring did not raise his gun but offered the target to Galland, who brought it down with his first shot. The king stag was usually reserved for Göring's sport alone; letting Galland bring it down was the Reich Marshal's way of rewarding him.

For Göring, this day in the woods with Galland was a welcome respite from the mounting pressures of the air war. Hitler was beginning to ask some embarrassing questions. The Führer had postponed the seaborne invasion of England but had given Göring the green light to subjugate it from the air. Now Hitler wanted to know why the Luftwaffe was apparently faltering, instead of finishing the job.

The Führer's annoyance was bad enough, but Göring was also having to cope with a new restiveness among the men of the Luftwaffe itself. Bomber crews were wondering aloud whether the British were psychic, so uncannily efficient had the RAF become in intercepting them on the way to their tar-

gets. Although the Germans knew about the enemy's radar network, they were unaware that the British had cracked the German code, thus making the RAF privy to the Luftwaffe's operational orders.

At the same time, the German fighter pilots were close to despair. Göring's latest whim had been to have the sturdy Me-109s fitted with two 500-pound bombs for hit-and-run raids on Britain. After some initial success through surprise, the 109s were increasingly being destroyed by Spitfires that were waiting for them as they came across the Channel. With bombs aboard, they were too slow and unwieldy to elude the British fighters.

More bad news lay in store for Göring when he and Galland got back to his hunting lodge later that afternoon. A message from Luftwaffe headquarters, reporting the results of the day's raid on London, shocked and dismayed him. Two wings of Me-109s had arrived over London with orders to rendezvous with a large force of Dornier-17s and Junkers-88s and escort them on their bombing runs over the capital. The fighters had waited over the target area until their fuel warning lights began blinking red, but the bombers had not appeared. Caught in an RAF fighter trap over the Channel and southern England, badly mauled by Spitfires and Hurricanes, the bombers had been forced to run for home.

The 109s, having used up most of their fuel waiting over London, were in no position to take on the enemy. They were obliged to scoot back to their bases in France, harassed every mile of the way by RAF fighters. Many of the 109s came down in the sea. Others glided down, tanks empty, for crash landings on the French beaches. In all, the Luftwaffe lost 55 planes—21 of them bombers—compared to only 28 fighters lost by the RAF.

"Göring was shattered," Galland said later. The success-oriented Luftwaffe chief simply could not understand the day's debacle, and Galland, blunt-spoken as always, undertook to enlighten him: "I assured him that in spite of the heavy losses we were inflicting on the enemy fighters, no decisive decrease in their numbers or in their fighting efficiency was noticeable."

Clearly, the Luftwaffe's strategy would have to be rethought. Since the start of the Battle of Britain, it had lost some 1,600 planes—more, Göring knew, than the Germans

King George VI and Queen Elizabeth inspect the wreckage of the north side of Buckingham Palace, damaged when an aerial bomb exploded on September 10, 1940. Ironically, the effect of the bombing of the palace was to boost the morale of the British by emphasizing the common plight of Londoners at all levels of society. As the Queen said, "I'm glad we've been bombed. It makes me feel I can look the East End in the face."

could afford. Even as he pondered this alarming number, it jumped higher. On September 30, another massive daylight operation over London resulted in the loss of 47 more German planes, to only 20 for the RAF. Galland's candid appraisal was proving to be painfully correct. However much the intensive bombing might be hurting the British on the ground, their efficiency in the skies remained unimpaired.

In October Göring made a decision that changed the course of the air war drastically. Henceforth his fleet commanders were to abandon round-the-clock attacks and concentrate on night bombing instead. The daylight raids had clearly proved too costly.

Flying at night, the Luftwaffe was bound to cut its losses, while continuing to inflict grave damage on Britain's economy. Moreover, the special terrors of night bombing would, no doubt, cause a fresh crack in the stiffening wall of British morale. And the change of strategy did succeed in posing tremendous new burdens for the RAF as well as the British people. Indeed no one could have foretold the incredible complexity of the problems that arose when the Germans shifted the full weight of their assault from day to night.

To begin with, air warfare by night was itself a relatively new art. At the start of this phase of the Luftwaffe's offensive, the RAF had only eight fighter squadrons—two of De-

fiants and six of Blenheims—that were assigned primarily to intercepting enemy bombers that came across the Channel after dark. The Defiants and Blenheims had been given night duty for a curious sort of reason—almost by default: because neither type of plane had proved very effective against the foe by day. Britain had no specialized night fighters at all, except for a few Beaufighters—a newer, faster plane than the Blenheim or Defiant. And Beaufighters were only beginning to come off the assembly line when the Luftwaffe switched its tactics.

The radar network, which had proved to be such a boon up to now, also posed some tricky new problems. The stations covered only the coastal areas, and the Luftwaffe's night bombers were penetrating deep inland, beyond the scope of the radar plotters. A radar set that could be fitted into a plane was devised to help offset this difficulty, but its range was no more than about two or three miles, as compared to a maximum of 150 miles for ground radar. And, in any event, the airborne sets were not to become generally operational until late in the year. Though some fighters had carried this equipment in the preceding months, most of the pilots sent aloft against the night incursions had to fly blind.

Britain's ground defenses, too, were hampered by the lack of inland radar stations. To warn of impending attack, the

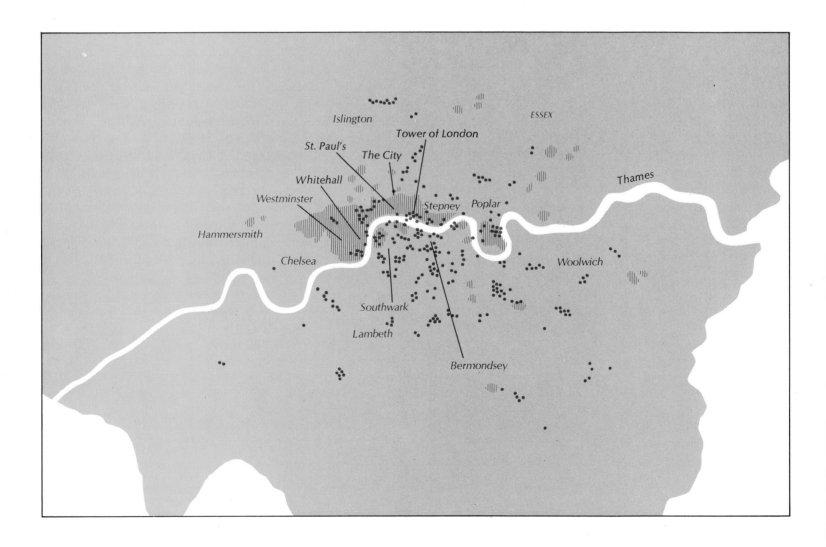

ground stations had to rely, instead, on sound locators. These varied in accuracy according to the state of the weather; moreover, they were unable to cope with the speed of many of the enemy planes. As one expert noted: "An aircraft flying at 20,000 feet and at 300 miles per hour would be one and a half miles farther on before its sound reached the listening apparatus on the ground, and five or six miles farther on before the burst of the shells."

Searchlights and antiaircraft weapons also were severely limited in their effectiveness. A searchlight's glare could reach no higher than about 12,000 feet, the fire of a heavy antiaircraft gun no higher than 25,000 feet, a light gun no higher than 6,000 feet. The Germans, of course, soon learned to turn such limitations to their advantage.

With all these inadequacies in the British ground and air defenses against night attacks, the immediate effect of the Luftwaffe's new offensive was to swing the course of the Battle of Britain back in Germany's favor. By night, for a while at least, London and other big cities lay wide open to attack, and the first German raids proved to be heavy, continuous and devastatingly effective.

To help their pilots zero in on targets, the Luftwaffe had equipped its fighters with an ingenious radio system known as *Knickebein*—crooked leg. From a radio-transmission tower on the French coast, a pilot would be guided along his course by a beam that sounded a continuous hum in his earphones. If he strayed from his course, he would hear a series of dots and dashes. Shortly before he reached his assigned target, a second beam, operating on a different frequency, would intersect the first beam, and the pilot would hear a different sound. He would then time his run from the point of intersection and, after a prescribed interval, release his bombs. The crooked-leg system was accurate to within about a square mile.

The British had known about *Knickebein* since the early summer of 1940, and had set their own scientific experts to work on countermeasures. Formed into a team under the innocent-sounding name of No. 80 Wing, RAF, these men were to prove a wellspring of electronic invention whose wizardry would have a considerable effect on the battle.

Planes were sent up to track and test out the Luftwaffe's beam system, and technicians climbed 350-foot-high radar towers along the coast of southern England. Precariously

perched there with radio receivers, they would listen in on the *Knickebein* signals to determine the source and frequency of the transmission. Countermeasures were then begun.

Hospital diathermy equipment, which transmitted high-frequency waves, was used at first. Installed in police stations and in mobile vans dispatched to target areas, the machines were turned on when RAF Fighter Command reported an incoming enemy plane. The sounds of these signals overpowered those of the enemy, making it impossible for the German pilot to hear the *Knickebein* beams.

Soon more sophisticated ways of interfering with *Knickebein* were found. By adapting some of their own radio beacons, the British were able to "doctor" the *Knickebein* signals by superimposing Morse code on the beam frequencies, thus misleading the pilot and causing him to overshoot his prescribed target.

British electronic trickery also played hob with another of the Luftwaffe's aids to navigation. To make certain that they were on course, the raiders calculated their position by tuning in to signals emanating from two medium-frequency direction-finding beacons the Germans had set up on the French coast. In this case, the British picked up and retransmitted so strongly that the original sound was disguised or distorted, throwing the pilots' calculations completely off.

At least one of the wizards' strategems was as ancient as war itself: the use of decoys, particularly areas constructed or disguised to simulate RAF ground installations, which had become a favorite German target. Knowing that second and third waves of enemy bombers used the fires that had been set by the first wave as a guide to their destination, British camouflage experts built about 70 dummy airfields, with flare paths and lights that were turned on as the raiders approached. Many a Luftwaffe pilot flew back to base unaware that he had wasted his bombs on a worthless target.

These technological successes not only reduced the damage done by the Luftwaffe, but also paid a great dividend in terms of morale. As the British grew more proficient at destroying the Luftwaffe's accuracy, the bombs of the night attackers spread, hit or miss, all across London. Thereafter, a debutante in Park Lane was as much in danger as a docker in Bermondsey—except, of course, that the deb still had better shelters to go to and better food to eat when the raids

were over. But even in that regard, the government was starting to get itself organized. Mobile canteens were formed and sent out to every bombed area. Local councils were ordered to start making their shelters more safe and sanitary. Recalcitrant local authorities were sacked and professionals as well as willing volunteers moved in.

Now that the whole population faced the same dangers, just about everyone felt better. Tubby Rosen, who had been planning a new march—this time on Buckingham Palace itself—admitted: "I don't feel so bad now that George and his flunkeys are getting it too." And in stylish Hampstead, a rich young war widow made an entry in her diary that any Cockney would have approved. Staring through her bomb-shattered windows, Rosemary Black wrote: "The papers now say that London has taken the worst punishment from bombing in the history of warfare, even worse than Rotterdam. We are all delighted to hear this."

Hundreds of antiaircraft guns now ringed London, and on Churchill's orders several batteries were brought into Hyde Park "where people can hear them blast off," as he put it. The deafening din, the sheer, hellish noise of the shells being pumped into the sky brought some measure of comfort to the citizens below. Those who remained in the streets rather than taking shelter were apt to cheer when they saw the shells bursting and the appearance in the searchlights of RAF night fighters on a hunt for the enemy bombers.

The constant sense of shared danger seemed to stimulate people and make them more friendly. Foreigners in the capital remarked that they had never before found the standoffish British so neighborly and communicative.

A new way of life was emerging in London. A number of polls recorded the changes. One, taken by a research institute in October 1940, set out to learn how much sleep Londoners had had the night before—a night of particularly heavy raids. Of those interviewed, only 15 per cent had managed more than six hours' sleep; 22 per cent, four to six hours; 32 per cent, less than four hours; and 31 per cent, no sleep at all. Remarkably, except for those whose homes had just been destroyed or whose relatives had been killed, most working people turned up at their offices or factories the following morning. Indeed, absenteeism was at a record low.

Another poll showed that during night raids 44 per cent of Londoners stayed in their homes or in makeshift shelters in their gardens, 44 per cent went to public shelters, and the remaining 12 per cent stayed with friends, wandered the streets, or made other arrangements. For most of the Londoners who used public shelters, this meant the Tubes, or Underground, the subway system whose tracks ran deep beneath the city and the River Thames.

Since the government still had not constructed the large, deep shelters that were needed, more and more people decided to take over the Tubes, and official efforts to prevent this soon had to be abandoned. The movement started in the East End and simply spread across the capital. Every night, as dusk fell and the sirens sounded the approach of the raiders, people would arrive with food, drink, blankets and babies, take the elevators or escalators down to the platforms below and settle in for the night. The trains kept running until around midnight, and travelers had quite a job picking their way among the bodies sprawled across the platforms. And though the situation in the Tubes was far better than it had been in the first makeshift shelters, some of the more sensitive passengers were still shocked by the reality of night life on these station platforms.

"Horrified by ghastly sight in the Tubes," wrote Rosemary Black in her diary after a night trip to her home in Hampstead on the Underground. "Seeing every corridor and platform in every station all along the line crowded with people huddled three-deep, I was too appalled for words. The misery of that wretched mass of humanity sleeping like worms packed in a tin—the heat and smell, the dirt, the endless crying of the poor bloody babies, the haggard white-faced women nursing their children against them, the children cramped and twitching in their noisy sleep. . . . Why, if I wanted to torture my worst enemy, I could think of no better Procrustean bed for the purpose."

Some Britons never lost this white-gloved perspective of the Underground shelters, but as time passed, more and more people from all levels of society came to see them in a far different light. The sculptor Henry Moore was excited and inspired when he first encountered the masses of people spread over the platform of Hampstead Station, the deepest in London and therefore one of the most popular. "The place was full of what have since been called Henry Moore reclining figures," he said. He immediately began

The shell of the cathedral at Coventry, gutted by German bombs, stands wreathed in a smoky haze after a massive air raid on November 14, 1940. Lasting 10 hours, the attack was the heaviest yet suffered by a British city. German raiders dropped hundreds of tons of bombs, razing 100 acres of homes and factories and leaving 554 dead and 865 wounded. But the city dug out; workers quickly returned to their jobs, even in roofless war plants, and the cathedral became a symbol of Britain's will to survive.

making sketches for a series of drawings that later became a celebrated part of the artist's *oeuvre*.

Even the Cockneys, so resentful at first, learned to like the comradeship and bonhomie of the Underground shelters. After the government's initial opposition to their use, officials began to accept the fact that if people were barred from the stations, they would break in anyway. So the use of the Tubes was made official, and extra toilets, first-aid posts and food supplies were moved in. So were sanitation units; one of the peculiar nuisances that they had to deal with was a plague of mosquitoes, which were spending the cold months in the cloying heat and fertile fleshy pastures of the packed station platforms.

Many of the stations' residents arranged their own amusements. Often a community sing would be going on. And there were always plenty of buskers around—the entertainers who in peacetime performed on the street for people standing in queues at theaters and cinemas. They performed in just as lively a fashion for their new audiences in the Underground. At Aldwych, in the center of the theater district,

A CRUSTY HERO AND HIS MORE CONGENIAL SUCCESSOR

The military leader who probably did more than any other to save Britain from invasion and defeat was blunt, far-sighted Air Chief Marshal Hugh Dowding. Head of the RAF's Fighter Command from July 1936 to November 1940, he pushed hard in peacetime for development of faster, more sophisticated fighters such as the Spitfire and the Hurricane. During the first, desperate months of the Battle of Britain, he skillfully husbanded his planes and pilots by dispatching them to attack the Luftwaffe in small, coordinated groups rather than by sending them off in a swarm.

Because of Dowding's tactics and foresight, the RAF took a fearful toll of enemy planes. But on November 25, 1940, when the battle had been virtually won, Dowding was abruptly relieved of his post in a telephone call from the Secretary of State for Air, Sir Archibald Sinclair.

As Dowding recalled years later, "He told me I was to relinquish my command immediately. I asked what was meant by 'immediately' and was told it would take effect within the next day or so. . . . I pointed out that it was perfectly absurd that I should be relieved of my command in this way unless it was thought that I had committed a major crime or something like that. But all I could get in reply was that the decision had been reached, and that was that, with no explanation for such a precipitate action being taken."

Dowding was aware that he had incurred the enmity not only of Churchill but of other powerful figures in the government. As he wryly put it, "There had been hanging over my head for a long time a whole shop-full of bowler hats." Moreover, there were men in the military who disagreed strongly with his battle strategy, despite its success. Some in Fighter Command believed their planes would be more effective attacking the Luftwaffe en masse. Others in the Air Ministry disagreed with Dowding's emphasis on fighters, and felt that England's best defense was not fighter planes, but bombers that could retaliate against the enemy's homeland.

No one of these people could prove Dowding was wrong; they just thought so. Nevertheless, he was out—replaced by the far more tactful William Sholto Douglas —having committed the major crime of being too hard-mindedly right too often with the wrong people.

DOWDING

DOUGLAS

When Air Chief Marshal Hugh (Stuffy) Dowding was relieved of the RAF's Fighter Command in November 1940, his successor was Air Vice Marshal William Sholto Douglas, a former fighter pilot, Deputy Chief of Staff of the Air Ministry —and a frequent critic of Dowding.

such famous stars as Laurence Olivier, Vivien Leigh and Ivor Novello would come down after their evening performances and present impromptu songs and sketches.

Soon some families grew so attached to their patch of station platform that they were reluctant to go back up to the streets when the all-clear sounded. Others insisted on using stations that were relatively close to the surface, despite warnings by the authorities that they were extremely vulnerable to direct hits. One such station was Balham, which was only 36 feet below the street, with a network of gas and water pipes, main sewers and electric wires above it. On October 14, a bomb dropped just short of the station and smashed the water, sewer and gas pipes. Some 600 people were sheltering on the platform below. The lights went out; water and sewage poured down and gas began to pump in. In the noisome darkness, panic erupted. Eventually, station officials with torchlights led 350 people through the shoulder-high water to the street. But 250 others drowned.

Balham was only one of several Tube disasters. At Bethnal Green station during an air raid a woman tripped and fell on the stairs. Those directly behind fell over her and the rest stampeded. Nearly 200 people were either trampled or suffocated to death that night.

But no disaster seemed to diminish the popularity of the Underground. The more vulnerable stations were gradually closed, and the others were strengthened against the danger of flood from sewers or the Thames. Cockneys continued to use them every night long after the major bombing raids had ceased, some until the end of the war.

As the autumn of 1940 passed, Göring still believed Britain could be brought down by bombing, and the night raids were intensified, not only in London but all over England. Large sections of the biggest cities were demolished; Glasgow, Manchester, Liverpool, Birmingham and Bristol all had the craters and scorch marks of repeated raids.

On the night of November 14, it was Coventry's turn. Coventry was a medieval city whose old timbered buildings dated back to the days of the legendary Lady Godiva in the 11th Century; its handsome cathedral had been built in the 14th Century. But Coventry had one of the biggest concentrations of armaments factories in the United Kingdom.

Controversy has since swirled over the question of whether the Churchill government knew of the German strike against Coventry in advance. One version contends that the British code-breaking and interception system inexplicably broke down. Another and more dramatic version is that the system worked all too well—but was deliberately disregarded. According to this story, Churchill had been warned at least three days before the raid that Hitler had given Göring a go-ahead for a massive attack under the code name *Moonlight Sonata,* and that the chief target was to be Coventry.

Allegedly, Churchill decided to do nothing beyond alerting the city's civil defense chiefs to be ready for extra burdens in the days and nights to come. The grounds for not evacuating the city were that emergency measures might make clear to the Germans that the enemy was reading their code. Thus Churchill—according to this version of the story—had chosen to preserve the security of Ultra, his code-cracking machine, and to risk the threat to a quarter million people of an unexpected mass raid. In fact, however, the British received no reliable evidence that Coventry was to be the target on the night in question. It was later learned that Churchill had actually expected a raid on London.

November 14 was a bright, moonlit night. Pathfinder aircraft blanketed Coventry with incendiaries, turning the hapless city into a mammoth beacon on which bombers coming up behind could unload. The bombers—437 Heinkel-111s —dropped 450 tons of both high-explosive and incendiary bombs; and by dawn, the heart of Coventry had been all but wiped out. The cathedral was devastated. So were all the hospitals. The timbered buildings had burned like straw. More than 50,000 structures were destroyed or damaged; 865 citizens were seriously hurt. A total of 380 people died in the raids, 165 of them so badly smashed or charred that they were buried in a common grave.

Only one of the 437 enemy bombers was shot down—a clue to the sorry state of night defenses at the time. Although the RAF flew 165 sorties, their night fighters, still not properly equipped with radar, intercepted only seven of the attackers—all without success. The one German plane that was lost was brought down by ground fire.

Moreover, during the bombing of Coventry, the Luftwaffe added a new dimension of terror: an awesome device called a parachute mine. Adapted from the magnetic mine which the German Navy had introduced against Allied shipping at the beginning of the war, the parachute mine was eight feet long and two feet in diameter. Weighing two and one half tons, it was packed with high explosives and descended by parachute silently and slowly from a great height. And even those who were close enough—and unfortunate enough—to see the black cylinder floating down had scant chance of escaping its shattering explosion once it made contact with the earth. When one went off, the entire area within a half-mile radius might feel the effects of the blast.

Right after Coventry, London felt the destructive power of the mines. At Portland Place, in London's West End, a parachute mine blew up a whole wing of the BBC building, destroyed a hotel and devastated the surrounding area. Others destroyed large tracts elsewhere in the capital—Chelsea, Hammersmith, and the ancient part of London, now its financial district, traditionally called The City.

When some of the mines failed to go off, the British responded to the terrifying technical challenge of defusing them. At first only a few naval men, experts in dealing with magnetic mines at sea, took on the job; but soon a small cadre of quickly trained specialists was assembled for the hair-raising task of deactivating the mines.

The technicians worked in pairs, their sole equipment a screwdriver to loosen the fuse, a ball of string to remove the fuse from a safe distance, and steady hands. One man kept his ear to the mine while the other tinkered. "The important thing when dealing with these mines," said one of the specialists, "was to realize that if you had to roll them over before you took the fuse out, you had to listen very carefully all the time. If you heard buzzing you ran like hell, and you had a maximum of 15 seconds to get away."

Compounding the hazards of the work was the fact that the unexploded bombs did not always come to rest in earth or building rubble. One of them hung by a fraying parachute from the biggest gas storage tank in East London, swaying in the breeze while it was being deactivated. Another landed on the electric train line on Hungerford Bridge, which spanned the Thames, but did not go off even though the electric rail welded it to the track. And as if all that were not enough, the Germans put booby traps inside the mines, placing a trigger fuse under the main fuse, which would set off an explosion if any but the most skilled and knowledgeable man tried to deactivate the main fuse.

With these lethal new engines joining the regular rain of bombs coming down upon Britain's cities night after night, life for most citizens acquired a highly emotional quality. Mass Observation, a research organization that measured public opinion, had its members send in weekly written reports about their own feelings, conversations and activities, and those of their neighbors. Most people honestly recorded that they were frightened by the noise and by the possibility of being buried by bombs. However a surprising majority also said that they had no fear of dying, providing it was a direct hit. Many added that they found the excitement of the blitz stimulating, especially sexually.

There were those who liked to walk the streets during a raid, getting a kick out of the noise of the explosions, the crack of antiaircraft fire, the rattle of shrapnel clattering on the rooftops and streets around them. According to Henry Moore, "It was a fascinating time. You could see the fires and the gaps in the buildings where the bombs had torn them, the patterns of twisted tramlines and the tangled overhead wires. I found it continuously exciting, and I sketched like a glutton."

Winston Churchill was another who liked to leave his underground air-raid shelter in Whitehall for the streets the moment bombs began falling. Attempts were made to stop him, because the risk of getting one's head blown off or losing a limb from shrapnel was great. Churchill's valet, a Royal Marine named Ives, tried to stop him from going out by hiding his shoes. Ives was angrily ordered to produce them.

"I'll have you know," thundered Churchill, "that as a child my nursemaid could never prevent me from taking a walk in the Green Park when I wanted to do so. And, as a man, Adolf Hitler certainly won't."

In contrast, some people were honestly terrified by the raids, but were even more afraid of giving in to their fear by fleeing the city—and their duty. They stayed there to work and endure. C. P. Snow, the physicist and writer, afterwards confessed: "When the bombs began to fall on London, I discovered that I was less brave than the average man. I was humiliated to find it so. I could just put some sort of face on it, but I dreaded the evening coming."

Snow envied the bravery of so many of his fellow citizens. "My landlady in Pimlico, for instance. She was a slattern with few qualities, but she was as brave as a lion. So were the clerks in the office, those I met in the pubs in Pimlico, and most of my friends. It made me feel worse."

Although the slaughter from the bombs turned out to be well below the toll of 600,000 that British experts had predicted at the start of the blitz, London and the other big cities in England were hardly desirable places to live and work in if you wanted to stay alive and in one piece. Any big raid was likely to kill a thousand or more Londoners and to injure five or six times that many; in the same raid 10 times that number would be made homeless.

The rubble-filled cities reeked with the acrid smell of burning. What people feared most was being buried under wreckage. To rescue people trapped by debris, yet another kind of craftsman made his appearance: the "body sniffer," who had developed the ability to tell from the smell whether there was a victim buried under a building, and whether that person was alive or dead.

The moment the Luftwaffe's raiders had plastered a heavily populated area, rescue gangs would begin digging down into the wreckage for survivors, stopping every now and then to listen for sounds or movements or groans. But when no sounds came, the "body sniffers" would take over, snuffling into the debris like dogs, ignoring the noxious odors of gas, sewage or smoke, until they would say: "Blood here." They would sniff harder and add: "Don't bother, blood stale, this one's a stiff." Or: "Fresh blood down here, and still flowing," in which case the rescuers would resume digging in the hope of reaching the victim in time.

On the night of December 29, as if to emphasize there would be no letup in pressure on Britain in the new year, the Luftwaffe unleashed one of its heaviest and most successful raids on London. The bombers concentrated on The City, the old heart of the capital, full of ancient churches and such landmarks as the Bank of England. The defense forces were caught off guard. It was a quiet Sunday night during the Christmas season. Most of those who normally firewatched in the area and manned the stirrup pumps and fire hose had taken a chance and gone home to their families —when a total of 244 German bombers dropped showers of incendiary bombs, starting fires on the wooden roofs of the buildings and sending flaming debris crashing down into the narrow, twisting streets.

Fire engines were soon on the scene, but the fires built up so fast and spread so rapidly that immense quantities of water were needed to quench them. The autumn season had been dry, and the Thames was so low that the fire engines soon drained the river down to its banks, and only a trickle of muddy water came out. Hundreds of venerable buildings and churches burned to the ground.

Of all The City's places of worship, only St. Paul's managed to escape more or less intact. The cathedral had maintained a 24-hour firewatch ever since the early raids, and with this one, every clergyman, chorister, verger and volunteer was on the job. Even so, the cathedral's great dome soon was afire. War correspondents gathered to watch, among them CBS correspondent Ed Murrow, who prepared to begin his nightly broadcast to America, with: "Tonight the bombers of the German Reich hit London where it hurts most, in her heart. St. Paul's Cathedral, built by Sir Christopher Wren, her great dome towering over the capital of the Empire, is burning to the ground as I talk to you now."

Luckily, he never had to broadcast those words. An army of volunteers managed to get the flames under control, and the cathedral was saved.

The ancient City itself was less lucky. For the second time in its history—the first time was in 1666—it was destroyed by a great fire. At an urgent Cabinet meeting on Monday, December 30, Churchill angrily shouted that this must never happen again. The British people were also angered by the ravaging of this particular beloved part of their capital. "It is so terrible," one woman wrote in her diary, "that because of sheer wanton neglect of the obvious precautions, millions of pounds worth of damage should have been done, and hundreds of brave men's lives risked and lost. . . . Are we a nation of utter imbeciles?"

Thus the people of Britain faced the new year with the ruins of The City still burning. But now they were more enraged than apprehensive and resentful—furious at their own bungling, but more deeply angry at the German attackers. There would be more bombs, more trials of courage and endurance before the battle was over. Yet the closing months of 1940 had forged among the British people a unity that, while it might not equal the Churchillian ideal, now seemed sufficient to withstand whatever else Göring and the Luftwaffe might have in store.

ORDEAL BY FIRE

Fire crews aboard a boat and on shore spray water pumped from the Thames into the blaze enveloping an East End brewery hit by incendiary bombs.

onnade of St. Paul's Cathedral as incendiaries rained down. "It's like the end of the world," said one.

Much of London had the same dreadful reflex that night, expressed in strikingly similar words. The East End, a jumble of docks, warehouses and Dickensian slums, burned so brightly the glow in the sky was seen 30 miles away. A Navy man piloting a small rescue boat down the Thames later that night said, "Smoke and sparks of all the fires swept in a high wall across the river. . . . It was like a lake in Hell."

On the riverbanks, fire fighters struggled to check the flames while the bombs were still falling. "One hit the end of the dock," said a volunteer. "Looking up for a split second, I saw a 30-foot length of timber sailing end over end above our heads." But as raid followed raid through the fall and winter of 1940, Londoners somehow got used to living in the middle of a nightly inferno of bombs. Each evening as the Germans came over, the British calmly took shelter in basements and especially in the Tubes, London's subway system. Belowground they developed a companionable existence—singing together, playing cards, nursing babies and reading, despite the cramped, fetid quarters, and the almost constant danger of being buried alive by a direct hit.

When the all-clear sounded, every Londoner knew he might emerge to find his home destroyed and his livelihood ruined. Yet this shared knowledge somehow drew them closer. And their comments on the destruction changed from horror to objective unconcern to outright ridicule of the whole catastrophe. After an early October attack, one raid-wise cab driver remarked, "I wouldn't mind except for the noise. It's the whistling of the bombs I don't like." Another witness lapsed into poetic imagery as he described the bombs falling "like black marbles from silver toys." An elderly charwoman walked half across London to find her place of employment a pile of rubble. She just grinned: "I've been scrubbing floors in this place for 16 years; I suppose old Hitler thought I ought to have a change."

A German bomber makes its run over a curve in the Thames River that encloses many of the city's vital East End shipping docks and warehouses.

A long queue of late afternoon refugees, at the entrance to the Kentish Town Underground station in north central London, waits to be admitted to shelter before the raids begin. As they became used to the raids, Londoners like these brought food, blanket rolls, suitcases and books to get them through the long night.

A Women's Volunteer Service matron reaches to take change from a boy who has just bought a mug of hot tea at an underground canteen. Behind her, a priest wearing an air-raid warden's helmet brings additional provisions to the counter. The W.V.S. was comprised of mostly middle-aged, middle-class women who not only served up refreshments, but helped with first-aid work in the underground shelters.

At a station underneath the Elephant and Castle section, just south of the Thames, Londoners attempt to catch some sleep on the subway platform

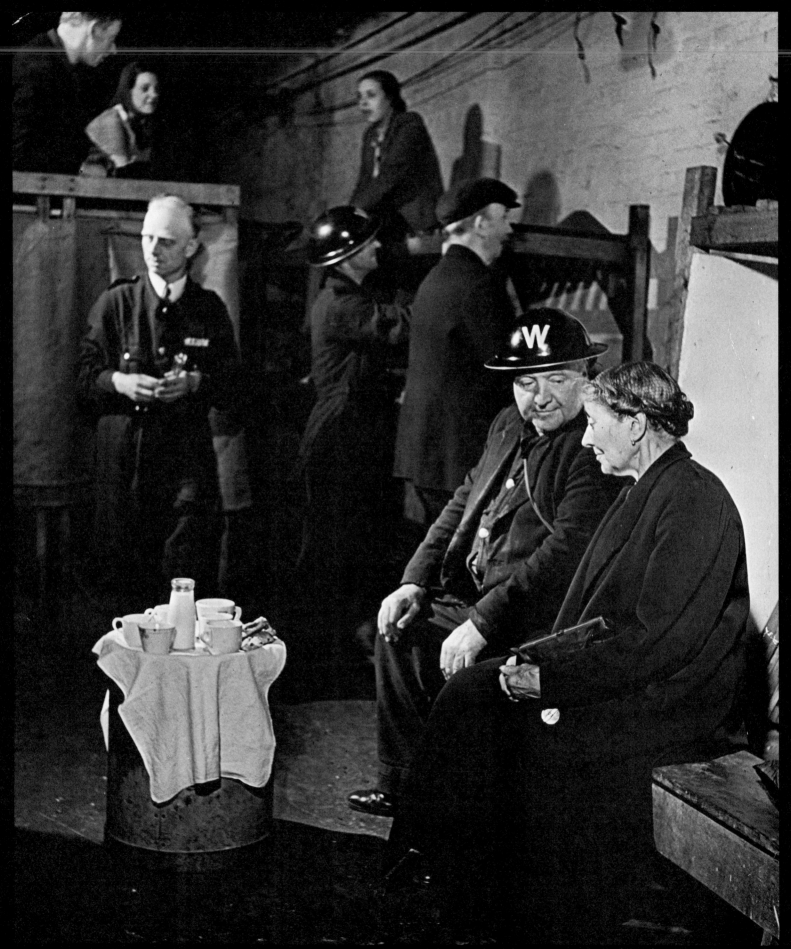

A warden and an elderly woman share some tea and raisin scones in an underground shelter. Behind them men play darts while others sit on bunks and chat.

Londoners settle down to spend a night in the basement of Dickins and Jones, a large store in Regent Street that opened its cellar as a public shelter

A drowsy group sing gets underway at a refuge in a working-class section of London

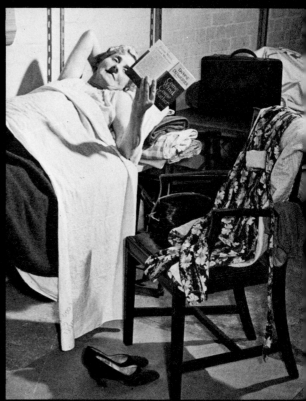

Lying on a makeshift bed, a woman reads at Dickins and Jones

The great dome of St. Paul's Cathedral rises
above the smoke and the flame of an incendiary
raid in late 1940. Despite the intensity of this
December 29 attack, in which 1,500 fires burst
out on the East End alone and incendiaries fell
directly onto the cathedral roof, St. Paul's came
through almost unscathed. A dedicated fire
watch, maintained in the church by volunteers,
snuffed out every fire bomb that hit the
cathedral before serious damage was done.

A bombed-out householder (right) scrambles to reach his clothes, still hanging neatly.

A fireman props his hose against a broken traffic beacon in the middle of Oxford Street, one of London's main shopping thoroughfares. In front of him, a portable sign warns passersby of "Dangerous Walls." In places where buildings were threatening to tumble to the ground, signs like this one diverted traffic and warned pedestrians not to approach.

Rescue workers, some of them wearing steel helmets marked with an identifying R, drag an injured woman from the cellar of her demolished house after digging for 18 hours to find her. The rescue squads, usually made up of plumbers, carpenters, electricians and others who knew their way around building sites, were tough and persistent. If the victim was a child, they would continue their efforts for days: one 12-year-old girl was saved from the ruins of her house after having been buried for 108 hours.

Seen from the north transept of St. Paul's Cathedral, London's core lies in blackened ruins. The dome of the Old Bailey—the city's ancient prison—is at left, to the right of it are the four spires of the Church of the Holy Sepulcher, and at the far right is the steeple of Christ Church in Newgate Street. Despite the visible destruction, very few people lost their lives in the devastation of this primarily commercial area of London.

Winston Churchill inspects the damage inflicted by incendiaries to the Debating Chamber of the House of Commons, the scene of some of his greatest triumphs. Though not positively identifiable, the man in foreground is believed to be Sir William Stephenson, also known as "Intrepid," a British master spy in World War II, and Churchill's friend.

Demolition and rescue workers use a long
wooden pole as a battering ram to knock down
a shaky wall in a residential section of London.
A chalked sign on a nearby building warns of
gas escaping from broken pipes—which
disabled or killed almost as many demolition
workers as did falling beams and masonry.

Repairmen in Oxford Street tape up the ends
of electric cables that have been severed by a
bomb blast as a temporary measure to make
the conduits safe until they can be respliced. In
the right background is Thomas Cook & Sons,
the world-famous British travel agency.

Wardens in business suits retrieve women's clothes from a damaged building in London's garment-manufacturing district. Behind them, fire fighters finish off their task of extinguishing a blaze started by a bomb that had landed at the end of the street only a few hours earlier.

A bombed-out East Ender piles what is left of his household—a sofa, a bedstead, bedding and a few rugs—on a horse-drawn cart. Hardest hit of all Londoners, many homeless East Enders looked for housing in other parts of the city, but the process of relocation was slow, and often hindered—at least in the early days of the bombing—by government red tape.

A neatly lettered sign assures the customers of business continuing as usual in a blasted suburban London shop.

Londoners drink tea at a windowless neighborhood restaurant, whose interior mirrors have somehow managed to survive the blitz

DON'T YOU WORRY I'LL B
AND WHEN IT'S ALL THRO
I'LL MEET YOU IN OUR AL
SO L   IT W   BE L

RALLYING THE HOME FRONT

British Army survivors of the evacuation at Dunkirk join a formally attired master of ceremonies in leading a round of patriotic songs in a London theater.

PROPS TO LIFT
THE BRITISH CHIN

Through the deadly and unremitting strain of the Battle of Britain, the British people responded with a mixture of determination, defiance and humor. On the ground, as well as in the skies, every resource was marshaled against the enemy, and virtually every aspect of life took on a patriotic tinge. Men and women seized at every device to bury their fear of the horror of the German air raids under a warm blanket of patriotic songs, cartoons, plays, theatrical reviews, posters, advertisements and films. Even the venerable English game of darts was altered *(right)* to give players a chance to take aim at their tormentor.

These morale-boosters were more than just the mass reflex of a people with its back against the wall. They were the carefully calculated creations of pitchmen backed by a government that knew something extra was needed to give the people a sense of common purpose and to tune out the daily litany of sirens, bombs and death.

The main weapon was humor. The stately BBC leavened ghastly war news with variety shows whose jokes were sometimes appalling, yet in the pressure cooker of besieged England, seemed awfully funny. (Girl in blacked-out train: "Take your hand off my knee. Not you. You!") Song writers also poked fun at the War, a ditty called "Kiss Me Goodnight Sergeant-Major" ("Sergeant-Major be a mother to me") being a good example of British irreverence.

Another side of the home-front war, promoted through government posters, told the populace how to cope with German spies. One poster exhorted men gabbing to a pretty girl to "Keep mum—She's not so dumb!" Others pushed food-saving drives or explained how to immobilize an auto so invading Germans could not use it—by removing the distributor head or carburetor, or emptying the gas tank. It was the cinema, however, that held the greatest appeal during the Battle of Britain. Films that depicted stalwart Englishmen facing nasty Nazis—and other ungallant foes dating back to the Napoleonic Wars—were featured in movie houses where millions watched their heroes in action, and were distracted for a while from the reality of the War.

In a cartoon published during the blitz, a pair of alert air-raid wardens momentarily allows a rare but revealing exception to strict blackout rules.

—FRED WILKIN—

"We'll give her another ten minutes, and then warn her."

In Plonk, a wartime version of darts, players aimed at Allied or Axis leaders, flags and weapons, and scored a bull's-eye for plonking the Führer.

"When you're up to your neck in hot water, be like the kettle and sing," urged one song cranked out during the blitz. The British heeded that advice with a constant outpouring of patriotic and defiant ditties that were sold as sheet music, sung in pubs and music halls, and played over the BBC. Among the hits was a paean to Britain's airmen called "He Wears a Pair of Silver Wings," and the sentimental ballad "Oh Soldier, Who's Your Lady Love?" A new demihymn bravely proclaimed that "There'll always be an England" ("And England shall be free/If England means as much to you/As England means to me"). And the spirit of the times was effectively captured in one song about the Home Guard, which wistfully complained that "There's a Home Guard Sentry at the end of Lover's Lane/So it's no place for lovers anymore. . . ."

THE PRINCE of WALES THEATRE
" LONDON'S FOLIES BERGERE "   Piccadilly Circus, W.1.

AN ALFRED ESDAILE
PRODUCTION

"REVUE
DES
ALLIÉS"

A NON-STOP FRENCH REVUE
IN ENGLISH

with

MR. GILLIE
POTTER

LONDON
PALLADIUM

TOP OF T

London's renowned musical stage thrived as never before during the blitz, with servicemen on leave flocking to the shows. The poignant warblings of popular songstress Vera Lynn (left) so moved British soldiers that they fondly called her "the sweetheart" of the armed forces. Shows at the Palladium and the Prince of Wales featured platoons of high-kicking hoofers in brief costumes with military or other patriotic themes. Perhaps most popular was the Windmill theater (right), a vaudeville house off Piccadilly Circus, where a man on liberty could drop in to watch chorines perform while statuesque show girls in military hats and not much else stood motionless on pedestals.

Save for Victory
Buy for Quality
JAEGER
JAEGER AGENTS EVERYWHERE

YOUR EVACUEES
Extra mouths to feed
To make the most and get the best
out of every scrap of meat
use
BISTO

AFTER DUTY—
15 MINUTES' PLEASURE
AND SATISFACTION WITH
A **CHURCHMAN'S** NO. 1

★ *It is now more than ever necessary to empty your packet at the time of purchase and leave it with your Tobacconist.* Churchman's No. 1 Cigarettes: a fine 15 minutes of smooth smoking. 10 for 10d., 20 for 1/8d.

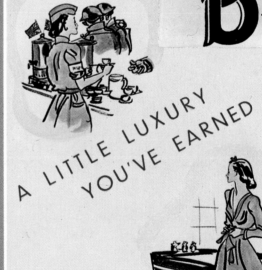

A LITTLE LUXURY
YOU'VE EARNED . . . .

Elizabeth Arden
SOAPS
FRESH FRAGRANT LASTING

My Good
My
GUINN

Advertising lent a helpful hand during the Battle of Britain. Uniformed cigarette smokers in ads exhorted customers to recycle cardboard packets. Clothing and soap manufacturers linked the quality of their products to thoughts of the war effort. Consumers of Guinness stout popped their helmets, while housewives learned how to benefit from a beef flavoring called Bisto. And although civilians could not buy automobile tires, the Dunlop people ran ads anyway, explaining military insignia so readers could recognize the ranks of the men who had preempted the rubber.

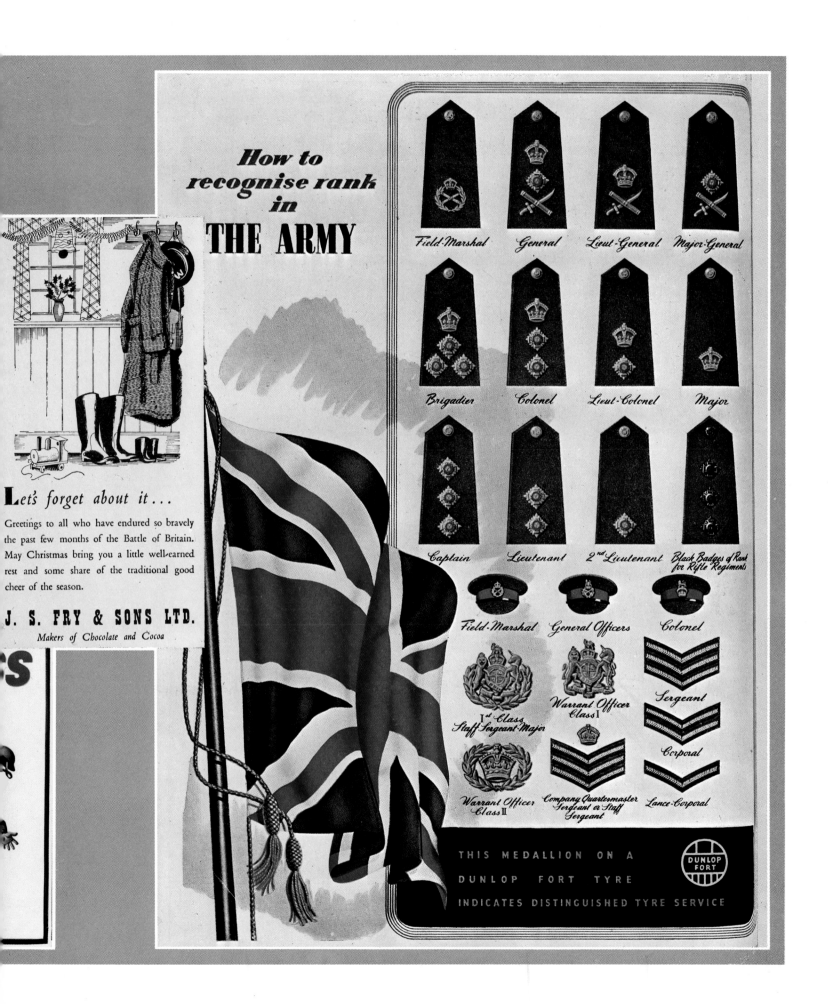

How to recognise rank in THE ARMY

Field-Marshal · General · Lieut-General · Major-General

Brigadier · Colonel · Lieut-Colonel · Major

Captain · Lieutenant · 2nd Lieutenant · Black Badges of Rank for Rifle Regiments

Field-Marshal · General Officers · Colonel

1st Class Staff Sergeant-Major · Warrant Officer Class I · Sergeant

Warrant Officer Class II · Company Quartermaster Sergeant or Staff Sergeant · Corporal · Lance-Corporal

THIS MEDALLION ON A DUNLOP FORT TYRE INDICATES DISTINGUISHED TYRE SERVICE

DUNLOP FORT

Keep mum
she's not so dumb!
CARELESS TALK COSTS LIVES

DONT TELL
AUNTY & UNCLE
OR COUSIN JANE
AND CERTAINLY NOT ——

BETTER POT-LUCK

with Churchill today

THAN HUMBLE PIE

under Hitler tomorrow

DON'T WASTE FOOD

In the Blackout

Although the door you've opened wide —
make sure it is the platform side

Bruce Angrave

Kill him—
with *War Savings*

There was a serious side to some of the posters appearing on subway walls, billboards and other public places. The threat of invasion, and the specter of spies lurking under—or in—the British bed, prompted the government to unleash a barrage of dos and don'ts that were plastered all over the home islands. Some posters pointed out the perils of becoming too intimate with sexy sirens who might be on the enemy's payroll. Others warned that TITTLE-TATTLE LOST THE BATTLE, or that even an aunty or uncle could not be trusted. Still others enjoined Britons to save food, curb unnecessary spending and be sure to leave the train from the platform side during a blackout.

NIGHT TRAIN TO MUNICH

CONVOY

Patriotic films depicting gallant heroes protecting England were a balm to besieged Britons in World War II. Potboilers like "Night Train to Munich," featuring Margaret Lockwood, Rex Harrison and Paul Henreid in Nazi uniforms, and "Convoy," starring Clive Brook and Stewart Granger, packed theaters all over England. But one of the most popular wartime films reached back into British history for inspiration. Called "Lady Hamilton," it was the favorite of Churchill and many other Britons, not so much because it featured a love affair betweenVivienLeigh and Laurence Olivier (right), as because Olivier played the dashing Lord Nelson, revered throughout Britain as his country's greatest naval hero.

LADY HAMILTON

6

The year 1941 began on a deceptive note. Just after the terrible bombing of London on December 29, the weather went sour, and the Luftwaffe was forced to slacken the pace of its attacks. Throughout the months of January and February the raids were much more widely spaced, providing a respite for the British people. The letup had a strange effect: instead of reviving people's spirits, it made their morale sag even further. Without the attacks to excite and distract them, people began to fret more about the increasing scarcity of gasoline and food. Butter and cooking fats, meat, eggs and tea were now all heavily rationed. There was just enough meat for an average family to dine on it once a week. The shortage of tea was particularly distressing.

In addition to these items, most of the British desperately missed having fruit or canned goods, which might have added a little variety to the stodgy food they were able to get on ration. One social worker in London wrote in her diary: "I'm just longing for some fruit but could not get any. I went out with the firm determination to spend a shilling per pound if necessary for apples, but to my horror there was not one in any shop in Notting Hill at any price whatsoever. The window seems to be full of turnips. . . . My friend, Mr. Booker, has hated onions all his life, but now he says that when once more we can get them he will eat the lot. I think we will all go on onion binges when the war is over."

It had been months since anyone had seen an orange or a banana. A wealthy woman in Hampstead came back from a day of driving an ambulance to find a note from her charwoman, who also did her shopping: "Dear Madam, there is no honey, no sultanas, currants or raisins, no mixed fruits, no sugar or saccharine, no spaghetti, no sage, no herrings, kippers or sprats (smoked or plain), no matches, no kindling wood, no fat or dripping, no tin of celery or tomato soup, or salmon. I have bought three pounds of parsnips."

On such days it was becoming all too easy for rich and poor alike to feel bitterly weighed down by the discomforts of life, the lack of heat in their homes, the blackout, the destruction all around. "We are in the dumps, and everyone is bad tempered," wrote another woman. "I almost miss the heavy bombing raids."

The truth was that the British people were tired. They had taken too much for too long.

Churchill sensed that what they needed was not encour-

FINALE FOR THE BOMBERS

agement or coddling, but a good jolt. And on February 9, 1941, he gave them one. In a radio address to the nation he warned that Hitler at last was planning to invade Britain, and that he would do so in the very near future.

"An invasion now will be supported by a much more carefully prepared tackle and equipment of landing craft and other apparatus," he warned, comparing the threat to that of the previous fall. "We must all be prepared to meet gas attacks, parachute attacks, and glider attacks, with constancy, forethought and practiced skill. . . . In order to win the war, Hitler must destroy Great Britain."

In fact, Winston Churchill knew that what he was telling his people was total nonsense. Code intercepts and other intelligence had informed him that Hitler had, in fact, abandoned any idea of an invasion. Churchill was simply reviving the invasion threat as a means of stiffening the backs of the wilting British people.

And they could not afford to wilt. Toward the end of February the weather improved, and heavy air attacks began again, with the German bombers concentrating now on cutting Britain's vital maritime supply links. At sea U-boats were stalking British ships with great success, and the Luftwaffe supported this effort by directing most of its attacks against shipyards and ports.

On two successive nights in mid-March, the small shipbuilding town of Clydebank, on the Clyde below Glasgow, was bombed to its foundations. All but seven of its 12,000 houses were damaged, and its inhabitants had to flee into the nearby moors. Bristol, Cardiff, Portsmouth, Plymouth and Southampton were blitzed repeatedly, Plymouth so often and savagely that many of its buildings were hit more than once and statistics on total houses hit or destroyed came to exceed the total number of the city's dwellings. London, on March 19, suffered its worst raid to date: 750 civilians were killed. Bombs rained on Hull, Newcastle, Belfast and Liverpool. Nottingham was badly hit. However, Derby, only 30 miles away, where the Rolls-Royce works was producing engines for fighter aircraft, escaped damage: a combination of electronic beam-bending and decoy fires led the attacking planes to dump their high explosives and incendiaries onto the Vale of Belvoir east of Nottingham, rendering hors de combat two chickens and two cows.

In April, bomb-weary Britons were hit with bad news from the Continent. First Yugoslavia and then Greece fell to the Wehrmacht. Was this a rehearsal, the British wondered, for the invasion of the British Isles about which Churchill had warned them? Their suspicions seemed to be confirmed when the intensity of the German air attacks on Britain reached a new peak in the second half of April. Coventry, Bristol, Belfast, Portsmouth and Plymouth were all devastatingly pounded. London was hit twice, each time with a greater tonnage of explosives than ever before; over 2,000 people were killed during the two night attacks, and 148,000 houses were damaged or destroyed.

These massive raids were indeed a prelude to invasion, but not of the British Isles. Their real purpose was to distract attention from Hitler's latest grand scheme: an all-out attack by land and air on the U.S.S.R.

By early May, secret orders went out from Göring's headquarters instructing the majority of the German bomber and fighter command, which had been hitting Britain, to prepare to move into Czechoslovakia and Poland in readiness for Operation Barbarossa, as the assault upon the Soviet Union was code-named. However, before the Luftwaffe pilots were informed of the decision to pack up and leave France and the Low Countries, they were given orders for one last, massive strike against Britain.

The idea was not only to inflict the maximum amount of damage, but to convey a message as well. During the past year, the RAF had been hitting cities in the Ruhr and had bombed Berlin several times. In early May the RAF hit Berlin particularly hard, and hammered away at Hamburg, Bremen and Emden as well. The Nazi High Command feared that the moment substantial Luftwaffe forces were committed to operating in Russia, the British would step up the intensity of their raids. Thus the Germans felt they must show Britain that such a policy would lead to ruthless reprisals. To give the British a foretaste of what would happen to them should they become overbold, a punishing attack on London was ordered for May 10.

One of the raid's most enthusiastic proponents was Hitler's Foreign Minister, Joachim von Ribbentrop. A passionate Nazi, he had been German Ambassador to London in the years immediately preceding World War II. And he had earned the resentment of the British people by insisting on giving the Nazi salute and shouting "Heil Hitler!" when he presented his credentials to King George VI. Subsequently he had behaved like an arrogant bully in all his dealings with the British government and people. (Even Ribbentrop's fellow Nazis referred to him as a "malevolent and mean-minded man.") And the British, in return, had missed no opportunity of snubbing or mocking him.

Thus Ribbentrop had come to regard the war as something of a personal act of revenge against the British government and people. He cherished one great ambition—to present himself in triumph at Buckingham Palace and there to force a chastened king and government to shout "Heil Hitler!" and give the Nazi salute. His fear was that the decision to attack Russia would, by draining away air power from the Battle of Britain, cheat him of his revenge. Ribbentrop had done his best to persuade Hitler to postpone the Russian attack until Britain was knocked out. He had failed, but he was to have a grudge raid in compensation.

On the morning of May 10, Ribbentrop came into his office in the Wilhelmstrasse and told one of his assistants, Erich Kordt, that the Russian campaign was about to be launched. He knew that Kordt was pro-British, loved London and had grieved over the continued bombing attacks on the city. So Ribbentrop quickly added, with wicked relish, that the Führer had agreed to a final raid against England before bringing the Luftwaffe back east.

"One last bombing, and it will be the heaviest of the war," he said. "The pilots have been given only one target." His face lit up and his pale eyes blazed. "London, London, London!" he cried.

The attitude of many Luftwaffe pilots had become more malevolent, too. Earlier, during the raid on Coventry, German fliers had been shocked at the fact that they were ordered to deliberately bomb civilian targets. But the RAF by now had been bombing German cities for many months and sensibilities had become blunted. Field Marshal Hugo Sperrle, commander of Air Fleet 3, supervised the operation, and as he put it later:

"We had ceased to be oversensitive about such things by that time. In any case, the odds had evened up. British cities were no longer helpless targets. They were dangerous places for an enemy plane to fly over, and my pilots were lucky to get back alive from operations against them."

Indeed, the RAF night fighters had become a real menace. The Beaufighters were equipped now with improved radar that allowed them to pick up enemy planes miles away, and to home in surely on their targets. They had already made many kills. Moreover, the British no longer needed their Ultra code-cracking system to tell them where raids were coming. A method of reading the Luftwaffe's directional beams had been so perfected that the British knew the moment enemy bombers were switched on to the target for the evening—which was some time before the actual raid. This enabled the British to alert civil-defense forces, to mobilize fire squads and medical units, to get their greatly strengthened antiaircraft batteries ready and also to tell the Beaufighters where to wait in the dark sky for the raiders.

For the climactic attack on London, the Germans had divided the city into three sectors. *Kampfgeschwader 2* (Bomber Division 2) under Colonel Johannes Fink, would take off from the fields around Cambrai in northern France and make for east London. Those of KG 53 under Colonel Stahl would leave from the Lille district to hit central London, and those of KG 4 under Colonel Hans-Joachim Rath would assemble at Soesterberg, near Utrecht, in Holland, and then make for south and west London. In addition to hitting certain tactical and strategical targets, they were instructed to destroy the ancient and historic center of Britain's capital. One of the fliers in the raid, a 25-year-old Austrian lieutenant named Baron Walther von Siber, had picked out a target of his own: Buckingham Palace. German fliers had been told that the palace was no longer off limits and that the first one to hit it would earn a Knight's Cross, to be pinned on him by Göring himself.

At 5 p.m. on May 10, Lieutenant Karl Fiebach of the Luftwaffe Signals Office telephoned his commanding officer for the order to switch on the radio beams for the night's operations. Given the go-ahead, he rang the operators at Station Anton at Cherbourg, Station Berta at Calais and Station Cicero at Fécamp. Then, at 5:10 p.m., Fiebach informed his commanding officer that the beams were on.

At the same moment, in England, the duty controller of No.80 Wing RAF, at a secret headquarters at Harrow-on-the-Hill, picked up his own telephone to speak, in turn, to RAF Fighter Command, Antiaircraft Command, the Royal Navy, the General Post Office (which controlled air-raid alerts in Britain), and the London Fire Service at its headquarters on the Thames at Lambeth. As each unit answered, he identified himself by a code name and number, and then said: "Hallo, sir. This is to inform you the beam is on London."

At London Fire Service headquarters, Deputy Chief Frank Jackson took the message with a feeling in his bones that something extraordinary was about to happen. The Luftwaffe recently had seemed to like bombing London on weekends; it was an effective terror tactic against civilians who yearned for respite and relaxation. Moreover, tonight the moon would be full, and the Germans preferred moonlight, because it gave their gunners a better chance to see night fighters coming at them. Jackson pressed a button on his intercom and said:

"All available pumps into London tonight. I want a thousand plus. And all men stand by, leave cancelled. This is an emergency." But a disappointment was in store for Jackson. There were not a thousand pumps—the professional term for fire engines—available. Heavy raids on Liverpool and

AN AMERICAN SPOKESMAN FOR BELEAGUERED BRITAIN

To millions of Americans nothing brought home the agony and defiance of Britain in the blitz so vividly as the nightly eyewitness radio broadcasts of Edward R. Murrow, CBS's chief European correspondent.

Authenticity was his trademark. Behind the deep, resonant, slightly sardonic voice intoning the familiar opening, "This . . . is London," listeners often heard the crump of bombs, the wail of sirens. Murrow took his audience with him onto London rooftops, along shattered streets, aboard minesweepers on the Channel, and into overcrowded bomb shelters.

"Off to my left," he reported one night as a Luftwaffe raider approached his rooftop post, "I can just see that faint-red angry snap of antiaircraft bursts. . . . Four searchlights . . . are swinging over in this general direction. The plane's still very high. . . . The searchlights now are feeling almost directly overhead. Now you'll hear two bursts a little nearer in a moment. There they are! That hard, stony sound."

Even more effective were his frequent low-key tributes to unsung British heroes like the soldiers he saw sifting rubble for possible blitz survivors: "They paid no attention to the bursts of antiaircraft fire overhead as they bent their backs and carried away basketfuls of mortar and brick. A few small steam shovels would help. . . . But all the modern instruments seem to be overhead. Down here on the ground people must work with their hands."

Homburg rakishly atilt, CBS reporter Ed Murrow strides past London's All Souls Church (right) and the BBC building from whose roof he often broadcast during bombings. Murrow stayed away from bomb shelters except in pursuit of news. "Once you start going into shelters," he explained, "you lose your nerve."

Hull during the week had drained off reserves, and there were only 700 machines on hand plus another 60 making their way back to London in convoy from the north.

If, as Jackson suspected, the raid tonight turned out to be "a dirty one," as the firemen called a fire raid, then 760 machines would not be nearly enough.

Londoners were old hands at air raids now, and few of them expected a quiet weekend, but all the same, pubs and restaurants were packed on Saturday night, and so were theaters and the movies. The most popular show in town was the New York hit *No Time for Comedy,* starring a couple of bright-eyed young stars, Rex Harrison and Lilli Palmer, and the new Commander-in-Chief of Fighter Command, Air Marshal William Sholto Douglas, had slipped into town from his outer-London headquarters to see them at the afternoon performance. Another American play, *Thunder Rock,* starring Michael Redgrave, was packing them in at the Globe Theatre nearby. The hit films were *Gone With The Wind* and *Kitty Foyle,* with Ginger Rogers. The cabaret star of the moment was a blonde Hungarian named Magda Kun, who seduced her audience with a beguiling song:

> I've got a cosy flat.
>> There's a place for your hat.
> I'll wear a pink chiffon negligée gown.
>> And I do know my stuff,
> But if that's not enough,
>> I've got the deepest shelter in town.

Luckily for the Saturday night crowds, entertainment in London closed early now, and most people were home by 10 o'clock. At RAF Fighter Headquarters at Bentley Priory, it was 10:15 when Sholto Douglas's assistant, Robert Wright, told the Air Marshal that the yellow warning had been given. The raiders were coming in.

Douglas ordered his night fighters aloft.

At 11 the air raid sirens began sounding over London.

What turned out to be the last mass bomber raid on the British capital during World War II began at 11:30 p.m. on Saturday, May 10, and lasted until 5:37 a.m. on Sunday, May 11. Five hundred and seven Luftwaffe planes took part in the attack, dropping a total of 708 tons of bombs on London —a deadly mixture of incendiaries, high explosives and parachute-borne land mines.

A tremendous barrage from London's antiaircraft defenses greeted the raiders. "You don't need gloves when you fly over London nowadays," one German pilot said. "Their flak keeps your hands warm." The RAF's night fighters shot down seven German planes and damaged three for the loss of one of their own. Among their victims was the Heinkel-111 flown by Baron von Siber, who never did get close enough to London to bomb Buckingham Palace. His plane was destroyed by a Spitfire over the Essex coastline and three of his crew were killed. Siber himself managed to parachute to safety. He spent the rest of the war in a POW camp.

The concentrated antiaircraft fire kept the raiders flying high, so that they could not pinpoint their targets. But, in the circumstances, this did not matter. They simply dropped their bombs somewhere over the capital, inflicting the worst

A Royal Engineers' bomb-disposal squad gingerly defuses a 1,200-pound delayed-action bomb that has gouged a crater near a North London hospital. Disarming such missiles called for high courage and iron nerves since the bomb's timing device could trigger an explosion at any moment. This particular bomb was safely defused and later detonated in Hackney Marshes, far from populated areas.

damage of the entire war to date. Not only the East End and The City of London, this time, but every section of the capital fell prey to swarms of incendiary bombs. Deputy Fire Chief Frank Jackson's suspicion was right; not all the fire engines he had managed to alert nor all the firemen could cope with it. Moreover, even if additional men and machines had been available, there was not enough water.

Geoffrey Blackstone, a divisional officer in the London Fire Service, was assigned to the Elephant and Castle district —named for a famous local tavern—in South London. His beat encompassed an important traffic circle linking all the bridge roads, and it included block after block of old houses and highly combustible warehouses. Within seconds after the sirens sounded their warning he was on his way to his post. He would have 20 pumps to work with as the bombs began to fall, and more later, when it became clear that his district was in critical danger. The situation was already bad by the time he got to the junction of the bridge roads.

"The stuff was beginning to drop," he said later. "Quite a lot of it. I soon began to realize that this was something a bit heavier than anything we had had before." The high explosive bombs had broken practically every water main around. For this, ironically, the mild English climate was as much to blame as the German bombers. In the absence of the severe frosts that plagued most of continental Europe, the water mains in England had been laid comparatively close to the surface; they were only three feet deep, and easily damaged. Now, when they were most sorely needed, they were useless.

"For a time we had the awful exasperation of lots of firemen, lots of pumps, lots of fires—but no water. Then a water unit arrived, which carried up to two or three miles of folded hose. It dropped a canvas dam and made its way to the Thames near Westminster Bridge. Four lines of hose were laid out, waiting for the water." The water was to be pumped from the river to the canvas dam or tank, then relayed by other pumps to the fires.

Blackstone headed for the Thames by car until stopped by a bomb that tore up Westminster Bridge Road. He got out and started walking along the hose lines leading to the river. "Here was a most disappointing sight," he recalled later, in a masterpiece of British understatement. "Fires were showering embers onto the hose which was lying flat without water, burning it and charring it so that when the water arrived it would be wasted." While bombs burst on all sides —those in the near distance falling with a long, low whistle and the closer ones sounding like a train going into a station —Blackstone ran into a colleague named Cruse, one of the heads of the Metropolitan Water Board. As in all raids, Cruse was in the midst of the action, doing everything he could to find water. "Cruse said he didn't know where there was an unbroken main, but he would do what he could to help. Seconds later he was disembowelled by a bomb splinter."

Blackstone went on to the pumps. Getting water out of the Thames was difficult at the best of times; now the river was at low ebb, and the water was out of reach of most of the engines on the embankments. Nevertheless the pump crew had managed to set up three pumps and link them to hose lines. "I told them it was no good—I had seen the hose and they would have to replace it. By now it was almost impossible to get past the fires on Westminster Bridge Road, and there was still no water." Finally the firemen got four new hose lines laid, and set about linking them to the pumps. Once the hose was filled with water, it would no longer be so vulnerable to embers. Desperately hoping that the water would start flowing before the new lines burned, Blackstone left the Thames pumps and hurried back through the blazing streets to the road junction.

The fire, he now saw, had spread down Newington Causeway and Newington Butts, and down the New Kent Road. A high explosive bomb had fallen onto a pump, wrecking it and killing the crew of five. They were lying in a pool of blood, half in the gutter and half in the fire engine. "Get those bodies out of sight!" said Blackstone crisply. A group of firemen carried them into nearby Skipton Street and covered them with canvas.

Superintendent George Adams, who was in charge of the whole South London area, told Blackstone that he now had 100 pumps available and ready to go to work. "We both smiled rather sourly. One hundred pumps, five men to a crew—500 firemen—and still no water." But then: "The four lines laid along the Westminster Bridge Road suddenly began to swell, and water poured into the large canvas dam. A ragged cheer went up from some of the firemen. There were blazing buildings on each side of us, and it was getting uncomfortably hot. Four large pumps already had their suctions lying in the dam, and as soon as there was a foot of water in it, they primed. The jets started literally throwing water on to the flames."

But no sooner had the firemen fought their way into one blazing warehouse than their jets died away. There was not enough water flowing into the dam to keep pace with the pumps. Working feverishly, the men laid out two more lines. Then a message from headquarters informed Blackstone that fireboats had been ordered to Westminster Bridge and Waterloo Bridge and were piping more water ashore.

Meanwhile, the high explosives were still falling. Three more firefighters had been killed in the vicinity of the Elephant and Castle. The whole of the night sky was lit up, and Blackstone estimated that at least 50 buildings in his sector were "well alight."

Many more were burning in other parts of London. Altogether 2,200 fires were reported during the night. Nine of these were so big that each raged over an entire acre of buildings; 20 other fires almost as big required over 30 pumps apiece to keep them from spreading uncontrollably. At least 37 others had more than a score of pumps pouring water onto them. For a while, about 700 acres of London were ablaze, roughly one and a half times the area engulfed by the Great Fire of London in 1666, when the capital as it then existed was all but destroyed.

The Tower of London was hit, and the Beefeaters in their traditional costumes walking its battlements overlooking the Thames had to man stirrup pumps and sand buckets to put out the fires. The Crown Jewels had already been taken out of their showcases in the Tower and spirited to a safer haven outside London.

The Houses of Parliament, Westminster Abbey, the British Museum, all were hit. Seven high explosive bombs ripped through the House of Commons, tumbling the galleries to the floor and mingling them with the wreckage of the member's green-leather padded benches and the canopied speaker's chair. A bomb pierced the clock tower, blackening and scarring the face of Big Ben. But the old clock was structurally unimpaired, and the famous chimes scarcely missed a peal. In Westminster Abbey the roof over the lantern in the center of the building was set ablaze by incendiary bombs and came crashing down into the choir and sanctuary. The magnificent oaken roof of Westminster Hall was pierced by bombs; Westminster School, which had educated Ben Jonson, John Dryden, Christopher Wren, Jeremy Bentham and Robert Southey, was severely damaged; the Deanery of Westminster, one of the finest examples of medieval architecture in England, was destroyed.

Most of the richest treasures of the British Museum had been removed, but incendiaries gutted the library and almost demolished the museum's Egyptian section. Other bombs hit Scotland Yard, the Salvation Army headquarters, and every main-line railroad station in London, including Cannon Street, Paddington, Waterloo, Euston, Liverpool Street, Victoria and Charing Cross. Every single church in The City of London was either badly damaged or entirely destroyed. In the Strand, one of the oldest and most beloved of the churches in London, St. Clement Danes, was reduced to a smoldering ruin. The great bells, which had long rung out the melody of the old nursery rhyme, "Oranges and lemons say the bells of St. Clement's," cracked asunder when they crashed to the ground. Five London hospitals were hit, one so badly that it had to be evacuated at the height of the raid. Other bombs fell on shops, houses, a warden's post, a shelter, a hotel, a cinema, a club.

One stick of explosives came down near Spurgeon's Tabernacle in Geoffrey Blackstone's district, dropping in the midst of the pump crews. To Blackstone, "there seemed to be blue-clad, fire-booted bodies everywhere. We sorted out the dead from the injured. There were five more dead." Ambulances were urgently needed for the living. The firefighters had no radio equipment, so Blackstone and his men tried to telephone for help. "We tried every telephone kiosk and every telephone in the buildings around. Not one line was live. There was a sense of isolation in this—to be in the middle of a great city whose communications had been disrupted." A despatch rider had to be sent with a message to HQ asking for ambulances.

"As usual the decision had been made to let certain buildings burn out and concentrate on what seemed worth saving," said Blackstone. "For some reason the Elephant and Castle pub seemed to have some symbolic value. This magnificent piece of old London stood on a sort of island site in the middle of the six-road junction. I had a sort of urge to

AN UNLIKELY EMISSARY FROM THE SKY

On the night of May 10, 1941, a solitary Me-110 came winging in low over Scotland. Its pilot was Rudolf Hess, Deputy Führer of the Third Reich, on perhaps the most bizarre mission of the War: a single-handed attempt to make peace. At 10:30 Hess found his objective: Dungavel House, southeast of Edinburgh, home of Douglas Douglas-Hamilton, Duke of Hamilton. Hess had seen the Duke in 1936 at the Olympic Games in Berlin, and had heard that he had access to Churchill and other high government figures. Hess cut his engines and bailed out, unarmed.

On the ground below, a Scots plowman, David McLean, heard the plane's engines, rushed out of his house, captured Hess and turned him over to the Home Guard. Hess asked to see the Duke of Hamilton. The startled Duke—an RAF Wing Commander —was notified and talked to Hess on May 12, later reporting to Churchill that Hess felt his flight would "show his sincerity and Germany's willingness for peace."

Hess was indeed sincere, but he was totally naive. The British regarded his peace feelers as demands for surrender, while Hitler, furious, wanted to shoot him. His mission a fiasco, the emissary of peace was jailed as an ordinary prisoner of war.

Farmer McLean assisted Hess out of his chute and handed him over to the local constabulary.

British newspapers trumpet the news of Rudolf Hess's capture—two days after the fact. Censors, wary of possible fraud, had withheld the news until German radio officially acknowledged the flight.

save it and perhaps wasted precious water and manpower on it. The fireman at the control point in the middle of the circus said, 'Cor, sir, what a wind—just our luck!' It was a perfectly still night, but the hot air rising from the fires all around was sucking cool air into the circus so that sheets of newspaper, sparks and burning rags were flying through the air around us.''

Flames licked at the roof of the Elephant and Castle, and smoke billowed through the intersection. While the pump crews were battling to control the blaze the station master at the Elephant and Castle tube station came up to Blackstone and said that there might be a bit of trouble in the tube because smoke was going down and the people sheltering below were getting frightened. Blackstone told him to go back and tell them they were perfectly safe, that the smoke wouldn't hurt them. But a quarter of an hour later the divisional officer's attention was sharply distracted from the raging fires by something he had never encountered before in all the London raids: signs of panic.

''Someone had decided that the tube station should be evacuated and the occupants, mostly women and children, were coming into the fire area. They came at a shambling run, children carried in arms or dragged screaming behind their mothers or grandparents. Fortunately there was little smoke in the streets, as the heat was funneling it upwards. But there was red heat; there were sparks, flying cinders, the rumble of falling stone and the sharp whistle of distant bombs.'' Watching the frightened people disgorging from the Underground station into the inferno, Blackstone felt enormous anger toward the faceless German men in the throbbing planes above.

Bone-weary and thirsting for tea, Blackstone made his way over to Skipton Street. There were 22 bodies now, only the boots visible under the tarpaulin. He counted eight pairs of leather boots and 14 pairs of rubber boots. London firemen wore fine leather fire boots; the auxiliary firefighters had cheap rubber Wellingtons. ''You are all equal now, mates,'' Blackstone thought. ''God forgive those who caused it.''

He looked at his watch. It was 5 a.m., soon it would be day; the raid seemed endless, he felt weary and almost disassociated. Mercifully, less than an hour later the all-clear sounded. Blackstone's work was not yet done; London was still afire; nearly 8,000 streets were blocked by fallen build-

ings and fire equipment. The firefighters' job was made harder by the morning rush hour. ''People were going to work and finding all vehicular traffic stopped by our lines of hose. Spectators rubbernecking after the raid crowded around, got in the way, stood on the hose. I heard one of them say to a station officer, 'Cor blimey, you 'aven't 'alf made a balls of this lot. I don't know what we pay you for.' ''

At 11 o'clock relief crews arrived. Geoffrey Blackstone got in his car and went home. As he drove slowly through the devastation he said to himself, ''I don't think London can stand much more of this, and I don't think I can.''

By a final count, 1,436 Londoners had been killed, some 1,800 seriously injured; for the survivors, it seemed almost more than they could bear. The wreckage of their beloved capital, the crumbled buildings and blackened monuments they saw all around them, aroused a terrible despair. One woman wrote in her diary:

''Just heard the terrible news that Westminster Hall was hit last night, also the Abbey and the Houses of Parliament. They saved the roof to a certain extent but some of it is gone. In the Abbey it is the Lantern. They thought at first that Big Ben had crashed to the ground. I cannot comment on such disasters. I feel we must have sinned grievously to have such sacrifices demanded of us. . . . There's bound to be further destruction, and there's not much satisfaction to hear of the treasures of the enemy being laid to waste in a similar manner. I don't wish it.''

Others affected indifference. ''I remember my friend Mary,'' wrote another woman, ''telling me that after she had been bombed out of her flat for the first time with the loss of all her clothes and belongings—and she has now been bombed out three times, including last night—she had simply not cared about her personal things ever since. There is the human inability to take in more than a certain degree of calamity, which is God's merciful tempering of the wind to the shorn lamb.''

An American correspondent in London, Larry Rue of the Chicago *Tribune*, saw two City gentlemen on the morning after the raid walking to work in black coats and striped trousers, bowler hats on head, briefcases and brollies in hand —but with blue stubble on their chins. They hadn't shaved.

''I began to really worry for the first time,'' Rue said, ''and to realize to what depths of their being the May 10 raid had shocked and shaken the people of London."

For days afterward, many other Londoners walked around in a semi-daze, dreading new trials to come. They assumed, reasonably enough, that the big raid was the beginning of an even more savage blitz.

Three weeks passed, and there were no more big raids, only gadfly attacks by isolated planes. But then on June 2 the British-held island of Crete in the Mediterranean succumbed to an attack by German parachute troops. Britons feared that now, surely their own island would be next. But another week went by, with still no raids—and no invasions. "WHAT'S HITLER UP TO?" asked a headline in the *Daily Express*. Others repeated the question: Was this a lull before the final storm? Was the invasion coming at last?

A select circle around Prime Minister Churchill, armed with decoded information, was well aware that there would be no more major raids after May 10. The reports from the Continent confirmed the news that the Luftwaffe was indeed on its way out of western Europe, and that new airfields to service the transferred planes and men were being opened in eastern Europe. But no one had told the British people. Two more weeks of quiet nights passed, yet Londoners were taking no chances. Thousands of civilians still packed into the Underground stations every night. Those who persisted in staying at home spent uneasy nights, wondering why things were so quiet.

Even some of the Luftwaffe units still operating against England believed that they were the vanguard of an invading army, and their belief was confirmed when Göring arrived in Paris after the fall of Crete and called a meeting of his unit commanders on the Western Front. He told them that their air attacks were the overture to the final defeat of Britain, and that stepped-up raids, plus intensified U-boat war, would now be used as a prelude to a landing.

Adolf Galland was one of those who were at the conference, and he was both convinced and impressed by the Reich Marshal's speech. But after the conference, Göring took him and Werner Mölders aside and, rubbing his hands with glee, said: "There's not a grain of truth in it." Then he confirmed to the two Luftwaffe aces that his speech was a bluff, whose aim was indeed, as later disclosed by Galland, "to hide the real intentions of the German High Command:

the imminent invasion of the Soviet Union." To Galland, Göring's revelation "was a paralyzing shock."

To the British people, it became an undreamed-of reprieve. On June 22, 1941, the German armies jumped off against Russia. Some people were sorry for the Russians, but most of them cheered the news. "IT'S MOSCOW'S TURN NOW," said a banner headline in the London *Evening News*, and Londoners commented: "Now we will see what *they* will do about it."

In an odd sort of tribute to the newly beleaguered Ally, the Windmill Theater put on a special show called *Moscow Nights* in which the nude performers wore fur hats on their heads and red stars on their navels. The prostitutes who haunted blacked-out Piccadilly began calling potential clients "tovarich."

As July gave way to August, and still no raiders came, Churchill confirmed—reluctantly, because he was afraid of a slump in morale now that the bombing was over—that the Luftwaffe had moved out the bulk of its forces.

"BLITZ OVER," said a newspaper poster.

And in truth the Battle of Britain was over, too. Although the war had a long and weary way to go, slowly the fact seeped into everyone's mind that so far as the dismemberment of Britain was concerned the danger was over; the United Kingdom was still there, united and free.

"We won," the British began to tell each other, in tones mingling surprise with pride.

There were Germans who would not agree with them, who would say, in fact, that there never was anything called the Battle of Britain. General Adolf Galland of the Luftwaffe, for instance, said later:

"All that happened was that we made a number of attacks against England between 1940 and 1941. Then we discovered that we were not achieving the desired effect, and so we retired. There was no battle, and we did not lose it." To which, much later, an RAF pilot who had fought against him in 1940 replied: "General Galland, do you know what happens in the tenth round of a boxing match, when one fighter is groggy on his feet, and his trainer throws in the towel, shouting: 'My fighter retires!'? Who has won the fight and who has lost it?"

The British people had no doubt whatsoever. They bore many bruises, but they knew who had thrown in the towel.

GERMANY'S FALLEN EAGLES

Home Guardsmen, rescue-squad members and police surround a downed and disabled German flyer. After a hospital stay the flyer was taken to a POW camp.

A PRETTY GOOD WAY TO SIT OUT THE WAR

"When my plane was hit," recalls Eckehard Priebe, a Luftwaffe pilot shot down during the Battle of Britain, "I bailed out, a bullet crease along my scalp, blood running into my eyes. But I came down safely, and the Home Guard was there to meet me. They were unfailingly kind."

Most downed German airmen who survived to become prisoners of war in Britain would have agreed with Priebe about the decency of their treatment. Part of it was undoubtedly due to Britain's desire to create a climate for the good treatment of their own men held in Germany. But a significant measure was the British sense of fair play.

At one POW camp, the colonel in command regularly visited his charges with a bottle of whiskey, handed out full glasses and toasted the Germans with the words, "It's a horrible war." But the truth was the POWs in England had fallen into a pretty good spot to sit out the War. Food was hearty and sufficient; the Germans were issued all the marmalade they could eat. Officers did not have to work; enlisted POWs were given cigarette money in return for jobs that ranged from construction to bomb disposal.

At first, however, some Germans were restless, arrogant —and not always so well treated. One former POW later complained about a "slimy captain," an army doctor whom he struck for refusing to X-ray a knee broken in a crash landing. And there were occasional escape attempts—though some tended to have the giddy overtones of later POW television stories. "Of course," said the injured airman, "we had our fun among ourselves." When British sentries in the camp called out, "All's well" from their posts, the POWs, busy digging escape tunnels, grinned and snorted, "Denkste!" —meaning, roughly, "That's what you think!"

Perhaps as a result of the generally fair and generous treatment, only a few POWs made serious efforts to escape; those who did were mostly unsuccessful. One thwarted attempt around Christmas of 1940 earned the escapee 14 days' solitary. But the authorities also saw that he drew his holiday wine ration, and they even sent a Tommy dressed as Santa Claus to the prisoner's cell.

On a blanket that hangs to divide a recreation room, a picture of Hitler shares space with a hand-drawn pinup tacked below a radio loudspeaker.

A captured German, with a typical airman's interest in all planes, works on a wooden model of a British Spitfire. A Hurricane he has finished stands at left.

German prisoners take afternoon exercise in the rain outside the converted factory where they were confined. Accommodations for prisoners of war ranged from country estates and hotels to tent compounds that were thrown up as the number of POWs passed 1,000 in late 1940.

A kibitzer and two chess opponents—one of them wearing gloves—discuss a match that is being played on a makeshift table in a chilly recreation room.

Prisoners sit down to the POW's standard meal of beef hash, potatoes and coffee, served on tin dishes in a converted warehouse. Prisoners had few complaints about camp food, which supplied them a daily 3,300 to 3,400 calories.

Rows of wooden beds in an enlisted men's dormitory lie spruced up for inspection. The issued gear included a mattress, two blankets, a canvas duffel bag for clothing, towel, toothbrush, shaving brush, shaving soap, comb, hairbrush—as well as tennis shoes to protect wooden floors from the Germans' own hobnailed outdoor boots. Though some captured officers also lived in dorms, many were housed in converted private homes.

Enlisted POWs supervised by a German naval officer (left), a British officer (center, rear) and a German noncom (right) move conduit pipes to low ground that is

Prisoners on an outside work detail shovel gravel for use in road repairs near their camp.

A noncom finishes a large-scale map of Europe to be used by the British War Office.

to be drained. For a 48-hour week, the men earned about $1.44.

Three men sweep their prison courtyard beneath windows masked with barbed wire.

A guarded column of POWs, with patches on their backs to make them conspicuous in escape attempts, marches to work past a pair of curious British women

and an excited dog. Sights like this aroused the compassion of many British civilians, who were forbidden to befriend the prisoners until later in the war.

BIBLIOGRAPHY

Andrews, Allen, *The Air Marshals*. William Morrow & Company Inc., 1970.

Ansel, Walter, *Hitler Confronts England*. Duke University Press, 1960.

Baldwin, Hanson, *Battles Lost and Won*. Harper & Row, Publishers, 1966.

Baumbach, Werner, *The Life and Death of the Luftwaffe*. Coward-McCann, Inc., 1960.

Briggs, Susan, *The Home Front*. American Heritage Publishing Co., Inc., 1975

Calder, Angus, *The People's War*. Pantheon Books, 1969.

Calvocoressi, Peter, and Guy Wint, *Total War*. Pantheon Books, 1972.

Churchill, Winston S.:
My Early Life. Charles Scribner's Sons, 1958.
Their Finest Hour. Houghton Mifflin Company, 1949.

The City of London: A Record of Destruction and Survival. Architectural Press (London), 1951.

Collier, Basil:
The Battle of Britain. The Macmillan Company, 1962.
The Defence of the United Kingdom. Her Majesty's Stationery Office, 1957.

Collier, Richard:
The City That Would Not Die. E. P. Dutton & Company, 1960.
Eagle Day. E. P. Dutton & Company, 1966.

Collins, James L., ed., *The Marshall Cavendish Illustrated Encyclopedia of World War II*. Marshall Cavendish Corporation, 1972.

Douglas-Hamilton, James, *Motives for a Mission*. St. Martin's Press, 1971.

Eden, Anthony, *The Reckoning*. Houghton Mifflin Company, 1965.

Fleming, Peter:
Invasion, 1940. Rupert Hart-Davis, 1957.
Operation Sea Lion. Simon and Schuster, 1957.

Frischauer, Willi, *The Rise and Fall of Hermann Goering*. Houghton Mifflin Company, 1951.

Fuller, Major General J. F. C.:
A Military History of the Western World, Vol. 3. Funk & Wagnalls Company, 1954.
The Second World War. Meredith Press, 1968.

Galland, Adolf, *The First and the Last*, translated from the German by Mervyn Savill. Henry Holt and Company, 1954.

Halle, Kay, *Irrepressible Churchill*. The World Publishing Company, 1966.

Irving, David, *The Rise and Fall of the Luftwaffe*. Little, Brown and Company, 1973.

Jablonski, Edward, *Airwar*, Vol. 2: *Terror from the Sky*. Doubleday & Company, Inc., 1971.

Jacobsen, H. A., and J. Rohwer, eds., *Decisive Battles of World War II: The German View*, translated from the German by Edward Fitzgerald. G. P. Putnam's Sons, 1965.

Jullian, Marcel, *The Battle of Britain*. The Orion Press, 1967.

Kendrick, Alexander, *Prime Time*. Little, Brown and Company, 1969.

Kesselring, Albert, *Kesselring: A Soldier's Record*. William Morrow & Company, 1954.

Killen, John, *A History of the Luftwaffe*. Doubleday & Company, Inc., 1968.

Latreille, André, *La Seconde Guerre Mondiale*. Hachette (Paris), 1966.

Leasor, James, *The Uninvited Envoy*. McGraw-Hill Book Company, Inc., 1962.

Liddell, Hart, B.H., ed., *The Other Side of the Hill*. Cassell and Company Ltd., 1951.

Mason, Francis K., *Battle over Britain*. McWhirter Twins, Ltd., (London), 1969.

Mason, Herbert Malloy, Jr., *The Rise of the Luftwaffe*. The Dial Press, 1973.

McKee, Alexander, *Strike from the Sky*. Little, Brown and Company, 1960.

Michaelis, Ralph, *From Bird Cage to Battle Plane*. Thomas Y. Crowell Company, 1943.

Michel, Henri, *The Second World War*, translated from the French by Douglas Parmée. Praeger Publishers, 1975.

Middleton, Drew, *The Sky Suspended*. Longmans, Green and Co., 1960.

Miller, H. Tatlock, and Loudon Sainthill, *Churchill, the Walk with Destiny*. The Macmillan Company, 1959.

Mosley, Leonard, *Backs to the Wall*. Random House, 1971.

Murrow, Edward R., *This is London*. Simon and Schuster, 1941.

Pelling, Henry, *Winston Churchill*. E. P. Dutton & Company, 1974.

Perry, George, *The Great British Picture Show*. Hill and Wang, 1974.

Price, Alfred, *Instruments of Darkness*. W. Kimber, 1967.

Richards, Denis, *The Fight at Odds*, Vol. 1. Her Majesty's Stationery Office, 1974.

Roskill, Captain S. W., *The War at Sea*. Her Majesty's Stationery Office, 1954.

Shirer, William L., *The Rise and Fall of the Third Reich*. Simon and Schuster, 1960.

Sims, Edward H., *Fighter Tactics and Strategy 1914-1970*. Harper & Row, Publishers, 1972.

Snow, C. P.:
Science and Government. Harvard University Press, 1961.
Appendix to Science and Government. Harvard University Press, 1962.

Taylor, A. J. P., *English History: 1914-1945*. Oxford University Press, 1965.

Taylor, Telford, *The Breaking Wave*. Simon and Schuster, 1967.

Thetford, Owen, *Aircraft of the Royal Air Force Since 1918*. Funk & Wagnalls Company, 1968.

Townsend, Peter, *Duel of Eagles*. Simon and Schuster, 1970.

Von der Porten, Edward P., *The German Navy in World War II*. Thomas Y. Crowell, 1969.

Webster, Sir Charles and Noble Frankland, *The Strategic Air Offensive Against Germany*. Her Majesty's Stationery Office, 1961.

Wheatley, Ronald, *Operation Sea Lion*. Oxford University Press, 1958.

Wheeler-Bennet, John W., *King George VI*. St. Martin's Press, 1958.

Wilmot, Chester, *The Struggle for Europe*. Harper & Row, Publishers, 1952.

Winterbotham, F. W., *The Ultra Secret*. Harper & Row, Publishers, 1974.

Wood, Derek, and Derek Dempster, *The Narrow Margin*. Greenwood Press, Publishers, 1961.

Wright, Robert, *The Man Who Won the Battle of Britain*. Charles Scribner's Sons, 1969.

ACKNOWLEDGMENTS

The index for this book was prepared by Mel Ingber. For help given in the preparation of this book, the editors wish to express their gratitude to Lieselotte Bandelow, Ullstein, Berlin; Deborah Beevor, archivist, Weidenfeld and Nicolson, London; G. V. Blackstone, CBE, Chief Regional Officer, National Fire Service (Ret.), London; Stan Bradbury, Chappell & Co., Ltd., London; Sue Bradbury, London; Basil Collier, Lewes, Sussex; Terence Charman, Rose Coombs, Edward Hine, R. E. Squires, Imperial War Museum, London; Major Georg Peter Eder (Ret.), Wiesbaden; Erica Fry, Jaeger Co., London; General Adolf Galland (Ret.), Bonn-Bad Godesberg; George M. Greenwell, Jan Mercer, British Film Institute, London; Villette Harris, Washington, D.C.; Dr. Matthias Haupt, Bundesarchiv, Koblenz; Dr. Gerard Hümmelchen, Archiv für Wehrforschung, Stuttgart; Werner Kiessling, Deutscher Heimkehrer Verband, Bonn-Bad Godesberg; William J. Kelly, Garden City, N.Y.; Peter Matthews, Arthur Guinness Son and Co., Ltd., London; Richard Mayne, Jersey, Channel Islands; Ron McCreight, Noel Gay Music Co., London; Lt. Col. Werner Schroer (Ret.), Ottobrun; Carol Toms, Guernsey, Channel Islands.

PICTURE CREDITS

Credits from left to right are separated by semicolons, from top to bottom by dashes.

COVER and page 1—William Vandivert from TIME-LIFE Picture Agency.

HITLER'S NIBBLE AT THE CHANNEL—6, 7—Bundesarchiv, Koblenz. 8—Alan Clifton © Carel Toms. 9—Courtesy R. H. Mayne. 10, 11—Carel Toms. 12, 13—E. Guiton, courtesy R. H. Mayne—Bundesarchiv, Koblenz; Carel Toms. 14 through 17—Bundesarchiv, Koblenz.

BRITAIN AT BAY—20—Imperial War Museum. 23—Imperial War Museum. 25—Hans Wild from TIME-LIFE Picture Agency—Wide World. 26—Fox Photos.

READY FOR JERRY—28, 29—London News Agency Photo Ltd. 30—Radio Times Hulton Picture Library. 31—W. Suschitzky from TIME-LIFE Picture Agency. 32—Radio Times Hulton Picture Library—Wide World. 33, 34, 35—Graphic Photo Union. 36, 37—Wide World. 38—William Vandivert from TIME-LIFE Picture Agency. 39—TIME-LIFE Picture Agency. 40, 41—William Vandivert from TIME-LIFE Picture Agency. 42, 43—Douglas Miller; Wide World; Keystone Press Agency Ltd. 44, 45—William Vandivert from TIME-LIFE Picture Agency.

THE PREFIGHT ODDS—48—Top from *The Narrow Margin*, reprinted by permission of Curtis Brown, Ltd., © 1961 Derek Dempster and Derek Wood—Bildarchiv Preussischer Kulturbesitz. 50, 51—TIME-LIFE Picture Agency; (inset), Flugblatt Sammlung Buchbender. 53—Profile Publications (2)—From *The Narrow Margin*, reprinted by permission of Curtis Brown, Ltd., © 1961 Derek Dempster and Derek Wood (2). 55—Profile Publications.

THE INTREPID MR. CHURCHILL—58, 59—TIME-LIFE Picture Agency. 60—Radio Times Hulton Picture Library. 61—TIME-LIFE Picture Agency. 62—TIME-LIFE Picture Agency. 63—TIME-LIFE Picture Agency—Imperial War Museum. 64, 65—London News Agency Photos Ltd. 66, 67—Radio Times Hulton Picture Library; UPI (2). 68, 69—TIME-LIFE Picture Agency. 70, 71—Imperial War Museum.

THE GRANDIOSE HERR GÖRING—72, 73—Library of Congress. 74—From *Hermann Göring*, by Martin H. Sommerfeldt, published by E. S. Mittler and Sons, Berlin, 1933. 75—Library of Congress. 76, 77—Library of Congress. 78—Bundesarchiv, Koblenz, except bottom right, Bildarchiv Preussischer Kulturbesitz. 79—Bundesarchiv, Koblenz. 80, 81—Ullstein Bilderdienst; Heinrich Hoffmann. 82, 83—From Stefan Lorant's *Sieg Heil!;* © Ernest Sandau, Berlin; Library of Congress—From Stefan Lorant's *Sieg Heil!* 84, 85—Bundesarchiv, Koblenz.

DAY OF THE EAGLE—89—Crown Copyright. 90—Wide World. 93—Map by Nicholas Fasciano—Imperial War Museum. 94—Cartoon by David Low, by arrangement with the Trustees and the *London Evening Standard*. 96—UPI. 98—no credit; Ullstein Bilderdienst.

EXODUS FROM THE CITIES—100, 101—Syndication International. 102—Wide World. 103—Radio Times Hulton Picture Library. 104, 105—Fox Photos—Hulton from Black Star. 105—Syndication International. 106, 107—Fox Photos except top left Syndication International. 108, 109—Wide World. 110, 111—Radio Times Hulton Picture Library; Syndication International—John Topham from Black Star. 112, 113—Radio Times Hulton Picture Library.

THE ATTACK ON LONDON—116—Photoworld. 119—Italian propaganda poster urging the destruction of London, 1940, courtesy Salce Collection, Museo Civico Luigi Bailo, Treviso. 121—TIME-LIFE Picture Agency; Flugblatt Sammlung Buchbender.

WAITING FOR THE SCRAMBLE—124, 125—Radio Times Hulton Picture Library. 126—Imperial War Museum. 127—William Vandivert from TIME-LIFE Picture Agency. 128, 129—Radio Times Hulton Picture Library except top left William Vandivert from TIME-LIFE Picture Agency. 130, 131—Radio Times Hulton Picture Library (2)—F.P.G. 132, 133—Radio Times Hulton Picture Library. 134, 135—Graphic Photo Union.

THE CRUCIBLE OF THE BLITZ—138—Cartoon by David Low, by arrangement with the Trustees and the *London Evening Standard*. 140, 141—Graphic Photo Union. 142—Map by Nicholas Fasciano. 144—Fox Photos. 146—TIME-LIFE Picture Agency; Black Star.

ORDEAL BY FIRE—150, 151—William Vandivert from TIME-LIFE Picture Agency. 152—Wide World. 153—Wide World courtesy *American Heritage*. 154—William Vandivert from TIME-LIFE Picture Agency—Syndication International. 155—Bill Brandt from TIME-LIFE Picture Agency. 156—Robert Capa, Magnum Photos. 157—William Vandivert from TIME-LIFE Picture Agency. 158, 159—UPI. 160, 161—William Vandivert from TIME-LIFE Picture Agency, except center Popperfoto. 162, 163—William Vandivert from TIME-LIFE Picture Agency; TIME-LIFE Picture Agency. 164, 165—William Vandivert from TIME-LIFE Picture Agency. 166, 167—H. Wild from TIME-LIFE Picture Agency; William Vandivert from TIME-LIFE Picture Agency.

RALLYING THE HOME FRONT—168, 169—Fox Photos. 170—Museum of London, courtesy Weidenfeld and Nicolson Archives. 171—Imperial War Museum, courtesy Weidenfeld and Nicolson Archives. 172—Derek Bayes, courtesy Collection of Sue Bradbury, reproduced by permission of Gordon U. Thompson Ltd., Toronto, on behalf of Campbell Connelly and Co. Ltd., London. 173—Derek Bayes, courtesy Collection of Mander and Mitchenson (2)—Derek Bayes, courtesy Collection of Sue Bradbury; Derek Bayes, courtesy Collection of Mander and Mitchenson (2). 174, 175—Popperfoto; Derek Bayes, courtesy Collection of Mander and Mitchenson (3) right, William Vandivert from TIME-LIFE Picture Agency. 176, 177—Derek Bayes, courtesy Collection of Jaeger; Mary Evans Picture Library (2); *The Illustrated London News*; Mary Evans Picture Library; Derek Bayes, courtesy Guiness. 178—Weidenfeld and Nicolson Archives. 179—Eileen Tweedy, Imperial War Museum. 179—Eileen Tweedy, Imperial War Museum except top right London Transport, courtesy Weidenfeld and Nicolson Archives. 180, 181—Twentieth-Century Fox—E.M.I., Elstree Studios, Ltd., Culver Pictures, Inc.

FINALE FOR THE BOMBERS—185—CBS. 186—Imperial War Museum. 189—From Stefan Lorant's *Sieg Heil!*

GERMANY'S FALLEN EAGLES—192, 193—Syndication International. 194—William Vandivert from TIME-LIFE Picture Agency. 195, 196, 197—Imperial War Museum. 198, 199—William Vandivert from TIME-LIFE Picture Agency. 200, 201—William Vandivert from TIME-LIFE Picture Agency; Imperial War Museum (2)—William Vandivert from TIME-LIFE Picture Agency. 202, 203—Wide World.

INDEX

Numerals in italics indicate an illustration of the subject mentioned

A

Aces, *98, 99, 116*
Adams, George, 187
Adlerangriff. See Eagle Attack.
Air-raid shelters: Anderson, *36-37;* in London hotels, 138; lack of, 136-139, 143, 145; life in, 147, 152, *154-157;* Tubes used as, 145-147, 152
Air raids: drills, *34-35;* effects on civilians, 136-139, 145-147, 148-149; first night raids on cities, 118-119; night bombing intensified, 142-143, 147. *See also* Berlin; London
Aircraft production, British, 52, 91; bombing of factories, 116, 117
Aircraft production, German, 52
Alderney, occupation of, 8
Anderson, Sir John, 36; bomb shelters, *36-37*
Antiaircraft guns, 143; in Hyde Park, 145
Automobiles, in blackouts, 30, 32

B

Bader, Squadron Leader Douglas, *98, 99;* experiments with Big Wings, 116; urges 12 Group to independent action, 115
Balloons, barrage, *153*
Barbarossa, Operation, 183
Battle of Britain: August, 91-92, 94-95, 97-99, 114-117; bombing of cities begins, 118-120, 122; Göring plan, 19-20; Hitler postpones invasion, 123; last major bomber attacks, 183-188, 190; objectives of both sides, 88; Phase One begins, 56-57; Phase Two begins, 91-92; planned phases, 56; postponed by Hitler, 20, 24; preliminary skirmishes, 27, 57; *Sea Lion,* 23-24, 56, 117, 123; September, 118-120, 122-123; women's participation, 27, *38-39, 40*
Battle of Britain Day, 123
Battle of the Channel, 57
Beaufighters, 142
Beaverbrook, Lord, heads aircraft production, 52
Bentley Priory: headquarters of Fighter Command, 56; operations room, *93,* 120
Berlin, bombings of, 118-119, 183
Big Ben, 188
Black, Rosemary, 145
Blackouts: preparations, 30, *32-33;* problems, 30, *32*
Blackstone, Geoffrey, 187; on last mass bomber raid, 187-188, 190
Blenheim fighter, 94
Body sniffers, 149
Bomb shelters. *See* Air-raid shelters
Bombers: Dornier-17, 47, *48;* Hampden, 118; Heinkel-111, 47, *48;* Heinkel-177, 47; Junkers-88, 47
Bombs, delayed action, *186*
Brauchitsch, General Walther von, 88; and *Sea Lion,* 24
British Museum, bombed, 188
Brook, Clive, *180*
Buckingham Palace: bombed in error, 139, *140-141;* designated target, 184

C

Cartoons: morale boosting, *170;* political satire, *94, 138*
Channel Islands, occupation of, *6-7, 9-17*
Children, evacuated from cities, *100-113*
Churchill, Clementine, *64-65*
Churchill, Winston, *58-71, 163;* announces imminent invasion to boost morale, 183; and bombing of Coventry, 147; and bombing of London, 118; on British resistance, 21; on civilian morale, 136; confirms Luftwaffe withdrawal, 191; in damaged House of Commons, *163;* on German propaganda leaflet, *121;* and code word *Cromwell,* 122; and Lindemann, 54; orders antiaircraft guns into Hyde Park, 145; orders bombing of Berlin, 118, 119; on bombing of Buckingham Palace, 139; on RAF pilots, 126; and RAF policy during blitzkrieg, 49-50; reaction to German peace feelers, 22; walks during air raids, 148; on women's participation, 41
Civilian morale: advertising and, 170, *176-177;* fear of air raids, 148; films and, 170, *180-181;* at final mass bomber raid, 190; games and, 170, *171;* humor and, 170; improvement as bombing risk spreads, 145, 149; in Liverpool, 139; in London's East End, 137-139; myth of, 136; national unity grows, 139; posters and, 170, *178-179;* and shortages, 182; songs and, *168-169,* 170, *172-173;* at start of 1941, 182; theater and, 170, *174-175*
Clydebank, bombed, 183
Codes: and bombing of Coventry, 147; British knowledge of German codes, 56, 95, 141; Ultra, 147
Communists, English, position on bombing of London, 138
Condor Legion, 86
Coventry: bombed, 145, 147; cathedral, *144;* factories, 147
Crete, invasion of, 191
Cromwell, 122

D

Deanery of Westminster, bombed, 188
Deere, Flight Lieutenant Alan, 86, 89
Defenses: against night bombing, 48, 184; antiaircraft guns, 143; of British coast, *23, 93,* 95; electronic, 143, 184; night, 142-143, 147; radar, 54, *93,* 95, 142, 184; searchlights, 143; sound locators, 143
Defiant, Boulton-Paul, 52; in dogfights, 88
Deichmann, Paul, 92
Delmer, Sefton, 26
Dive bombers: Junkers-87 (Stuka), 49
Dogfights, 88; of August 15, 97; during summer, 86-89, *90*
Donaldson, Squadron Leader E. M., 99
Dornier-17, 47, *48*
Douglas, Air Chief Marshal William Sholto, *146;* and May 10 air raid, 186
Douglas-Hamilton, Douglas, and Rudolf Hess, 189
Dowding, Air Chief Marshal Sir Hugh, 50, 91, 117, *146;* conserves forces, 89; on day of first raid on cities, 120; on objectives of both sides, 88; opposed by Leigh-Mallory, 115, 116; and RAF policy during blitzkrieg, 50; relieved of post, 146; on start of *Eagle Attack,* 91-92; on task of RAF, 57

E

Eagle Attack, 56; authorized, 91; begun, 92, 94; battles of early August, 94-95, 97-99; second stage, 114-123
Eagle Day, 27, 91, 92, 94; losses, 94, 95; number of sorties, 94
Electronic warfare, 143, 183; improvements, 184; jamming, 143; radio beam guidance, 147, 183, 184; retransmission of navigational beams, 143
Elephant and Castle, during air raid of May 10, 187-188, 190
11 Group, 56; bases bombed, 115, 116
Evacuations: of children from cities, *100-113;* of invalids and old people, 102
Evans, Sir Edward, *34-35*

F

Factories: absenteeism, 145; in London's East End, 137; workers visited by pilots, *116,* 117. *See also* Aircraft production
Fiebach, Karl, 184
Fighter planes: Beaufighter, 142, 184; Blenheim, 94, 142; British production of, 52, 91; Defiant, 52, 142; dogfights during summer, 88-89, *90,* 91; fuel injection for, 52, 55; German production, 52; Hurricane, 52, *53;* Messerschmitt-109, 49, *55,* 141; Messerschmitt-110, 49; night, 142, 184; Spitfire, 49, 52, *53,* 57
Fink, Colonel Johannes: assigned to close Straits of Dover, 56; battle of the Channel, 57; leads first attack on Eagle Day, 92; on raids of May 10, 184
Flame Fougasse, 23
France, signs armistice, 21
Freya, 54

G

Galland, Major Adolf, 57, *98, 99;* on air tactics, 86, 89; on Battle of Britain, 191; and Göring, 99, 114, 139, 141, 191
Germany: cities bombed, 118-119, 183; objectives of air war, 88; peace feelers to Britain in 1940, 21-22; production priorities in 1940, 47
Germany, air force (Luftwaffe): attacks on British radar stations, 95; battles of August, 94-95, 97-99, 114-117; begins bombing of cities, 119-120, 122-123; begins *Eagle Attack,* 91, 92; bombers, 47, *48;* bombing accuracy reduced, 143; bombs Buckingham Palace in error, 139; bombs Coventry, 147; bombs London in error, 118; bombs ports, 183; concentrates on Eastern Front, 191; concentrates on night bombing, 142-143; disposition of air fleets, 54, 56; dissension over *Eagle Attack,* 92; dive bombers, 47, 49; Eagle Day, 92, 94-95; efforts to lure RAF to battle, 88-89, 91; fighters, 49; hero pilots, 98; last mass bombing air raids, 183-188, 190; losses on Battle of Britain Day, 123; losses through September, 141-142; management, 47; mines British ports, 92; morale, 49, 139, 141; night bombing adopted, 142; ordered to prepare attack on U.S.S.R., 183; prepares for Battle of Britain, 21; quality of aircraft, 47-49; radio guidance to targets, 143; rescue of downed pilots, 87, 96; sorties, 88; strategy in Battle of Britain, 56; strength in early part of war, 46-47, *48,* 57; tactics against radar, 91, 116; as vanguard of *Sea Lion,* 24
Germany, army of: invades Crete, 191; invades U.S.S.R., 191; masses troops on Channel during summer, 88; occupies Channel Islands, *6-7,* 8, *9-17;* and *Sea Lion,* 24
Germany, navy of: prepares for Battle of Britain, 21; and radar, 54; in *Sea Lion,* 24; U-boat attacks on shipping, 183
Goebbels, Joseph, *78;* and propaganda leaflets, 121
Göring, Emmy, *80*
Göring, Field Marshal Hermann, *20, 21, 72-85;* addiction, 19, 74; announces bombing of London, 122; ceases major attacks on radar stations, 95; celebrates promotion to Reich Marshal and decoration, 26-27; decides to concentrate on night bombing, 141-142; on Eagle Day, 94; attempts to lure RAF to battle, 88-89; first plan for Battle of Britain, 18-20; hunts with Galland, 139, 141; intensifies bombing in August, 114; and Messerschmitts,

Printed in U.S.A.

THE HOUSE THAT MATH BUILT

HOUSE MATH

TIME LIFE for Children ®

ALEXANDRIA, VIRGINIA

ALL ABOUT
I LOVE MATH

The *I Love Math* series shows children that math is all around them in everything they do. It can be found at the grocery store, at a soccer game, in the kitchen, at the zoo, even in their own bodies. As you collect this series, each book will fill in another piece of a child's world, showing how math is a natural part of everyday activities.

My family thinks I'm lost. But I'm having a purr-fectly great time. Look for me near the end of the book.

What Is Math?

Math is much more than manipulating numbers; the goal of math education today is to help children become problem solvers. This means teaching kids to observe the world around them by looking for patterns and relationships, estimating, measuring, comparing, and using reasoning skills. From an early age, children do this naturally. They divide up cookies to share with friends, recognize shapes in pizza, measure how tall they have grown, or match colors and patterns as they dress themselves. Young children love math. But when math only takes the form of abstract formulas on worksheets, children begin to dislike it. The *I Love Math* series is designed to keep math natural and appealing.

Talk about fast food— you won't believe how I got this snack! See my story on page 48.

How Do Children Learn Math?

Research has shown that children learn best by doing. Therefore, *I Love Math* is a hands-on, interactive learning experience. The math concepts are woven into stories in which entertaining characters invite children to help them solve math challenges. Activities reinforce the concepts, and special notes offer ways you can have more fun with this program.

We have worked closely with math educators to include in these books a full range of math skills. As the series progresses, repetition of these skills in different formats will help children master the basics of mathematical thinking.

What Will You Find in *House Math*?
In this book you will tour a wacky mansion where math challenges about time, geometry, patterns, numbers, and measurement abound. You'll analyze a malfunctioning food computer in a kitchen of the future; solve logic problems about neighborhood dogs; learn about the patterns and symmetry of quilts; and think spatially as you search an old house for a missing cat.

After you read *House Math*, take a math tour of your own house. What patterns do you see in tiles, rugs, and curtains? How many steps or windows or doors are in your house? What shapes can you find in the roofline or in the walkway? Which room is the largest, which one is the smallest? Are you surprised to find that your own home is full of math? Doesn't it make you want to say:

I LOVE MATH!

The Editors
Time-Life for Children

Table of Contents

THE HOUSE THAT MATH BUILT

When Tracy and Brad arrived at the Math House it looked just as it did on the back of the Math Cereal box. They had entered the Calculate-O's Math Cereal contest 6 weeks ago and couldn't believe it when the invitation arrived in the mail.

CONGRATULATIONS
TRACY AND BRAD
You have won the math contest!

Answer this riddle, and you may enter the Math House.

RIDDLE: What did one wall say to the other wall?

MATH FOCUS: ADDITION, SUBTRACTION, TIME, SOLID AND PLANE SHAPES, LENGTH, AND PATTERNS. By solving problems, children practice a variety of mathematical skills and concepts.

Encourage children to point to each answer as they proceed from room to room in the Math House.

"Greetings, children. Do you have the answer to the riddle?" asked the guard.

"Is it **I'll meet you at the corner?**" answered Brad.

"That's it," said the guard. "You may now enter the Math House. But first, here are the Math House rules. There are 5 rooms in the Math House. There are 5 questions in each room, and there are also 5 answers. Tell the guard which answer goes with each question, and you may then go to the next room."

Brad and Tracy turned and walked into a ruby-red hall, the strangest place they had ever seen.

MORE FUN. Have children make up their own questions about pattern, time, shape, and size in rooms around their own house.

If there are 11 big hats and 9 small hats, how many hats are there altogether?

How many more big hats than small hats are there?

If there are 8 hats with big dots and 4 hats with small dots, how many hats have dots?

How many hats do not have dots?

If there are 9 hats with feathers, how many hats do not have feathers?

TO THE
**TIME
ROOM**

8 HATS

12 HATS

20 HATS

11 HATS

11

TO THE
MEASURING
ROOM

square

cylinder

cube

rectangle

circle

**What shape
is the
refrigerator door?**

**What shape
is the
cookie jar?**

13

What color is the missing floor tile?
What color is the missing wallpaper flower?
What color is the missing shower curtain circle?
What color is the missing shower curtain ring?
What color is the missing rug stripe?

YELLOW

ORANGE

GREEN

BLUE

RED

18

EXIT

A House Made to Order

These photos show a house being built. But they're all mixed up. You can put them back in the right order.

Take 6 little pieces of paper. Mark them 1, 2, 3, 4, 5, and 6. Then put the paper marked 1 on the photo that shows what happened first. Put the 2 on the photo that shows what happened second, and so on.

MATH FOCUS: LOGICAL THINKING AND ORDINAL NUMBERS. By describing the sequence of a picture story, children apply reasoning skills and use positional number words.

Have 6 small pieces of paper and a pencil available for each child. First have children describe what is happening in each scene. Then have them put the numbered pieces of paper on each scene in order, explaining their reasoning for deciding on that order.

Which picture shows what happened last?

MORE FUN. Children can choose a household activity (such as getting up in the morning) and draw 6 sequential scenes depicting that activity. Then they can cut out the scenes, mix them up, and challenge others to arrange them in the correct order.

Who lives in this house?

Take a look at the kitchen. It's someone's birthday! How old do you think that person is? Does this family have any pets? What else in the kitchen gives you a clue about the family who lives here?

Now take a look at the bathroom, and then the front hall. How many people are in this family? How can you tell?

Look at the room with the bunk beds. How tall are the kids who live there? What do they like to do?

Look in the garage. What does the car tell you about this family? How many different sports do they play? What are they?

Now look around the rest of the house. Does this family like music? What other hobbies do you think they have?

Let's see how good a detective you can be. Can you figure out who lives in this house?

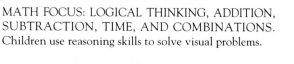

MATH FOCUS: LOGICAL THINKING, ADDITION, SUBTRACTION, TIME, AND COMBINATIONS. Children use reasoning skills to solve visual problems.

Ask children to point out the visual clues that enabled them to answer each question.

22

MORE FUN. Have children draw a detailed picture of a
room in their home and then have someone tell what
the clues in the room show about who lives there.

23

Jack is 5 years older than Harry. How old is Jack?
Margaret is 6 years younger than Harry. How old is Margaret?
The party began a half-hour ago. What time did the party begin?
Harry's birthday is circled on the calendar. When is it?
Is there a balloon for everyone at the party?
Harry has opened 3 gifts. How many more does he have to open?
How many gifts did Harry get in all?
How many flavors of ice cream are on the counter? How many types of toppings? How many different sundaes could Harry make with 1 flavor of ice cream and 1 type of topping?

25

Sew Beautiful

"Wow, Grandma, did you really make these quilts?" asked Joey.

"How did you figure out how to fit all the pieces together, Grandma?" asked Lisa.

"That was the fun part," answered Grandma. "I spent a long time thinking about how to put all the shapes and colors together. The one on our laps is called a crazy quilt. That means that the pieces of fabric are not arranged in a pattern, but in a crazy way."

"What about that one hanging on the wall?" asked Joey. "That one doesn't look crazy at all."

"You're right, Joey," said Grandma. "That one has a pattern and symmetry. Symmetrical quilts have one half that matches the other."

MATH FOCUS: PLANE SHAPES AND PATTERNS. By making their own "quilts" from construction paper, children explore the relationships of shapes and patterns.

Have available blue, green, yellow, and red construction paper, pencils, scissors, and glue. Draw the grid as shown on page 28, and help children cut out the colored squares and triangles.

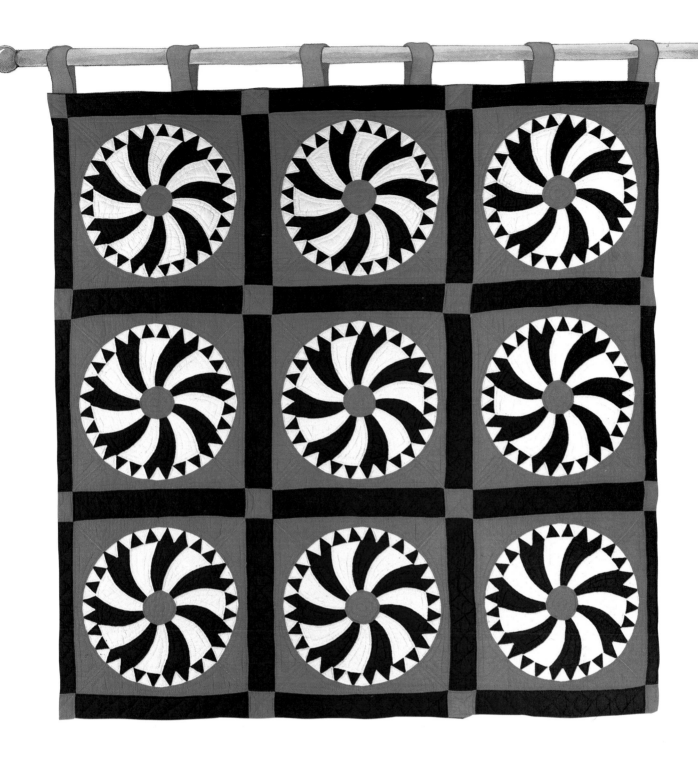

Name all the shapes you see in this quilt.
Are there more triangles or circles?
Are there more big circles or little circles?

How do the shapes fit together?
What patterns do you see?
What name would you give this quilt?

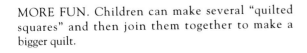

MORE FUN. Children can make several "quilted squares" and then join them together to make a bigger quilt.

"Look, Lisa!" cried Joey. "I found the quilting scraps Grandma told us we could look for in this trunk. I want to make a funny quilt."

"I'm sure it will keep you in stitches for a long time," laughed Lisa.

Create your own quilting kit.

1. Cut these shapes out of colored construction paper:

• 3 blue two-inch squares

• 4 red triangles
  (two-inch squares cut diagonally)

• 4 green triangles
  (two-inch squares cut diagonally)

• 4 yellow triangles
  (two-inch squares cut diagonally)

2.

Draw a six-inch by six-inch grid on a piece of colored construction paper.

3.

Glue all the shapes on your grid in a pattern or in any fun arrangement. When you are finished, give your quilt a name.

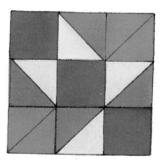

Here are 4 quilts made by using all the
shapes in the kit.

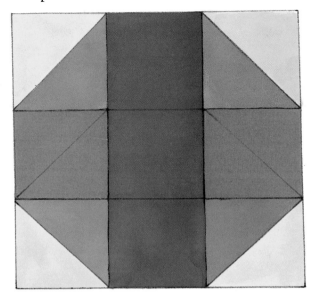

What patterns can you find in each one?
Which quilts are symmetrical?

How is your quilt the same as these quilts? How is it different?
Did you know you could make so many different quilts using
the same pieces?

THE CASE OF THE SQUARE GARDENERS

Professor Guesser's favorite time of year was spring. She loved to rake and hoe and dig and plant. But like most apartment dwellers, Professor Guesser didn't have her own yard. She had to share a yard with the other people who lived in her building.

So on this April morning, Professor Guesser waited patiently in line while the building manager assigned garden plots to those who wanted them. The manager handed her a map of all the available bits of land. Plot 7-C was circled in red.

MATH FOCUS: AREA. By using the same unit of measure to compare two garden plots with different shapes, children discover that they cover the same area of ground.

Point out that the same unit of measure—Professor Guesser's frame—is used to measure both plots, so that it is easier to compare their sizes.

The professor followed the path until she found the plot marked 7-C. It was a small rectangular plot. But it was big enough for the tomatoes, peppers, and squash she had already started from seed in the egg cartons on her window sill.

"Positively perfect," thought Professor Guesser. She put down her square frame and dumped the portable garden tools out of her backpack. She began to work the soil. When she had finished raking, she used her square frame to mark off sections in her garden. Then she counted the squares. "1, 2, 3, 4, 5 . . ."

Her counting was interrupted by Alma Morales and her cousin Paco, who both lived on the third floor. They were arguing over their two garden plots. Alma's father was listening to them patiently.

MORE FUN. Have children draw 3 other garden plots that each have an area of 12 squares but are different shapes than those shown in the story.

The professor went to see what all the fuss was about.

"Oh, Professor Guesser! How nice it is to see you. Maybe you can help us with our problem," suggested Señor Morales.

"Whose garden plot is bigger, mine or Paco's?" asked Alma.

"I don't know for sure because they are different shapes," said Professor Guesser. "One is short and fat and one is long and skinny."

"Then how can you help us?" asked Paco.

"Don't worry," said Señor Morales. "The professor is a professional problem solver! I'm sure she will think of something."

Professor Guesser studied the two plots for quite a while. She looked them up and down. She walked around them. At last she said, "I have an idea! Wait here. I'll be back in a jiffy!"

How do you think Professor Guesser will solve this problem?

The professor went back to garden plot 7-C, got her square frame, and jogged back to the children's gardens.

"What's that for?" asked Paco.

"I use it to plan my garden. I put one tomato plant, or two pepper plants, or one squash plant in each square section," explained the professor. "But we will use it to find out if your garden plots are the same size or not."

Professor Guesser knelt down and pushed the frame into the soft black soil in Alma's garden. It made a perfect square. Then she carefully made a second square right up against the first.

Hurry! Hurry, children!

"I see what you're doing," said Alma. "May I try it?"

"Of course," said Professor Guesser. She stood up, gave the frame to Alma, and brushed the dirt from the knees of her pants.

Alma took the frame and busily made squares in her garden until she ran out of garden. When she was finished, she had one row with twelve squares in it.

"It's my turn now!" shouted Paco excitedly. He took the frame from Alma and began to make squares in his garden.

How many squares did Alma mark off in her garden?

34

Do you think Paco's garden will have more squares, fewer squares, or the same number of squares as Alma's?

Paco made three rows with four squares in each row. When he was finished, he stood up and scratched his head. "Now what do we do?" he asked.

"You dig!" gasped Señor Morales.

"No, you don't dig yet. You compare the amount of space each plot takes up!" said Professor Guesser. "Count the number of squares in each plot."

"I have twelve squares in my garden," said Alma.

"I have twelve in my garden, too," said Paco. "Our gardens take up exactly the same amount of space."

"Now you can dig," said Professor Guesser with a smile.

"Gracias, Professor Guesser," said Señor Morales. "¡Muchas gracias!"

"You're welcome! De nada!" said Professor Guesser.

GARDENS GALORE!

Look at all of these gardens! They take up a lot of ground space, don't they? How much space does Garden A take up? Did you say 4 squares? You're right! Can you find another garden that takes up the same amount of space?

Did you say Garden D? Right again. Garden A and Garden D are shaped differently but each one takes up 4 squares of ground. See if you can match the other pairs of gardens that take up the same amount of ground space.

A

B

C

D

MATH FOCUS: AREA. Children find pairs of garden plots that are shaped differently but cover the same area of ground.

Point out that the same unit of measure—Professor Guesser's frame—is used to measure all the plots, so that it is easier to compare their sizes.

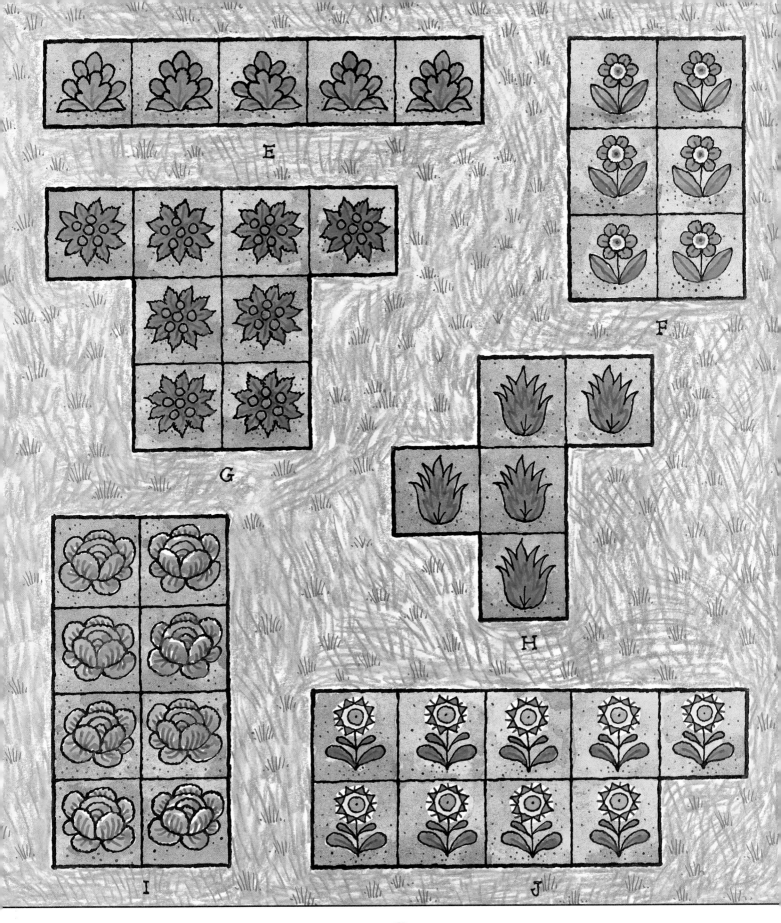

E

F

G

H

I

J

MORE FUN. After children have matched each pair of gardens, have them draw a third garden plot for each pair, making it have the same area but a different shape from the ones shown on these pages.

37

Is your home in this poem?

People in all kinds of places
Live in different dwelling spaces.
They live in cabins, yurts, or caves,
Or up on stilts near ocean waves.

**Cabin! High rise! Houseboat! Dome!
I love living in my home!**

In igloos live the Eskimos.
They stay inside in bitter snows.
Ice blocks stacked into a dome
Make a warm white winter home.

**Cabin! High rise! Houseboat! Dome!
I love living in my home!**

MATH FOCUS: LENGTH (HEIGHT), ESTIMATION, ODD AND EVEN NUMBERS, AND PATTERNS. By solving visual problems, children practice a variety of mathematical skills and concepts.

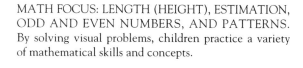

38

Tell children that a yurt is a dome-shaped tent made of skins, used by nomads in central Asia.

A lighthouse high up on a bluff
Warns the ships where seas are rough.
It flashes signals with its light
To keep ships safe and sound at night.

**Cabin! High rise! Houseboat! Dome!
I love living in my home!**

A ranch house on the open range
Has one floor. That isn't strange.
They'd make them bigger if they could
Find a lot more trees for wood.

**Cabin! High rise! Houseboat! Dome!
I love living in my home!**

*Which is taller, the ranch house or the house on stilts?
Which homes have flat walls? Which have curved?
About how many more ice blocks need to be stacked
on the igloo to finish it—about 5, 25 or 250?*

MORE FUN. Have children draw two homes with varying numbers of windows, doors, floors, and architectural shapes and then analyze their similarities and differences.

Just like books upon a shelf,
No row house stands all by itself.
Because they stand so close they meet,
Many can fit on a city street.

**Cabin! High rise! Houseboat! Dome!
I love living in my home!**

Do you think your house could float
Along a river like a boat?
This houseboat's in no big hurry,
Traveling down the old Missouri.

**Cabin! High rise! Houseboat! Dome!
I love living in my home!**

A tree house is a secret spot
To play in when the weather's hot,
Or sleep in on a summer night
And tell ghost stories by flashlight.

**Cabin! High rise! Houseboat! Dome!
I love living in my home!**

*What would be the number of the next
 row house on the right?
Does your home have more windows
than the houseboat?*

40

So many people live inside
Apartment buildings tall and wide!
Each floor is like a neighborhood,
Encased by bricks and glass and wood.

**Cabin! High rise! Houseboat! Dome!
I love living in my home!**

A home of any shape and size,
From tiny hut to huge high rise,
Is where your heart is. And it's true.
Just ask the woman in the shoe.

**Cabin! High rise! Houseboat! Dome!
I love living in my home!**

*How many floors does the apartment
building have?
What kind of home would you like to
live in when you grow up? Why?*

41

*Some of the window shades in the apartment
building are halfway down and some are all
the way down. What is the pattern? Find the
two windows that do not fit the pattern.
Which one should show a half shade? Which
one should show a whole shade?*

2B OR NOT 2B

Isaac, Kathy, and Carl were drawing a chalk picture on the sidewalk. Petunia, who delivers flowers for Daisy Chain Florist, came out of their apartment building.

"What's wrong, Petunia? You look worn out!" Kathy said.

"Of all the places I deliver to, this building takes the most time," Petunia explained. "Five people ordered flowers, and all they told me on the phone was their street address and their last name."

"But the names of the people who live here are on the doors of their apartments," Isaac said. "Couldn't you find them?"

"I found them OK, but there are 6 floors in this building with 4 apartments on each floor. I had to look for the names on every door. Today it took me an hour to make my deliveries, and now I am out of flower power."

MATH FOCUS: LOGICAL THINKING AND SPATIAL SENSE. By describing the positions of apartments in an apartment house, children learn to use a code.

Discuss with children the picture of the layout of the apartments on page 44.

"What if we made a code that tells where the people live so you know right away which apartment to go to?" Carl suggested.

"That would be great, but I guess you'd better ask the building manager," said Petunia.

"Well, the building manager is my dad, " Isaac said. "He's been getting complaints from delivery people lately. He'll be glad to have us help."

"OK, Petunia," Kathy said. "Here's a drawing of the building. Tell us what would help you make your deliveries faster."

"I guess I'd like to know what floor the people live on," Petunia said.

"What if we gave each floor a number?" suggested Carl.

"That's a great idea. How about floors 1, 2, 3, 4, 5, and 6?" said Petunia.

"OK. We'll start at the bottom with 1," said Kathy. "What else, Petunia?"

"I'd like to know where each apartment is so I don't have to wander around looking for it," answered Petunia.

MORE FUN. Children can create another code for identifying apartments; possible suggestions might include terms such as *left, right, front,* and *back.*

"We could use another number," suggested Isaac.

"No, that's too confusing," said Carl. "We should use something else."

"A color?" asked Petunia.

"Colors are not in a special order like numbers," Kathy said.

"I know! How about letters of the alphabet?" asked Isaac.

"Perfect!" Carl said. "We can use the same 4 letters to tell where each apartment is on each floor."

"Like A, B, C, and D?" asked Petunia. "And the 'A' apartment will be in the same place on every floor?"

"Exactly," said Kathy. "On each floor, the A and B apartments will always face the street, and the C and D apartments will always overlook the backyard."

"But if Mrs. Jones orders roses, how will she know what number and letter to tell Petunia?" asked Isaac.

"We'll put the numbers and letters on their doors," said Carl.

"I think Dad has a whole box of numbers and letters in the basement. They were here when we moved in," said Isaac.

"Let's go look," said Kathy.

Soon Isaac, Kathy, and Carl were sorting through the box, picking out the letters and numbers they would need.

6
5
4
3
2
1

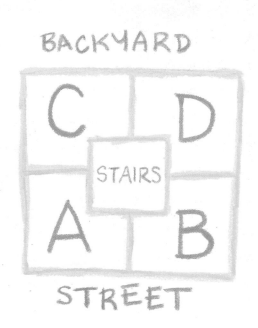

"I'll put a 2 and an A on this door because we're on the second floor and this apartment faces the street," said Isaac. "This is fun!"

"My turn!" said Kathy. "I'll put 2C on this door because we're on the second floor and this apartment overlooks the backyard."

What number and letter belong on the other two doors on this floor? What numbers and letters belong on each door on the fourth floor? On the sixth floor?

A few days later the kids saw Petunia leaving their building.

"Hey, Petunia!" cried Isaac and Carl.

"Hi, kids! I broke a record today: 5 deliveries in 5 minutes!" she said.

"You're the fastest petal pusher around!" yelled Kathy as Petunia rode away.

Where in the World Am I ?

I live at 123 Maple Street,

in the city of St. Louis,

in the state of Missouri,

in the country of the United States,

on the continent of North America,

MATH FOCUS: PATTERNS AND RELATIONSHIPS.
Children explore the relationships of different
geographical areas.

46

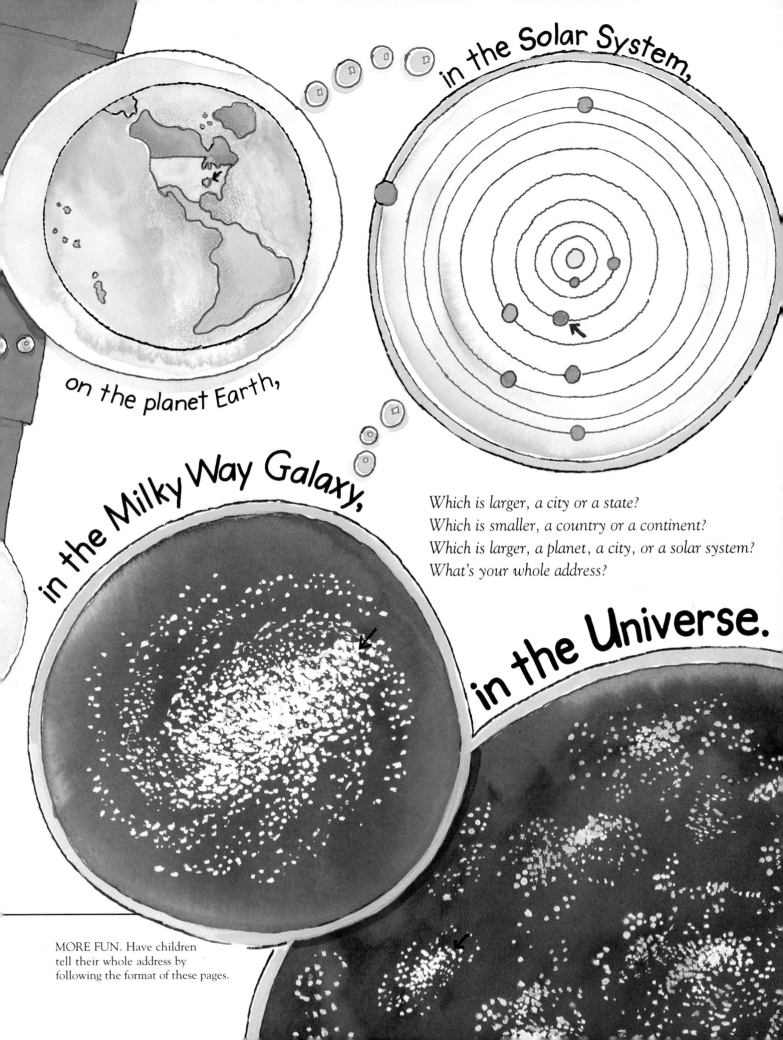

on the planet Earth,

in the Solar System,

in the Milky Way Galaxy,

in the Universe.

Which is larger, a city or a state?
Which is smaller, a country or a continent?
Which is larger, a planet, a city, or a solar system?
What's your whole address?

MORE FUN. Have children
tell their whole address by
following the format of these pages.

The Kitchen Magician

A PLAY IN TWO ACTS.

CHARACTERS:
ZACK: A 14-year-old boy
MRS. XENON: His mother
MR. XENON: His father
CURIOSITY: The family's pet cat
THE GANG: Seven of Zack's friends
TV ANNOUNCER
NARRATOR

SETTING: It's the year 2222 in the artificial rain forests of southern Nevada.

MATH FOCUS: PATTERNS AND RELATIONSHIPS. By comparing what comes out of a function machine to what was ordered from it, children learn to recognize patterns and relationships, a fundamental principle underlying mathematical operations.

As you read the story, have children first point to the food that was ordered and then point to the food that actually came out of the machine.

ACT 1: SCENE 1: (July 6, 8 o'clock at night)

NARRATOR: Let's listen in as the Xenon family watches TV.

TV ANNOUNCER: It slices! It dices! No 23rd-century home should be without the handy dandy Kitchen Magician 5000, the computer food processor of the future. Just push a button and PRESTO, your food is ready! A different menu will be sent to your home every six weeks or so. The first menu is free!

ZACK: Cool.

MRS. XENON: I want one.

MR. XENON: Me, too.

CURIOSITY: Meow!

MRS. XENON: Quick, what's the number?

MR. XENON: 1-800-EAT-5000

MORE FUN. Have children think of a rule, tell three food orders and results, and challenge others to guess the rule. Possible rule: You will get the item to the left of the item ordered.

49

ANSWERS. On page 50 the machine gave the item below the item ordered; on the top of page 52 the machine gave the item to the right of the item ordered; on the bottom of page 52 and on page 53 the machine gave the item above the item ordered.

SCENE 2

NARRATOR: The Kitchen Magician 5000 has been installed in the Xenons' home. The family is in the kitchen eager to use the wonderful new machine.

ZACK: How does it work?

MRS. XENON: Just press the button and anything you want will come out here. (She points to the opening on the front side of the machine.) Watch, I'll show you. I feel like having a slice of pizza and a glass of iced tea. (She pushes the appropriate buttons.)

BING, BOING, BING, ZIP, ZOOM, CRUNCH, CLICK!

NARRATOR: PRESTO! Mrs. Xenon's lunch is ready.

MRS. XENON: Mmmmm. Delicious!

ZACK: Cool.

MR. XENON: No 23rd-century home should be without one!

NARRATOR: Curiosity comes into the kitchen and paws a big red knob at the base of the Kitchen Magician hoping to get a bite of food herself.

ZACK: I want a plate of spaghetti and a carton of milk.

NARRATOR: Zack pushes the spaghetti button and the milk button. The food appears in a few seconds. But instead of spaghetti he gets fruit salad, and instead of milk he gets a tofu burger.

ZACK: Something's wrong, Pop! What happened?

MR. XENON: I don't know, son. Try to get me a turkey sandwich.

NARRATOR: Zack tries the turkey sandwich button to see what will happen. Instead of a turkey sandwich he gets a bowl of wonton soup!

ZACK: Whoa, Pop. Major problemo!

Can you figure out what the machine did?

What food will the machine give if Zack pushes the omelet button?

Which button should Zack press to get spaghetti? Which should he press to get milk?

Which button should Zack press to get Mr. Xenon's turkey sandwich?

51

MR. XENON: The machine gave us what was *under* the button that was pushed. Maybe we need to adjust something. Let's see what happens if I turn this red knob.

NARRATOR: Mr. Xenon turns the red knob and then pushes the button for a turkey sandwich.

BLAT, BORP, BLOOP!

MR. XENON: Wrong again! A tossed salad!

ZACK: Let me try for a plate of spaghetti and a carton of milk one more time.

NARRATOR: Zack crosses his fingers and presses the buttons.

BLOOP, BLAT, BORP!

ZACK: Oh, no! A tofu burger and a glass of orange juice! I think you turned the knob too far.

What did the machine do this time?

MR. XENON: You try turning the red knob, Zack.

NARRATOR: Zack turns the red knob. He pushes the spaghetti button and the milk button.

ZACK: Yikes! I was supposed to get spaghetti and milk, but I got a grilled cheese sandwich and a glass of apple juice instead!

MR. XENON: I'm going to try for my turkey sandwich again. I think I know what's going to happen to my order.

What do you think Mr. Xenon will get?

MR. XENON: Would you look at that—a glass of orange juice! Just as I thought.

What did the machine do this time?

NARRATOR: Mrs. Xenon returns from the solarium where she has just finished her lunch.

MRS. XENON: What's going on here?

MR. XENON: What's going on indeed! Does anybody know? Do you know? What is the Kitchen Magician 5000 doing to everybody's orders?

ZACK: I'll tell you what's going on, Mom. Your new Kitchen Magician is wacko, that's what's going on.

MRS. XENON: I'm the engineer in the family. Let me fuss with it.

CURIOSITY: Meow!

NARRATOR: Curiosity paws the red knob again. Mrs. Xenon sees the knob and gives it a huge twist. Then she pushes a couple of buttons. Something unexpected happens.

BING, BOING, BLAT, BORP, BONG, BEEP, BURP!

ZACK: Cool! Now I see how it works!

NARRATOR: Instead of one plate of spaghetti, out come a hundred! Instead of one carton of milk, out come a hundred! Instead of one turkey sandwich, out come a hundred! The more Mrs. Xenon pushes the buttons, the more food comes out of the machine!

ACT 2: (15 minutes later)

KNOCK, KNOCK, KNOCK!

ZACK: Come on in.

MRS. XENON: Zack, what's this?

ZACK: You mean, "*Who's* this?"! These are my friends: Jerf, Nebula, Rashid, Kork, Milo, Sparky, and Bob.

THE GANG: HI!

MR. XENON: Do any of you know how to fix one of these?

ZACK: Don't sweat it, Pop. We don't have to fix anything! The machine works great! We're going to crank that red knob to the max 'cause it's...

THE GANG: PARTY TIME!

NARRATOR: Zack turns the red knob as far as it will go. Mr. and Mrs. Xenon call their friends over, too.

ZACK: The Kitchen Magician 5000! No 23rd-century home should be without one.

THE GANG: COOL!

NARRATOR: Curiosity eats up all the scraps and has a *purrrfectly* wonderful time.

CURIOSITY: Meow!

55

Dan's in the

There are four doghouses, each a different color: blue, green, red, and yellow.

A different kind of dog lives in each house: a poodle, a bulldog, a collie, and a dachshund.

Each dog has a different name: Dan, Jan, Fran, and Van.

Tip: On 8 small pieces of paper, write the kinds of dogs and their names. Place each one on the correct house as you go along.

Use the clues below to figure out which house each dog lives in. Then figure out each dog's name. Who's Dan? What color is Dan's house?

1. The poodle lives in the blue house.

2. The collie lives to the right of the poodle.

3. The dachshund lives to the left of the bulldog.

MATH FOCUS: LOGICAL THINKING. By selecting items that satisfy given conditions, children use reasoning skills to systematically solve clues.

Help children write the 4 types of dogs and the 4 names on slips of paper. Children can then place each piece of paper on the appropriate house as they solve each clue.

56

Doghouse!

4. Jan lives in the yellow house.

5. Fran does not live next to the blue house.

6. Dan is not a poodle.

57

ANSWERS. Van, the poodle, lives in the blue house. Dan, the collie, lives in the green house. Fran, the dachshund, lives in the red house. Jan, the bulldog, lives in the yellow house.

Paw Prints in the Dust

Usually Seefer Cat was a very good cat. She washed her smooth gray coat and her four white paws every day.

She never let milk stay on her little black mustache.

And when Donna and Sam put her to bed in her basket, she curled up, put her long stripy tail around her, and went to sleep.

But not tonight. Someone had left a window open. Seefer was never allowed to go out alone, but tonight was a night for adventure. Out she went.

MATH FOCUS: SPATIAL SENSE. Children develop spatial sense by exploring relationships of objects in space through the use of the words **on, in, out, down, inside, outside, high, low, above, under, left,** and **right.**

58

Reread page 58 to remind children of Seefer's attributes. Have children find Seefer and then tell how the family in the story should move through the house to reach her.

As she walked past a dark old house, Seefer heard some strange noises. She walked up the front steps to get a better look. She heard something go, "Whoo, whoo," and then something else go, "Rrrow, rrrow." What was inside that house? She had to find out.

So she slipped in the open front door, bumping it a little with her tail as she stepped into the hall. *Creak, creak.* Seefer shot into the air and bounded up the stairs, leaving her paw prints behind her in the dust.

Meanwhile, Donna and Sam were looking high and low for Seefer. They looked above the refrigerator and under the sink.

"Come here, Seefer!" called Sam.

"Seefer, where are you?" called Donna.

"She must have gotten out," their father said. "We'll have to go outside and look for her."

"Let's go," said their mother. "I'll take a flashlight. It's dark outside."

MORE FUN. Children can make up their own questions about the picture on pages 60 and 61 and challenge others to solve them.

When they reached the old house down the road, Donna asked, "Could Seefer be in there?"

"Well, some cat is in there," said Sam. "Look, I see paw prints."

Seefer's family followed the paw prints up the steps and through the door where they found a houseful of cats and other surprises. What can you find in this old house?

How many cats are to the right of the owl?

How many cats are outside the house?

How many cats are inside the house?

Are there more cats inside the house or outside the house?

Find the cat hiding under the rug.

How many cats are in the trunk?

How many spiders can you see on each floor? How many spiders can you see altogether?

Is the picture on the third floor to the left or to the right of the stairs?

Is the owl above or below the second floor?

Where is Seefer?
Which way should the family go to find her?

Calculator CAPERS

Pick any number from your zip code.
Enter your number on the calculator.
Add 5.
Subtract 3.
Add 5.
Subtract 7 and then press =.

Let's use our zip code in this calculator game. The answer should be the same number we start with.

This time we can use our address. The last number on the screen should be 1.

Pick any number from your address.
Enter your number on the calculator.
Add 4.
Subtract 1.
Add 6.
Subtract 8.
Subtract the number you started with and then press =.

MATH FOCUS: ESTIMATION, ADDITION, AND SUBTRACTION. By using a calculator to perform number tricks and solve problems, children practice estimating, adding, and subtracting.

Help children use the calculator, and remind them to press = to find the answer.

A = 1	J = 1	S = 1
B = 2	K = 2	T = 2
C = 3	L = 3	U = 3
D = 4	M = 4	V = 4
E = 5	N = 5	W = 5
F = 6	O = 6	X = 6
G = 7	P = 7	Y = 7
H = 8	Q = 8	Z = 8
I = 9	R = 9	

This one uses the name of our street. Guess if it's worth more than 30 points or less than 30 points.

Enter the value of the first letter of your street name.
Add the value of the next letter.
Keep adding the values of the letters until you have entered the value of the last letter.
Press =.

Enter the value of the first letter of your city or town.
Add the value of the next letter.
Keep adding the values of the letters until you have entered the value of the last letter.
Press =.

Do you think our city name is worth more than our street name or less?

Now that you've gone to town on this game, figure out what the name of your state is worth. Is it worth more than or less than your city or town name?

MORE FUN. Children can compare the value of their street name with the value of a friend or relative's street name.

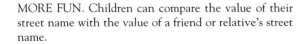

TIME-LIFE for CHILDREN®

Publisher: Robert H. Smith
Associate Publisher and Managing Editor: Neil Kagan
Assistant Managing Editor: Patricia Daniels
Editorial Directors: Jean Burke Crawford, Allan Fallow,
    Karin Kinney, Sara Mark, Elizabeth Ward
Director of Marketing: Margaret Mooney
Product Managers: Cassandra Ford,
    Shelley L. Schimkus
Director of Finance: Lisa Peterson
Financial Analyst: Patricia Vanderslice
Administrative Assistant: Barbara A. Jones
Production Manager: Marlene Zack
Production: Celia Beattie
Supervisor of Quality Control: James King
Assistant Supervisor of Quality Control: Miriam Newton

Produced by Kirchoff/Wohlberg, Inc.
866 United Nations Plaza
New York, New York 10017

Series Director: Mary Jane Martin
Creative Director: Morris A. Kirchoff
Mathematics Director: Jo Dennis
Designer: Jessica A. Kirchoff
Assistant Designers: Daniel Moreton, Judith Schwartz
Contributing Writer: Anne M. Miranda
Managing Editor: Nancy Pernick
Editors: Susan M. Darwin, David McCoy

Cover Illustration: Troy Viss
Cover Photograph: John Lei/OPC

CONSULTANTS

Mary Jane Martin spent 17 years working in elementary school classrooms as a teacher and reading consultant; for seven of those years she was a first-grade teacher. The second half of her career has been devoted to publishing. During this time she has helped create and produce a wide variety of innovative elementary programs, including two mathematics textbook series.

Jo Dennis has worked as a teacher and math consultant in England, Australia, and the United States for more than 20 years. Most recently, she has helped develop and write several mathematics textbooks for kindergarten, first grade, and second grade.

Judy Heard is an elementary school teacher in the public school system of Fairfax County, Virginia. She was a first-grade teacher for almost 14 years, and currently teaches math in grades 1 through 6. In 1990, she was awarded the Virginia Elementary Math Teacher Award by the Virginia Council of Teachers of Mathematics. In 1991, the National Science Foundation presented her with the Presidential Award for Excellence in Teaching Elementary Mathematics, an award given each year to one teacher from every state.

Illustration Credits: Diane Blasius, pp. 22–25; Liz Callen, pp. 46–55; Al Fiorentino, pp. 20–21, back end papers; Ron LeHew, pp. 56–57; Don Madden, pp. 22, 24, 30–37, 58–61; Jane McCreary, pp. 26–29, 42–45, 62–63; Frank McShane, pp. 38–41; Troy Viss, pp. 6–19.

Photography Credits: Pages 6–19, John Lei/OPC; 27, Merikay Waldvogel.

First printing. Printed in U.S.A.
Published simultaneously in Canada.

Time Life Inc. is a wholly owned subsidiary of THE TIME INC. BOOK COMPANY

Time-Life is a trademark of Time Warner Inc. U.S.A.

For subscription information, call 1-800-621-7026.

Library of Congress Cataloging-in-Publication Data

The house that math built : house math/[the editors of Time-Life]
      p.   cm. — (I love math)
    Summary: Shows the importance of early math skills through original stories, poems, riddles, games and hands-on activities.
    ISBN 0-8094-9986-X
    1. Mathematics—Juvenile literature. [1. Mathematics. 2. Mathematical recreations.] I. Time-Life for Children (Firm) II. Series.
QA40.5.M97   1993
510—dc20   93-25398
                                         CIP
                                         AC

HOME SWEET HOME!

The Number of Players: 2–4

The Object of the Game: To pass through all 4 rooms of the house.

The Playing Pieces: A different playing piece for each player; a pair of dice.

The Play: Each player puts a playing piece on START. Players take turns throwing one die. The player who throws the lesser number goes first. The play then continues to the left.

Players take turns throwing both dice and subtracting the lesser number from the greater. The player moves forward that number of spaces.

The Winner: The player who gets to FINISH first wins the game. The exact number is not needed to reach FINISH.

Math Concepts: Determining greater and lesser numbers. Subtracting numbers up to 6.